Bardot

Also by Willi Frischauer

TWILIGHT IN VIENNA
THE NAZIS AT WAR
GOERING
HIMMLER
THE NAVY'S HERE (*with Robert Jackson*)
THE MAN WHO CAME BACK
EUROPEAN COMMUTER
GRAND HOTELS OF EUROPE
ONASSIS
THE AGA KHANS
DAVID FROST
MILLIONAIRES' ISLANDS
BEHIND THE SCENES OF OTTO PREMINGER
NICKY'S HEART
JACKIE
MARGARET: PRINCESS WITHOUT A CAUSE

Bardot

An Intimate Biography

Willi Frischauer

LONDON
MICHAEL JOSEPH

For Nicky, with love

First published in Great Britain by Michael Joseph Ltd
52 Bedford Square, London WC1B 3EF
1978

ISBN 0 7181 1744 1

Typeset and printed in Great Britain by
Tonbridge Printers, Kent and bound by
Redwood Burn Ltd, Edinburgh

Introduction

When Brigitte Bardot says, 'I will not be held to what I said last year – or yesterday,' I suspect that she may not want to be held to that statement either. A creature of moods who lives for the moment, she has never revealed more of herself than what she thought and felt at the time, and much of what she has said over the years was coloured by the demands of publicity and image-building. While rejecting the Bardot legend, she has astutely helped to perpetuate the Bardot myth, and, for someone so anxious not to be tied down, has been remarkably consistent in this respect.

Because I set out to discover the reality behind the legend and the myth I have concentrated on what Brigitte did rather than on what she said and have quoted her only to put her words into the context of her actions. Although I do not entirely accept the simplistic view that Bardot is a creation of the media, the running commentaries which have accompanied her from her beginnings are an integral part of her story. The world's most photographed woman, her face and her body have been implanted on our minds by a generation of film and press cameramen but these images are not always a reliable mirror of her personality.

First on the scene with a deep analysis of the Bardot phenomenon was Simone de Beauvoir, Jean-Paul Sartre's companion. In her apotheosis, *Brigitte Bardot and the Lolita Syndrome,* she defended Brigitte against philistine attacks, but has since denounced 'women who have the misfortune to find sex with men so pleasurable that they become more or less dependent on them' – which sounds like a stern criticism of the Bardot ethos.

It is impossible to convey Brigitte's character without taking account of the views of Roger Vadim, her first husband and mentor and director of her most successful films, although he has not made many new revelations in his entertaining autobiography, *Memoirs of the Devil*; or the amusing glimpses which Curd Jurgens, the continental star, gives of her in his life story: . . . *Und Kein Bischen Weise* (. . . And Not a Little Wise). The well-known show-business writer Peter Evans has produced an excellent portrait, *Bardot, Eternal Sex Goddess,* and Tony Crawley's *Bébé* is the most comprehensive account to date of the French superstar.

Brigitte's work and life are so closely integrated that some of her films seem an extension of her life and some of her personal pursuits seem to mirror the characters she has portrayed. A sex symbol *par excellence*, she has, on screen as in life, for better or worse, pushed back the frontiers of permissiveness and helped to break down the barriers of narrow bourgeois morality earning for herself a place in contemporary social history. As a result, her private life and loves command as much attention as her career.

Writing about Brigitte Bardot, living so long with such a seductive subject on my mind, has been a stimulating experience. As with my previous biographies, I owe much to my wife's help, advice and constructive criticism. Thanks are also due to Brigitte's many friends and acquaintances, as well as one ex-husband, who have added light and shade to my canvas and filled in the gaps in my personal experience, although other evidence has on occasions forced me to modify or amplify their accounts. I have respected the anonymity of all who did not want to appear ingratiating or sound derogatory.

London 1978 | Willi Frischauer

I

'. . . And the Devil Created Bardot'

Brigitte Bardot floated down the Champs Elysées to keep an appointment. Her impact was immediate. 'First the walk – what the French call *la démarche*. Never again have I seen such a walk. As if she was carrying a basket of fruit on her head. The long neck surging up from the collar-bone like a question mark. The features, the cheek-bones, the big over-full mouth might belong to a coloured girl – like a trick picture Gauguin might have painted in Tahiti after waking from a dream of the Bretagne. For the skin is light, the hair blonde as wheat. How does she manage to be so attentive when her whole demeanour seems to say: "These people talking – what's it to do with me? Let me go back to my cosy bed or the sun and the beach!" She is tall, taller than most of the men who stop and stare. . . .'

The brief pen-picture which captured Brigitte in 1955 when she was barely twenty-one is as valid today. Few of the professionals who have sharpened their imagination and their vocabulary to convey their first stunning experience of the exquisite creature have matched the impulsive spontaneity of this bumbling outburst from a dilettante writer (albeit an expert on nubile females), Curd Jurgens, the charismatic Teutonic mime with the acquired Viennese charm. Jurgens partnered Brigitte on her explosive arrival on the world film stage (in *Et Dieu Créa la Femme*); Americans celebrated him as 'the man who made Bardot', although all he did was to lend his time, prestige and box-office appeal to help two unknown young Frenchmen to raise the finance for the project that launched Bardot on her extraordinary career.

Et Dieu Créa la Femme, produced by Raoul Lévy and directed by Roger Vadim, though indifferently received in France, extracted millions of dollars from the pockets of American audiences and, in the passage of time, put Brigitte Bardot on a pedestal alongside Greta Garbo, Marlene Dietrich, Marilyn Monroe and Jane Fonda who entered the fray as 'America's answer to Brigitte Bardot.' It was Vadim who guided Bardot as her Svengali, Rasputin, Frankenstein, Machiavelli – some of the fanciful epithets attached to him – but not as her Professor Higgins because she never was the kind of urchin that needed house training. In the end Vadim happily settled for yet another sobriquet – *'le Diable'* from which it was but a short step to promote the young star with an intriguing extension of the film's title – '*. . . et le Diable créa Bardot.*'

Vadim, of whom more later, encapsulated some of her characteristics with journalistic flair and wit: 'I met her in the summer of 1949,' he wrote in a handout to launch a Bardot film, *La Lumière D'en Face*. 'She was fifteen and a half years old, with a face in which sensuality combined with candour. She danced and still went to school. She received the best education in the world but she swore like a trooper.' After a siege of two years Vadim married her. He said that, like all children brought up in war-time, she was more advanced than children of previous generations, but had blank spots. Though she knew Egyptian history down to the smallest detail, he had to teach her that rats don't lay eggs and that the moon always presents the same side to the earth.

'She cannot fry an egg,' Vadim sighed but added that she covered the chairs and divans at home as well as a professional could. She used to drive her car in Paris with all the assurance of a taxi-driver but feared – still fears – spirits which become invisible monsters. To protect her from these monsters when he was working late, Vadim bought her the cocker spaniel, Clown: 'Here in order after Clown is what Brigitte likes most in the world: other dogs, birds, the sun, money, the sea, flowers, period furniture, grass, kittens and mice.' Vadim was not sure where she placed him but thought, perhaps, between the grass and the kittens.

On a more intellectual level, Brigitte liked Mozart, Beethoven, Tchaikovsky, good mambos, blues which make her stretch voluptuously, songs in which sensuality is expressed without sloppiness. And when asked why she so often had a melancholy air, she used to reply: 'I would have liked to have lived in the days of the horse and carriage.'

London, Pinewood Studios, 1954. Starring in *Doctor at Sea*, directed by Ralph Thomas, with Dirk Bogarde and James Robertson Justice, Brigitte has a scene in which she is seen taking a shower. The point is to suggest that she is in the nude – what else? – but the producer thoughtfully provides an ingenious garment which allows her alluring contours to show while protecting her modesty. Brigitte is puzzled. Discarding the camouflage, she plays the scene as God created her. A little sniggering, raised eyebrows, much delight and a lot of talk. No actress before her had bared her breasts, her whole body, before a British camera crew. 'Why on earth not?' Brigitte asks.

Nudity and Bardot were soon synonymous. Her 'ravishing bosom' inspired Simone de Beauvoir who also enthused about her lascivious walk and wrote: 'Seeing her dance, a saint would be tempted.'

From nudity to immorality was but a short step in the public imagination. Sexual extravagance and promiscuity, their name was Brigitte Bardot. What in the current jargon is at worst 'a liberated woman' was 'a scarlet woman' in the context of twenty-five years ago. She seemed to identify with the titillating characters she portrayed on the screen and, indeed, insisted that, as Juliette in *Et Dieu Créa la Femme*, she played herself. Her tumultuous private love life, much in the public eye, proved her point. Having started Bardolatry – the Bardot craze – with a cover picture which first brought 'BB' (only identified by her initials) to the attention of a film producer, *Elle* magazine rhapsodised some time later: 'Her perfect body seems to reinforce a purity which she no longer possesses but which is yet unchanged. With her inciting hip movements she manages to create a poetry which is undeniable and deeply stirring.'

Bardot is a myth. She is not what she is but as the world chooses to see her. Over-sexed and wicked yet 'so fresh, so healthy, so honestly sensual that it is impossible to discover any trace of Satan in her.' This, according to Simone de Beauvoir, is exactly why she appears all the more diabolical to women who feel humiliated and threatened by her beauty. Serge Gainsbourg who was very close to her at one time waxed lyrically about Bardot's boots which went up to her thighs 'like two chalices for her beauty.' General de Gaulle, who was rather susceptible to a woman's charm (he once said that all he wanted to bring back from the United States was Jacqueline Kennedy), told Brigitte: 'We are enchanted to see you. "Enchanted" is the only word!'

In the trend-setting *Et Dieu Créa la Femme* one character says: 'That girl can drive men wild.' She seemed to offer herself to every man on screen – and in the audience. When she danced her famous mambo, she looked as solitary as a strip-tease dancer on a bar-room table. That, it was said, was why they stamped her as a whore and took their revenge by traducing her. A discarded lover, Gigi Rizzi, said: 'BB is not a woman for marriage', which is true and false because she has been married three times but parted from all her husbands and – who knows? – may yet repeat the exercise. 'Brigitte is very childish,' according to Henri-Georges Clouzot, one of her directors; others elaborated: 'She has the spontaneous dignity and seriousness of a child.' Not even promiscuity, others insisted, detracted from her dignity.

This is how an anonymous lover described being with Bardot: 'She is so beautiful, so exquisitely desirable. Day and night, on every occasion, whether joyful or sad or bored. She is so desirable that life with her becomes an inferno of lust. Nothing can stop you approaching her, disturbing her because you live in constant fear that it could all end a minute later. I believe all men have exhausted her patience. She can drive them all mad. I was mad while we were together.' Marguerite Duras, the novelist, adds: 'If Bardot is attracted to a man she goes to him at once. Nothing stops her. It makes no difference whether she is in a restaurant, at home or visiting friends. She disappears with him without another glance at her escort. In the evening she returns. Or she does not.' Marguerite Duras' conclusion: 'Naughty, lazy, constantly involved in love affairs, that's Bardot, our little girl.'

This sounded fanciful until I talked to Gunter Sachs, the handsome, personable, German-born Swiss playboy-industrialist who told me how he first met Brigitte Bardot and became her third husband. In the summer of 1966 he went with friends to the Vieille Fontaine restaurant near St Tropez where Brigitte was dining with a party. They were at different tables but their eyes met and their glances criss-crossing the room spun a spider's web in which he was caught, in which both of them were caught. 'We were both unattached that evening,' Sachs recalled. There were some exchanges between the tables – St Tropez habitués don't stand on formality – until Brigitte and Gunter left together.

'It was instant love,' Sachs went on to say, making a careful distinction between 'falling in love', a state which, in his experience, lasts a matter of weeks, and reaching the haven of 'loving each other' which comes later. Before they had progressed from phase one to phase two, within five weeks of their first encounter, they decided to marry. They had, as we shall see, a good time together but it is not wholly hindsight if I maintain that it could not last or, perhaps, that it was too good to last.

Flitting across life as ephemerally as her images on the screen, Bardot rarely lingers for long. But while neither infatuations nor marriages last, she is loyal to her friends among whom she counts two of her three husbands (one retired hurt). Like Roger Vadim, Gunter Sachs, who parted from her after less than two years of marriage and has since acquired another wife, speaks of Brigitte with affection and respect.

Ex-husbands, ex-lovers are haunted by the memory of Brigitte who has branded her label – BB – deeply into their soul. With some it smarts like an open wound, others carry it proudly as a badge for life. At least one has built an international career on a passing association with her. In the public mind she has progressed from the intimate 'Bébé', so appropriately combining her initials and the affectionately onomatopoeic French word for baby. Usherette of the permissive age, symbol of female emancipation, she has even, quite inappropriately, been drawn into the discussion about 'women of violence' – the urban guerillas and terrorists of the seventies among whom women like Ulrike Meinhof and Leila Khaled played an increasingly dominant role.

These cruel, unfeeling molls turned gang leaders, it was suggested (*Der Spiegel*, August 1977), were just one step on from the Brigitte Bardot who, in her 1965 film *Viva Maria!*, was shown – with Jeanne Moreau – as a militant behind a machine-gun. It is a malignant growth on the beautiful body of the Bardot myth. Her passionate stand against violence in Algeria, her temperamental defence of animals (seals, for instance) against the cruelty of man testify to genuine, old-fashioned compassion and could not be further removed from the soulless habitat of de-sexed female bank robbers, kidnappers and assassins trying to demonstrate their sexual equality – or superiority – with a loaded gun in their hands.

What is also remarkable about Bardot is her effect on some women who are as powerfully, as sensually, attracted to her as men. Jane Birkin, the boyish British girl who has become an unlikely sex-symbol in France, was offered the part of a young woman (in the film *Don Juan*) who falls in love with Bardot: 'I accepted immediately,' Jane Birkin said, 'just to be in bed with Bardot. She is the most utterly perfect woman. There's not a fault. God knows, I looked. Even her feet are pretty.' Jane Birkin is not a lesbian – she lives with Serge Gainsbourg – nor has any jealousy detracted from her admiration for Bardot who was her predecessor in Serge's affections.

My own first impression of Bardot was the impact of her absence. It was in the mid-fifties when BB (Bébé) was the living embodiment of the latest literary sex-symbol, the fashionable juvenile *femme fatale* in the mould of Nabokov's Lolita, the nymphet, the child-woman (successor of the notorious *demi-vierge* of the twenties who was generous and versatile with her sexual favours but denied her suitors and herself the final consummation). In the same tradition, Françoise Sagan, in her fabulously successful *Bonjour Tristesse*, had just created the teenage Cécile, a spoilt and pampered brat who becomes involved in her father's love tangle. When Otto Preminger acquired the film rights in the much acclaimed French novel, Bardot was the obvious choice to portray the character. Françoise Sagan was delighted but it did not happen.

Bardot would not play – Vadim advised against it – and Preminger had to make do with his young American discovery, Jean Seberg (who blossomed into a star only after escaping from his tutelage). Visiting the location just down the road from St Tropez, Françoise Sagan watched the performance of the director and his American protégée with demonstrative disdain. I spent an hour with her on the set but she hardly exchanged a word with Preminger. Had Bardot not been in everybody's mind, the director and little Jean Seberg might have got away with it. Without Brigitte, the production seemed doomed from the start. The film was a flop. Bardot, Sagan and, indeed, *Bonjour Tristesse* have been all but obliterated from Preminger's mind as a bad memory.

Brigitte adopted St Tropez and has since spent most of her summers in a fine house she built for herself, an elusive attraction protected from the curious by high garden walls behind which she relaxes in her favourite attire – no clothes. She was already a celebrity among the celebrities who made the French Riviera their home from home. I remember her in these early days, pursued by photographers, going to see Pablo Picasso at his villa and studio in Cannes where he was at work decorating pottery. It was a memorable encounter, like a reunion although the two had never met before. She seemed to have long inhabited Picasso's fantasies. As with Gauguin's work which came to Curd Jurgens' mind when he first saw Brigitte, the women in Picasso's paintings strangely resembled this vibrant, pulsating, natural phenomenon.

Coming face to face with the incarnation of his imagination, Picasso looked startled; his fingers itched for a chalk or a brush to commit the living Bardot to canvas. A few deft strokes conjured up a striking sketch which, like many of Picasso's portraits, penetrated his subject more incisively than many a film or photograph. But, however instructive, it was but one view, captured but one instant in a scintillating life with so many facets that it becomes an adventure to explore it. It was in this spirit that I went in search of the real Brigitte Bardot.

II

Ugly Duckling

The pale skin smudged by blotches, a recurring nervous rash; the small face distorted by a brace which, while coaxing recalcitrant front teeth into line, pushed the lips forward into an Afro-Asian bulge – an ugly duckling. Long after the lips had settled into the suggestive pout and the child had grown into a lissom, long-limbed girl, Brigitte Bardot looking despairingly in the mirror did not like what she saw. She continued to think of herself as ugly, and four dozen starring roles, elevation to sex-symbol of her time, the consuming adoration of a vast regiment of men and the envy of millions of women have apparently not reconciled her to her looks. The fan magazines dubbing her 'the gorgeous Peke' (or Pekinese) did not help. Just one of her many hang-ups.

It requires no Sigmund Freud nor any of his latter-day disciples who compile psychograms of the famous without putting them on the couch, to trace Brigitte's characteristics and problems to her mother's womb, to parents with starkly contrasting outlooks who yet both loved her in their own ways and tried to raise her as any normal girl in an all too conventional environment.

Although Louis and Anne-Marie Bardot (née Muscel) inhabited a solid bourgeois world at home in their luxurious apartment at 35 avenue de la Bourdonnais in Passy, the French capital's prosperous eighth arrondissement, when early in 1934 Totty told Pilou (the Bardots' nicknames for each other) that she was expecting their first child Europe was already threatened by turmoil – the rise of Hitler and the Nazis in Germany, the threat of civil strife in France itself.

For Pilou, a well-to-do industrialist with an orderly, orthodox mind, the instability was unsettling beyond the effects it might have on his highly profitable enterprise in Aubervilliers producing liquid gas and acetylene. Would his baby be born into a period of unrest, revolution, war? Whatever the portents, he ploughed on with his business, stuck stubbornly to routine in a household which worked with clock-like precision. With her artistic temperament and background – dancing and acting studies in Milan where she grew up, frustrated theatrical ambitions, a suppressed urge to break out from domestic monotony – Totty took the ominous signs more lightly although the prevailing tensions were bound to affect her in her delicate condition and transmit themselves to the child she was carrying.

Yet, when her time came on 28 September 1934, the midday sun glowed as brightly as the radiant mother and the delighted father who pushed all other thoughts into their subconscious. The baby girl, looking fit and healthy and weighing in at well over seven pounds, was received with uninhibited joy by both parents. They named the little mite Brigitte, the name of Totty's favourite doll. It was fondly abbreviated to Bri, and, baby-talk-wise, Bri-Bri (such was the impact of the grown-up Bri-Bri that Gunter Sachs called Christian, his son by his next wife, Chri-Chri). On the baby's head, only a few wisps heralded the pile of blonde hair which, together with the pout, became Bardot's trademark. The eyes were big but sleepy, the limbs strong and well formed.

Of Bri-Bri's childhood there is very little to report, except these were momentous times in the world at large. She was two years old – too young to register the historic event which troubled adults in this critical period – when the Wehrmacht marched into the de-militarised Rhineland, four when Hitler invaded Austria and when French Premier Daladier joined Chamberlain, Mussolini and Hitler at Munich to sell the Czechs down the river, and five when the war broke out. With a world convulsed by war and with parents preoccupied with the precarious situation, Bri-Bri's infant mind developed a self-sufficiency and defence mechanism which became second nature to her. Her apparent immunity against trouble, her habit of ignoring problems was impressive but artificial and deceptive and did not help to resolve them. From a tender age Bri-Bri did her own thing which was as little as possible. Unlike many children who hate to share their parents' affection with a newcomer, she was not disturbed by the arrival of a sister, Mijanou (christened Marie-Jeanne) in 1939, though relations were not always sisterly when the girls grew up.

War deprived Bri-Bri of her English nanny who was forced to leave, though not before instilling into her little charge a feeling for the English language. A French governess took her for walks in the Bois de Boulogne where the child would not really have been aware that many of the men they encountered were in uniform – German uniform.

War or no war, Pilou's firm prospered and the German occupation of Paris damaged his business interests not a whit. Like most wealthy upper-middle-class businessmen, he did not become embroiled in personal conflict with the military or civil authorities of the victorious *boches*, and his aloofness could be conveniently interpreted as either contempt or indifference. It was a time for all good Frenchmen at his social level with family and business responsibilities to look after their own, which Louis Bardot did extremely well.

The new Bardot apartment at 1 rue de la Pompe near the intersection with the avenue Paul Doumer was, if anything, more luxurious than the one into which Bri-Bri had been born. Tasteful, elegant furniture, a spacious nursery crammed with toy animals was shared with a live kitten, Crocus, first of a long line of pets on which Brigitte came to lavish more love than on most humans.

Whenever Brigitte talked about her childhood she never admitted to any disturbance below the surface of a scrupulous and smooth routine. She was ministered to by the family's two servants but imprisoned by a discipline which status-conscious French parents imposed on their infants: conducted to mother's presence in the morning after having been scrubbed, brushed and fed; discouraged from making a fuss of father and not encouraged to speak to him unless spoken to; and instructed at home until she was old enough to got to school. She did not as yet revolt against the strict timetable which rigorously governed her life and interrupted her play – breakfast at the stroke of eight, lunch at one, dinner at seven with an afternoon stroll in between – but her resentment against the tyranny of the clock became evident in adult life. Impossible to count the times she was an hour or more late for appointments or missed them altogether. She often says she was a lazy child, but in fact she attended to her lessons and her little domestic chores conscientiously. When Vadim remarked about the effect of the war on Brigitte's generation, he must have included the even more unsettling post-war period as a factor in his character analysis.

Exhibiting early some of the traits of the beguiling, confusing creature into which she grew up, Brigitte's manners, instilled by governess and parents, were impeccable in small things. In a wider sense she came to be totally indifferent to convention, impervious to reproach and contemptuous of other people's view of her. Enticingly loving with friends and animals whom she spoiled with her surfeit of unassimilated affections, she soon started to ride rough-shod over the feelings of others, baffling most of her companions whose translation from coveted lover to insufferable nonentity was swift, bewildering and final. The overwhelming impression she made on others went hand in hand with the failure of others to make any impression on her. Casual relationships left not the slightest mark. (Mike Sarne, pop star turned film director, having indiscreetly admitted to a brief fling with her, recalled a friend telling him that he had mentioned his name to Bardot two years later. Her reaction was typical: 'Mike – who?')

But was she not anxious to impress? She has said that she was so ambitious because she wanted to compensate for her ugliness, but anxiety about her looks, at first intense and painful, degenerated into a habit and a fad or at best a means of provoking reassurance. Vadim remembers her spending hours before the mirror with tears in her eyes until he swore that she was more alluring than any other woman he knew. It was, of course, not as unusual as she pretended for a little girl to need glasses; nor was she the only child of her age whose teeth were corrected by a brace.

With parents unwilling or unable to show a great deal of affection – a hint of French Victoriana – Brigitte, much against her natural inclinations, kept her emotions bottled up; like the compressed gases her father produced, they were bound to explode sooner or later. In the meantime, the little girl with the smooth exterior and self-contained, aloof demeanour was a bundle of nerves. Her skin erupted with ungainly, persistent eczema, a psychosomatic symptom which aggravates the problem that causes it in the first place.

As a matter of course, Pilou sent Bri-Bri to Hattemar, an exclusive, expensive, conventional private school which did not encourage children to be 'different.' Individuality was frowned upon, to depart from the pattern was regarded as an offence against the unwritten rules. In school as at home, Bri-Bri's personality, like her teeth, was ruthlessly forced into line. While Pilou fondly hoped that his gawky elder daughter would emerge as a well-marked butterfly and settle on a desirable young man from a good and prosperous family, Totty harboured secret thoughts of a theatrical career for both her daughters to make up for her own unfulfilled ambition. If father insisted on the traditional schooling for upper-class girls, mother would steer at least Bri-Bri towards loftier opportunities. In the first instance, she arranged for Bri-Bri to receive dancing lessons from a member of the Opera Ballet, from which she graduated to Madame Bourget's small dancing studio and, before long, to the Conservatoire Nationale de Danse.

For Brigitte, dancing was like a release from invisible shackles. Such was the exhilaration of free movement that she flowered, her lithe body taking off on a magic carpet of weightlessness. Her teacher, Boris Kniaseff, was delighted and it is to him that she owes her incomparable walk: feet moving gracefully forward, toes touching the ground before the heel, the body whipping elastically in rhythm, the whole movement inspired by the joy of cheating gravitation. Floating on air. There was nothing artifical about it. Once she had acquired the knack, it became second nature, sensual, sexual, long before such instincts were fully awakened.

Unremarkable, almost lethargic, an increasingly reluctant pupil at school which was a burden and a bore offering no prizes, Brigitte found the mornings in the classroom only bearable because afternoon dancing sessions beckoned as an outlet for her artistic talents. She came to life when she donned her leotard and put on her ballet slippers. At school she made few friends. In dancing classes she chummed up with like-minded girls, the talented, tiny Leslie Caron among them.

Entering upon her teens and maturing fast in troubled, unsettled post-war Paris, Brigitte was not beautiful by any means, could hardly be described as good-looking – though the Bardot mythology has carried the tale of her 'ugliness' too far. As a dancer, she was stylish, inspired, with a kind of beauty which more handsome girls of her age found elusive. Boys queued up, attracted by her animal innocence, but, though her parents were too old-fashioned to enlighten her about the mysteries of sex, she was not as innocent as she was later made out to have been, and knew only too well what the boys were looking for. She may have been uncertain about the procreation of mice but was by no means ignorant about the behaviour of the human ape.

Had they involved themselves more deeply with Brigitte's puberty, Bardot *père et mere* might have changed the course of the cinema's history – for the worse. Feeling that she was discharging her duty as a mother by giving the girls a comfortable home, a good education and a sound code of behaviour – no gallivanting at night, curfew only slightly extended on Saturdays and Sundays – Totty was instead looking for something to occupy her own time, profitably if at all possible.

In the event, she opened a boutique in the rue de la Pompe and recruited her wide circle of friends and acquaintances as customers. The girls, Brigitte more so than Mijanou, wore clothes well, and Brigitte at fourteen was a well-groomed, attractive walking advertisement for the dresses, hats and accessories her mother offered for sale. Totty had taste, imagination, a touch of showmanship and ideas. She chose her moment well. With the fashion industry a cornerstone of French economic reconstruction, everything was geared to restoring *haute couture*, giving it a 'new look'.

Operating in the wake of the big houses, Madame Bardot kept a keen eye on newcomers to the fashion scene and was particularly impressed by a young modiste, Jean Barthet, whose creations were on show in her shop. When the designer planned a fashion show, Totty came up with a novel idea. Why not engage a dancing mannequin to display Barthet's work with each design representing a dancing step – *entrechats, jetée battue,* and so on? Barthet was enthusiastic.

Totty's choice of a suitable mannequin was her daughter. Some accounts have suggested that Barthet's enthusiasm faded rapidly when he saw Brigitte. Not true. He had met Totty's daughter before and, what's more, by this time (1948) Brigitte was already a piquant, sexy girl. Like de Gaulle a little later, Barthet was totally enchanted. Brigitte carried out her assignment like a practised performer. She was a natural. Rehearsals at the Drouand David Gallery gave scope to her latent talent and on the day Barthet's clever hats enhanced her provocative face and figure. Her dancing was riveting and her 'innocence' nipped sales resistance by jealous matrons in the bud. Women were not as yet disturbed by her questing expression and hint of insolent aloofness which became part of the Bardot mystique. She was an instantaneous success with the fashion writers, one of whom was quick to recruit her for *Jardin des Modes*, a popular magazine which was planning a cover and layout on teenage fashion. Would Madame Bardot allow her daughter to model for the feature?

The Bardots have since made much of their doubts, their heart-searching, their reluctance to let Brigitte be lured into the 'dangerous' realm of fashion. Pilou had serious misgivings because, in his view, the word 'mannequin' or 'model' – fashion or photographic – covered a multitude of sins. It was an outdated prejudice. There was nothing ambiguous about models in the year when many of them acquired social status, when Prince Aly Khan first set eyes on Bettina, the sensational Jacques Fath mannequin, who modelled a wedding dress for his bride Rita Hayworth and not much later became her successor in his affections. Within a few more months, leading fashion models ruled the roost – and several stately homes – in English society. Brigitte, who had long wanted to be a ballerina, began to dream of a career as a mannequin.

In spite of Pilou's protest, Totty supported her daughter which did not make for domestic peace. The whole performance of agonising doubts, tests of strength between father and mother, angry obstruction and reluctant approval was repeated when Madame Lazareff, editor of the big circulation magazine *Elle*, homed in on the new discovery to replace a cover-girl who had defaulted on her contract. Brigitte on the cover of *Elle*! That would be fame indeed. But there was still the problem of a schoolgirl's face prominently displayed on every news-stand in the country. A problem, yes – but there was a solution. The Bardots decided they would let Brigitte pose as long as her name was not disclosed. Madame Lazareff suggested a compromise: 'If not her name, we shall use her initials.' And so BB was born.

III

Enter Vadim

When the Bardots opened the door of their apartment in the rue de la Pompe to Roger Vadim, they unlocked the gilded cage in which they had brought up Brigitte. It took her some time to struggle free but once she had flown out she was never recaptured.

In the late forties, Vadim – full name Roger Vladimir Plemiannikov – son of a White Russian who had settled in France, was an impecunious, would-be novelist and film writer. His hopes were pinned on the script, *Les Lauriers Sont Coupés,* which he had submitted to Marc Allegret, a respected film maker to whom Simone Simon, first of the screen's child-women, owed her stardom (in a film shown in the year of BB's birth). While waiting for Allegret to make up his mind, Vadim made himself useful to the director as best as he could.

Times changed– as Marc Allegret's name faded from prominence, Vadim rose to fame; and, once married to Brigitte, he was hailed as her discoverer which was unfair to Allegret. It was he who picked up a copy of *Elle* with BB on the cover and was captivated by the unusual face, the expression of innocence which yet suggested hidden passion and a rare personality: 'Get her!' he told Vadim, or words to that effect. Like most film directors, he expected any girl to come running when he lifted a finger.

Vadim soon discovered the full name behind the intriguing 'BB' tag. But when he looked more deeply into her background, he discovered that BB was not a run-of-the-mill cover girl who would jump at the chance to meet a director. Considering the standing of the Bardots, Vadim decided on a formal approach and sat down and wrote a note to Madame Anne-Marie Bardot: 'M. Marc Allegret would be delighted to meet your daughter in connection with a project he would like to discuss with you. . . .'

He thought it wiser not to be too specific; no mention of a film test, no hinting, as film scouts are wont to do, at the prospect of a glittering career such a meeting could open up for BB.

The arguments which the note provoked in the Bardot family went on for days and days and spilled over into a weekend at the family's Norwegian-style chalet at Louveciennes, near Versailles. If fashion was not what Pilou wanted for his daughter, films were utterly beyond the pale. But Marc Allegret had already given Leslie Caron a test – she was currently dancing in Roland Petit's ballet, *La Reconte*. Totty was tempted. She persuaded her husband to agree to a non-committal meeting with the director.

Madame Bardot was taken a little aback when the great Marc Allegret presented himself at the apartment accompanied by the writer of the letter whose appearance could only reinforce her husband's doubts and prejudices about the practitioners of the movie business. Vadim has described how he saw himself on the occasion of this visit, his first encounter with Brigitte – a thin, taciturn boy of nineteen, without a tie, a character out of a Dostoyevsky novel who nevertheless appeared to enjoy life. That his hair was weirdly long and unruly did not improve the impression he made on the Bardots.

While Totty devoted herself to Allegret whose legendary charm quickly won her over, Brigitte surveyed the younger man with amiable curiosity. She was barely fifteen but behaved like a practised seductress. Without taking her eyes off Vadim, she slipped out on to the balcony making it quite obvious that she expected him to follow her.

In the sitting-room, Totty argued that her daughter was not really suitable for the cinema. On the balcony, Brigitte and the unconventional young man – according to Vadim's poetic recollection – engaged in the kind of dialogue of which Bardot films were made. I quote Vadim's version:

'I love balconies,' she said.

'Why?'

'Do you have to have a reason for loving?'

Si non è vero ben trovato. Brigitte does not remember it this way; it may not have happened like this but the reality could not possibly improve on Vadim's account. As he saw her, she seemed to have stepped right out of the pages of his first, as yet unpublished, novel, *The Wise Sophie*, the personification of his principal character – much as Picasso came to see her as one of his earlier portraits come to life. How many artists seem to have a Bardot tucked away in their subconscious!

The upshot of this fateful afternoon was that Brigitte was greatly attracted to Vadim and that Madame Bardot, impressed by Allegret, agreed to let her daughter have a film test. Although Totty persuaded herself that nothing would come of it and that it would not be a good thing if the matter went much further, she thought that Brigitte would not forgive her if she stood in her way. However reluctantly, she wanted the girl to have at least a chance to try. It was arranged that Vadim should explain what Brigitte would be required to do and rehearse her: 'Shall we say next Wednesday after her dancing class?' Madame suggested and Vadim said: 'Next Wednesday and the Wednesday after that and a third or fourth time if necessary.'

On the following Wednesday, Brigitte hurried straight from dancing class to the address in the avenue Wagram which Vadim had given her. Without a home of his own, he was living with his friend, the actor Daniel Gélin and Gélin's wife, Danièle Delorme – in the absence of his hosts to all intents and purposes a bachelor pad. As a vehicle for Brigitte's test he chose a scene from *Les Lauriers Sont Coupés*, his plan being to concentrate on her acting and her diction. Neither he nor Brigitte seems to have concentrated as hard as they might have done. Brigitte was alluring, seductive with the natural instinct of a nubile adolescent. As for Vadim, the sexual appeal of his new protégée was at odds with his artistic requirements.

As they rehearsed, Vadim playing opposite her, he was in turn fascinated and frustrated, enchanted and indignant. Brigitte lacked discipline and application, and, like the sex kitten she was, seemed more inclined to play than to work. Some of their sessions were exasperating and confusing. She talked delightfully but did not enunciate properly. Her acting was non-existent. She could not be other than herself, gloriously so, but as yet she was no actress.

Vadim marvelled at her transformation when he went to see her dancing. The dedication, the passion, the grace! If only she showed a tenth of it at their rehearsals! She was so accomplished, her mirror reflection seemed to lag behind her. From the beginning he, too, saw her as 'a creature made to fly.' At the moment it was more important that she should learn to act. Vadim staked his own future on her – if she made it, Marc Allegret and his producer Pierre Braunberger would have to go ahead with his script.

Against all odds, he coaxed her and tried to mould her in the image of the character he had created. Aching for the day of the test to come, he was yet fearful that it would end in disaster. It did. With Marc Allegret behind the camera, Vadim and Brigitte acted out their scene. The result was so disappointing that Braunberger put the Vadim project in cold storage. Vadim says that this is where he consigned Brigitte Bardot. In truth, he could not forget her.

She was in his mind as he continued his Bohemian existence, bursts of activity following idle days and weeks in Left Bank *boîtes*; working on film scripts alternating with periods when all he did was to exercise his charm on the free-living, free-loving girls of the Quartier Latin. Not that he would admit it to himself, but the girl he was searching for was Brigitte. He convinced himself that she had not forgotten him either – and he was right. Compared with the pale youngsters of her circle, Vadim, even as their brief encounters faded into the misty past, was a life force. Perceptive for her age, she could sense that his languid, indolent manner disguised great talent and a strong intellect.

Brigitte would not say much about the course of events which brought them together again except that school became more intolerable as final examinations loomed ahead like unattainable mountain peaks. While much in her mind, Vadim seemed almost as elusive; he was, in fact, drifting, mostly penniless, from one day to another, ambitions thwarted, with only one fixed purpose

– to find Brigitte again. One idle Saturday, he summoned up – not courage, he had plenty of that – energy and will-power to do something about it. Why not telephone her? Doubts troubled him. She was probably not at home, anyway; or, if she answered, had most likely forgotten his name; or, at best, might ask him decorously to tea and then dismiss him. It was not a promising situation, threatening only another set-back, yet in his despondent, fatalistic frame of mind he was craving for an adventure even if it ended in failure. What, to a Russian soul, could be more gratifying than rejection?

With the last coin in his pocket he dialled the Bardot number (JASmin 82 86) from a telephone kiosk. Brigitte answered. Why not come round, she asked. Her parents were away but her grandmother was with her: 'I look forward to seeing you,' she said. To Vadim it sounded like an invitation to love. He went to the rue de la Pompe where Brigitte received him with open arms. She introduced him to her grandmother and to a young man who appeared to be her current boy-friend. Having cast a critical eye over the newcomer with the long straggly hair and bare feet and sandals, the grandmother withdrew but not, Vadim chuckles, before telling Brigitte's boy-friend to keep an eye on him – and the family silver. The youth's mind was on other things. The strange visitor was obviously not after the silver but after Brigitte. Conversation between the unequal trio was desultory but Brigitte spoke with her eyes and Vadim responded with his. When he left, she went with him to the lift. In her uninhibited way she put her lips to his. The kiss sealed an affair of the heart, the mind and the body which added a chapter to the history of the cinema.

Vadim could not keep away. When he called again, her grandmother telephoned Totty to warn her that Brigitte was clearly infatuated with this unsuitable young man. Mijanou, a wicked little spoil-sport, kept her ears pricked to their whispers. They were talking about films but what Mijanou picked up were Vadim's unorthodox views on love, sex, morality – it sounded very daring. There were strong existentialist elements in Vadim's raw ideas when he talked of the immortality and immorality of his generation.

If his ideas did not go far beyond the general run of Left Bank theories and practices, in the arid bourgeois atmosphere of the rue de la Pompe they seemed sensational and outrageous. Brigitte was highly receptive because much of what he said coincided with her natural inclinations. She was as absorbed by Vadim's accounts of his earlier life, his thumbnail sketch of his White Russian father who had had a hard time maintaining himself as an exile in Paris, playing the piano in night clubs and less savoury establishments until he married a French woman, took French nationality and managed to obtain some minor consular appointments which took him, his wife, Vadim and a younger sister to Egypt and Turkey. Back in France, Vadim, just turned eight, had seen his father collapse over the breakfast table and die.

Vadim made it sound tremendously exciting and adventurous, peppering his tale with spicy incidents such as the occasion when he and his sister were kidnapped in Turkey – they were released unharmed without payment of ransom which his father could not have afforded anyway. There was his mother's struggle to provide for her children, their move to the South of France where they lived way beyond their means until Vadim, still in his teens, struck out on his own in Paris, none too successfully, he admitted. Fringe journalism, odd jobs for film men, always working on scripts and novels. Brigitte was transported into another world – her parents soon realised that she was hopelessly in love with Vadim (and he with her).

Pilou's angry disapproval of her young man could not break the spell. It made Brigitte unhappy, rebellious and resentful of the atmosphere of reproach which pervaded her home. Almost every day, she left school before the end of the last lesson to meet Vadim and was often late for dancing classes. Making her weary way home, she could see Pilou looking out from the balcony across the intersection of the rue de la Pompe and the avenue Paul Doumer to see whether her boy-friend, 'that dreadful Vadim,' accompanied her home. Brigitte suffered; 'I cried oceans,' she said later. She cried in school, cried even while dancing, much to the disgust of her teacher who tried in vain to conjure up the dancer's obligatory smile on the lips of his talented pupil. The tiresome rashes disfigured her face. Arguments about Vadim poisoned her relations with her parents although she was generally fond of them. She was getting desperate. To pacify her, Pilou relented as far as to permit Vadim to come to the apartment and even take her to the cinema chaperoned by Mijanou who often sneaked on big sister: 'Vadim kissed Bardot in the Métro.' It sparked off more rows.

Had the irate father known how much farther Brigitte and Vadim had already gone he would not have contained himself; as it was the explosion could not be long delayed. Vadim moved from the Gélin home to a furnished room of his own in the Quai d'Orléans overlooking the Ile Saint Louis. Brigitte was a regular visitor and, when her parents went to the country for their ritual weekends, spent the odd night with her lover. 'One day in paradise,' says the poet, 'is not too dearly paid for with eternal night!' Brigitte reversed the line – for her, Vadim recalled, one night was worth a lifetime. 'What was the best day in your life?' she was asked at a later stage. 'It was a night,' she answered without a moment's hesitation. What marred their togetherness was Brigitte's nerves, the tension, her fear of discovery and more quarrels at home, her father's threats not to let her see Vadim again. The walls of her home closed in on her as if it were a prison. Vadim's dingy little room spelled freedom.

When she and Vadim were apart she dreamt of escape, spent much of her time in her room writing him letters which laid her tortured soul bare. They were passionate, erotic beyond the average teenager's sexual fantasies. (All her life she has found release in writing: 'Her love letters are literary masterpieces,' Gunter Sachs told me.) She signed her epistles to Vadim 'Your little Sophie', to identify with the heroine of his novel. Totty knew instinctively that her daughter was Vadim's mistress but would rather bite off her tongue than rouse her irascible husband. She had good reason to keep quiet. Pilou, at first only dimly aware of what was going on, soon came to suspect the worst. One morning he stormed into Brigitte's room brandishing a revolver: 'If Vadim has seduced you, I shall kill him!' he screamed. Brigitte was terrified. She sought refuge with her mother who questioned her closely about her relationship with Vadim. Brigitte lied bravely: 'I'm innocent, I am not his mistress!' Dutifully Totty played the heavy mother: 'If you were stupid enough to do such a thing and your father did have the courage to kill Vadim, I would do it myself.' In her heart she knew it was too late.

No stranger to melodramatics himself and often flirting with death, Vadim, if anything, made Brigitte feel even worse. Pilou's threats were fuel for his morbid thoughts which communicated themselves to his youthful paramour – Brigitte was not even sixteen – until her despairing pursuit of happiness became a race with death. Ahead of her time, she was liberated in the sense of the seventies but thought that the prize of liberation was – a man. If she could not have Vadim, life was not worth living. Still, her parents would not allow her and Vadim to become engaged – why, the man did not even have a job, had no fixed income, no means of support, no future.

Vadim was actually no longer the no-hoper his ragged appearance suggested. Recognising his potential, Marc Allegret drew him ever closer into his orbit, even took him to London to work with him on a film (*Blanche Fury*) and kept him busy with other projects. While it did not impress the Bardots, the storming passion and growing distress of their daughter forced them to retreat. When Brigitte, day after day, repeated her plea to be allowed to marry, Pilou and Totty established a new line of defence: 'Not before you have your baccalauréat!' or, 'Not until you are at least eighteen.' By that time, they hoped, this absurd infatuation would have abated. Brigitte was not appeased. To her, eighteen months seemed an eternity; two years meant never.

To Vadim she still seemed child-like with a child's mentality, but she was very much a young woman. She no longer found solace in dancing and, looking for an excuse to hang up her slippers, measured her budding breasts and decided that she was getting too top-heavy to make it as a ballerina. Her rounded bosom and the hour-glass waist with the long legs added up to a delightful figure oozing sex; sadness gave her eyes a soulful dimension, an irresistible mixture. She could not pursue her dancing career, anyway, because it would keep her away from Vadim.

As the months went by slowly, tortuously, almost unbearably, Brigitte deteriorated. The recurring eruptions on her skin testified to her tortured mind. Every week brought a new confrontation at home. When Marc Allegret asked Vadim to go to England with him again, Vadim pleaded with the Bardots to let Brigitte come along but they refused. After the brief separation Vadim came up with an even more disturbing plan. He had decided to escape from the distractions of Paris and go to the South of France to write in peace. They had a tearful farewell and he went off accompanied by the haunting memory of the utter despair in Brigitte's moist eyes.

That evening the Bardots went for a drive around Paris to see the illuminations which signalled the city's return to business and pleasure as usual. When Brigitte, not for the first time, refused to join the family outing, Totty thought no more about it. As soon as she, Pilou and Mijanou had left, Brigitte sat down and wrote a brief note addressed to her parents. Life was intolerable, she wrote, she did not want to go on. She put the tear-stained letter on the kitchen table, turned on the gas stove, knelt down and put her head into the oven. She soon lost consciousness.

The tragedy of the vibrant, talented, attractive girl driven to this act of desperation, some of her friends felt, was compounded by the self-serving reactions of those around her. Although the Bardots had gone off quite cheerfully, Totty, as she later explained to an interviewer, had 'a maternal presentiment' and decided to return home. Another explanation put forward was that Mijanou, shivering in the evening cold, had asked to be driven back to collect a coat (or, alternatively, a scarf). Vadim, at the same time, was in the train 'full of misgivings' and haunted by Brigitte's eyes which, he later thought, had tried to tell him that she was at the end of her tether. He almost left the train, he said, at the first stop but only 'almost'. He had not yet, as he put it, learned to recognise the instinctive feeling which later told him whenever Brigitte was in serious danger.

As Vadim steamed on, the Bardots returned to the apartment where they found Brigitte lifeless on the kitchen floor. They called a doctor who administered oxygen and revived the hapless girl. Pilou and Totty were as puzzled as they were perturbed by Brigitte's behaviour in the wake of her traumatic experience. She seemed withdrawn and apathetic. Was she now reconciled to waiting until she could marry Vadim at eighteen? The suicide attempt left a deep wound on her mind. Vadim, too, found her a changed person and felt that she had lost some of her vitality; others thought that suffering had given her greater depth.

What is certain is that the tragic incident deepened her spirit of rebellion against the antiquated moral standards her parents tried to impose on her. Father was the chief culprit yet, strangely, dutiful respect for her parents was so strongly ingrained in her that she bore him no grudge. The target for her rebellion was his philosophy and morality which she blamed for her predicament. Her attitude to sex appears in this light as a personal revolution against authoritarian bourgeois oppression. 'Vadim took me out of my bourgeois prison,' she said looking back on this sad phase in her young life. Once free of her parents, she would live by her own rules. She would be married – to Vadim, of course – but would not allow marriage to dominate her any more than the parental home.

Vadim, too, felt that Brigitte's tragedy had accomplished something – it had broken down the last barrier to her happiness with him, and she could look forward to a new chapter in her life. For a man with a Bohemian reputation, his reaction was nothing but practical. At last the road into the future was wide open. There was no time to lose. Although she was less than enthusiastic, he pressed Brigitte to launch out on her acting career at once. He felt her vibrations so powerfully, he never doubted for a moment that others would come to see her as he did. To begin with he enrolled her in René Simon's drama school to which film scouts often turned in search of new talent. Wherever he went, Vadim talked about this gorgeous, inspired creature who would soon become his bride, and saw to it that film people who mattered became familiar with her name.

Gallantly, he later insisted that Brigitte had made it all on her own – the only assignment actually that came her way was to pose, reluctantly it seemed, for photographer Alexandre Choura for vacuum cleaner and electric shaver advertisements which appeared a few times in the press but were kept under wraps until they surfaced again twenty years later. In the face of evidence to the contrary, Vadim dismissed suggestions that he had been hawking Marc Allegret's test film of Brigitte around until one director – Jean Boyer – caught Brigitte's spark. Boyer was mounting the production of a film entitled *Le Trou Normand*, the name of a village inn. Vadim took him to see Brigitte at drama school, and Boyer promptly offered her the part of a young girl caught up in an intrigue about the ownership of the inn who, in the end, leaves the village to take up an acting career. Brigitte's reward was modest, some £300, but it was a role which would enable her to be almost herself. Since Vadim was in favour, she accepted. Her parents no longer dared to interfere.

Without any practical experience, the apprentice actress naively expected that all she would have to do was to walk in front of the camera, speak her lines and act her scene. But once shooting started she found the technicalities of film making utterly uncongenial. Most of her time on the set was spent standing in the wings. Waiting, waiting, waiting. Snatches of dialogue cut off in mid-emotion, repeating each scene once, twice, three times until she was drained of all feelings. Although she played herself, it was difficult to get into the mood, frustrating to have to switch off again and recreate the atmosphere after every interruption. She was bored, tired, not herself which was the greatest loss. She felt she was not doing her best, not performing as well as she could, not looking as good as she would have liked – it was the same with every film she was to make.

Le Trou Normand was a minor venture which made no great

impact but the critics liked the newcomer. The film had a brier run in France, was not shown in Britain, and imported into the United States only when Bardot became a star and a phenomenon no longer judged by ordinary standards. The favourable critical reaction enabled Vadim to get Brigitte another engagement almost immediately. It was the leading part in the film *Manina, la Fille Sans Voile* – and veilless is how she appeared in it. Pilou, who had watched his daughter's progress as a film star with growing misgivings, demanded the right to see and censor the film. He objected violently to a brief scene in which Brigitte appeared in the nude and threatened to sue the producers. Although they made a few small cuts to gain his grudging approval, he was the loser. While the devil in the guise of Mephisto in Goethe's *Faust* described himself as the force that always wills the evil and always creates the good, Pilou willed the good and created the evil he hated.

IV

The Making of Madame Plemiannikov

The first time I heard of Vadim was in the autumn of 1952 when his name cropped up in a small Paris bistro where I spent some evenings with Jean Roy and David Seymour, both established photographers closely associated with *Paris Match*. Among the young writers on the magazine with whom Jean and David had dealings and drinks was Roger Vadim, but neither they nor I knew that he had joined *Paris Match* only because Monsieur Louis Bardot would not let him marry his daughter unless he took up regular work. The magazine paid Vadim some £80 a month, not a princely salary but, then, jobs were easy to come by. Pilou also instructed Vadim to transfer from the Orthodox Church to the Roman Catholic faith. Vadim would not let such minor obstacles stand in the way of Brigitte's happiness.

He might not have attracted much attention among his eminent colleagues on the magazine had he not been talking so persistently and persuasively about Brigitte Bardot, his protégée – fiancée was not a word to bandy about in such company – whom he described as a phenomenally handsome, exquisitely talented young dancer and actress. Brigitte's photographs, which he produced on every possible occasion like a conjurer drawing a rabbit from his hat, bore him out. To the expert eye of his friends, the face in the photographs exuded a magnetism which belied sour comments (made at a later stage) that it was fame which made Bardot attractive and not her attraction which made her famous. The pictures reflected her provocative instincts but little of the vaunted 'innocence' on which Vadim harped incessantly to heighten the impact. At best it was provocative innocence, the lure of a Lolita.

Once Vadim had become a Catholic and a wage earner (his job with *Paris Match* lasted fully three months), and as soon as

Brigitte reached her eighteenth birthday on 28 September 1952, Pilou and Totty resigned themselves to the inevitable. They bought or, according to Vadim, lent the young couple a small flat in the rue Chardon-Lagache which was still without furniture and fittings three months later when, on 20 December, Roger Vladimir Plemiannikov and his bride came together on the steps of the Town Hall of the sixteenth arrondissement, at the corner of the avenue Henri Martin and rue de la Pompe, just down the road from the home of the Bardots.

Throughout the wedding formalities Brigitte was giggling because the mayoress who conducted the ceremony sounded stilted and pompous, extolling the marriage as a symbol of Franco-Russian friendship; Brigitte saw her father getting redder and redder in the face with rage – rage and Pilou went together even on such a joyous occasion. What infuriated him was the implication that his daughter was marrying a Russian. Then the mayoress pronounced Brigitte and Vadim Monsieur and Madame Plemiannikov.

A few weeks later, Vadim told friends the story of his wedding night. Because the new apartment in the rue Chardon-Lagache was still unfurnished, it was arranged for him and Brigitte to spend the night with her parents. The newly-weds were about to bed down together in Brigitte's room when Pilou appeared and ordered his son-in-law to the dining-room where a camp bed had been made up for up for him. Until next day's church ceremony, Brigitte was not married in his eyes. Although she was livid, wanted to up and move to a hotel at once, Vadim persuaded her to let her exasperating father have his way. Next morning they travelled to Auteuil where the marriage was consecrated in church with Marc Allegret as Vadim's best man. 'After God had given us His blessing,' Vadim recalled, 'M. Bardot added his.'

A brief honeymoon in the French Alps – Brigitte loved winter-sports and still spends most winters at Le Chouan, her chalet at Meribel – the Vadims moved into their apartment although it lacked the basic ingredients of a home. As there was no bed they slept on a mattress on the floor. Much of the new Madame

Plemiannikov's time in the next weeks and months was spent scouting around for cheap, second-hand chests, tables, chairs, curtains. She settled down to a dreary routine, went shopping at local stores like a good housewife. From the kitchen where she was struggling to concoct simple meals – within the range of her very limited ability – she kept an eye on her husband hoping to catch a sign of appreciation. It did not materialise. All this domesticity! Her preoccupation with menial chores went against Vadim's grain. This was not the Brigitte Bardot he was interested in – Bette Davis, it so happens, had a similar problem with her husbands; and Marlene Dietrich drove some of her admirers to distraction with her *Hausfrau* habits.

Soon, and ever more frequently, Brigitte admitted defeat at kitchen stove and sink and demanded to be taken out to dinner – she still prefers restaurants to home cooking. To save her embarrassment, Vadim went with her on the town even when he would have preferred a quiet evening at home, food or no food. All the while his disenchantment grew apace with her almost maniacal emotional dependence on him and his approval. In the event he said, politely using the plural 'we' although it was largely he, 'we were exhausted' by the years of waiting, and drained by the protracted effort to break down Pilou's resistance. But if victory in the battle to conquer Brigitte as a wife seemed empty, control of BB as a star of the future made it all worth while.

For her part, Brigitte gave little thought to her career, could not be bothered to worry about the next day, far less about the more distant future. Her notion of marriage was simplistic. She was desperately in love and love was all that mattered. She wanted her man around morning, noon and night, and, as Vadim claimed, was upset if he let on that she did not always shine in his dreams. As so much in Brigitte's life, this was a passing phase – difficult to fix the time-span reliably – of no more than nine to twelve months. Gradually, her storming love gave way to doubt, impatience, restlessness. When she confessed a little later that as a lover her husband had not lived up to her expectations, her comment seems to have been about quantity rather than quality, but she was probably to blame for word getting around that Vadim, who fascinated women as few other men, was 'a lousy lover.' Vadim's friends retorted that Brigitte was to blame on all counts – she had been far too demanding until she suddenly lost interest.

One way or another, as so often happens, the marriage was no sooner properly consummated than it began to lose its momentum. Another element contributed to Brigitte's discomfiture and confronted her with a dilemma which recurred in various forms to plague her. Instead of craving a father figure as so many young girls, she was, for some time to come, attracted by men who were the opposite of Pilou – Bohemian, casual, unsteady, unpredictable, uninhibited by preconceived notions, sexually lax, even promiscuous. Vadim, however, insists that he was never unfaithful to his young wife, even when, a couple of years later in Rome, he and Brigitte shared a bed with Ursula Andress all three of them naked; he did not touch the other girl, whatever the rumours which followed the appearance of the trio, still totally unclothed, on the balcony.

While Vadim eminently fitted her specifications, Brigitte's unorthodox inclinations were at odds with her bourgeois background which still influenced her strongly and which, except in sexual matters, she could never gainsay. More frequently than she would admit to herself she reverted to Pilou's type. Money was a case in point. While Vadim was indifferent to money and cared little about earthly goods, she hoarded every sou with excessive bourgeois thrift except for brief bursts of incongruous silliness when she spent a small fortune on taxis to hunt down a bargain that saved her a few francs.

Vadim was gloomy by nature and irritated by Brigitte's craving for perpetual happiness. Constantly pondering the darker side of life, he was blinded when his young wife pulled back the curtains expecting twenty-four hours of sunshine. He could not, would not live up to it. The honeymoon was lasting too long, and when Vadim's clouds obscured her sun, she held him responsible if she shivered in the cold. In spirit she was already off in search of a partner with a sunnier outlook who measured up to her ideal and could provide her with instant and constant bliss. Having changed after her abortive suicide attempt, she changed again after – what turned out to be in the end – her abortive marriage.

The collision of two such diverse characters set complicated psychological processes in motion. There is little doubt that Vadim's failure to sustain admiration for Brigitte for days and nights on end intensified her inferiority complex which affected every move she made. Not that he was immune to her charms – quite the reverse – but he expected her to take his feelings for granted. She did not. If she could not seduce him with her body three times a day, she would flaunt it at every opportunity before others and harvest the adulation she craved.

Thus, while it is the received wisdom among analysts of the Bardot phenomenon that Vadim exploited her body for professional purposes and incited her to orgies of nudity on the screen as if he had unfrocked an unwilling disciple, Brigitte's own exhibitionism has been played down. Very frequently it was she who was anxious to show off her stunning physical assets. Vadim could only be blamed because what happened – or did not happen – between them at home intensified their quest to find satisfaction elsewhere. It was not so much a matter of Vadim, the Devil, leading her astray as of Brigitte, the Eve, forever offering the apple of temptation to all who cared to take a bite.

This does not mean that Brigitte's exhibitionism did not suit Vadim's artistic and commercial objectives. It was marketable, enhanced her prospects. While lackadaisical in his sexual efforts, he was indefatigable when it became a matter of advancing her career. Even when they were alone, he never stopped for a moment directing, correcting, advising, motivating her, channelling her sexuality into patterns which producers and directors treasured as a rare asset. To capitalise on that breathtakingly graceful walk, to exploit that adorable craned neck, to suggest heaven and hell with those expressive limbs, to lure every man with heavy lids opening tantalisingly slowly to reveal the magnetic eyes. . . . The basic material was hers, of course, nature's gift, but it was put together and packaged by Vadim.

The marriage did not go smoothly. They rowed and they loved with wild abandon, often at the same time. They fought like cats – there is something feline about Vadim's masculinity. They sulked and made up and fell out again. It was hectic at all times, Brigitte rising from deep gorges of despair to high plateaux of delirious pleasure only to end up in the dumps again. Brigitte's marital duties still included providing treatment for Vadim's various ills. To cure his backache – slipped disc? – she acted as her husband's unqualified osteopath and manipulated his vertebrae into position by standing on his back as he lay prone on the floor. I would not have believed this tale had not Donald Zec, the popular film writer, described for me how, some years later, arriving for dinner and an interview at Vadim's home, he watched Vadim's third wife, Jane Fonda, performing the same medical service for her suffering spouse.

As to Vadim and Brigitte the signs were on the wall although Vadim continued to plan, plot and scheme to promote the fledgling star. With a journalist's knack which he acquired during his brief fling with the profession, he used every trick of the trade to convert the smallest item of interest into the biggest number of column inches in the press. He promptly leaked Pilou's outburst against *Manina* and his threats to sue the producers. Brigitte's reputation as a daring hussy prepared to show cinema audiences more of a woman's body than they had hitherto been allowed to see was quickly established; it was many years before Vadim bothered to defend himself against the accusation that he had been hawking her body around (with all manner of innuendo). Yet he did see her as a temptress and a tease. His formula for Brigitte was: 'You are going to be the respectable married man's unattainable dream.'

There was as yet not much chance of married men, other than Vadim himself, dreaming of BB. Few even knew that she existed. She did not make much of an impact in her next film, *Les Dents Longues*, except for her own teeth, long since released from the firm brace, causing that provocative, suggestive pout. *Les Dents Longues* was largely a one-man, family effort by Daniel Gélin who wrote the script, directed and played the lead opposite his wife Danièle Delorme. Brigitte's appearance was fleeting, her partner in the brief scene – Roger Vadim.

Not much luck either with her next assignment, a slightly bigger role in a farce, *Le Portrait de Son Père*. What made these two forgettable endeavours worth while was the opportunity they gave Vadim to rehearse his wife in the arts and crafts in which he had instructed her before the directors took over. Brigitte's contribution to the second film was noteworthy only because it did not require her to show off her body which remained virtually unnoticed. The year was 1953. Beyond the circle of her friends, Brigitte was as yet undiscovered.

Withal, two more parts had already been lined up for her by the determined Vadim who was also busy with enterprises of his own so that the couple spent less time together than was good for their tenuous marriage. If the new films did not augur too well for the young starlet, *Act of Love* was at least produced by Anatole Litvak, connoisseur of sexy starlets who would not have overlooked Bardot even if she had not been cunningly manipulated into his presence. Though Brigitte's part was again miniscule, Litvak's French-American co-production (released by United Artists) was the big time. Script writer Irwin Shaw, well in with Vadim's journalistic friends, soon went on to greater things. Brigitte's contemporary, Dany Robin, was in the cast which included Kirk Douglas, American heart-throb and the first international star to cross her path. 'I was nervous at first,' she said later, but it was she who made Kirk Douglas nervous and rather angry before long.

Had it not been for Kirk Douglas receiving an invitation to the Cannes Film Festival of 1953, the annual gathering of the international film clans would have been beyond Brigitte's reach. But Vadim was alert to the opportunities the festival offered to an aspiring young actress and when the Litvak-United Artists publicity department put up funds for a few minor members of the cast to accompany the star, he made sure that Brigitte was one of those chosen. At worst she would enjoy a few days at the beach and at the Carlton Hotel where, in the trade's jargon, it all happened.

Accompanied by Vadim, she travelled to the South of France only vaguely aware that, two years earlier, Pier Angeli had been propelled to stardom – and into Kirk Douglas' arms – by the flash-lights of a hundred photographers at Cannes; and that, at the previous year's festival, another Italian pin-up with the tongue-twisting name of Gina Lollobrigida, completely unknown outside her own country, had found similar favour with the media and been instantly engaged to star in an American film with Humphrey Bogart, Jennifer Jones and Kirk Douglas. Could lightning strike three times?

Vadim promptly went to work on his journalist friends showing them photographs of his protégée only a husband could have taken in those days and hinting broadly (Tony Crawley reports) that there were more in his 'strictly private' collection and even these were nothing compared to seeing her in motion. They took the hint and found Brigitte quite as attractive as Vadim had promised. According to a story which probably originated in Vadim's fertile imagination, Brigitte told the photographers that she could not afford to stay much longer whereupon they clubbed together and paid her room at the Carlton for another week. A likely tale! The cameraman with whom I was in Cannes took scores of pictures of Bardot but did not part with a single franc.

'And now . . .' wrote Leonard Mosley, one of Britain's leading film writers at the festival, 'and now watch what happens to a French girl called Brigitte Bardot!' What happened was that the US Navy appeared off-shore in the magnificant shape of the aircraft carrier *Midway* to show the flag where it could not be missed, and to play host to the world's best-known film stars. On the appointed day, they were wolf-whistled aboard the imposing carrier by pop-eyed sailors, their noisiest cheers greeting the busty Lana Turner, the delicately beautiful Olivia de Havilland, the dainty Leslie Caron and the aggressively sexy Sylvana Mangano, with less raucous clapping reserved for mere males such as Edward G. Robinson, Mel Ferrer, Gary Cooper and Kirk Douglas.

Promenading on deck in their finery, smiling their widest smiles, gesticulating prettily in the direction of the lenses, the stars were girding themselves for the traditional the assualt by the cameras. Instead, incredibly, the photographers slunk away, slowly at first, one by one, turned their backs on the galaxy of stars, came together in a tight phalanx and, accelerating and rudely pushing through the throng, homed in commando-like on a slip of a girl in a raincoat. Self-confident and perfectly composed she let the raincoat slip from her shoulders, tossed back her head and sent her pony-tail flying, revealing a little-girl outfit fit to burst and drawing the cameras towards her like an irresistible magnet.

All eyes were on her. Flashlights exploded, shutters clicked accompanied by exclamations which sounded like mating cries. Bewildered onlookers did not know her name but soon took up the photographers' chant: 'Brigitte! Brigitte!' It was Brigitte and no one else. Kirk Douglas was upset because they would not take his picture until he joined her on the beach. Next day her face and figure covered the front pages of magazines and newspapers around the world. Brigitte Bardot had arrived.

V

Brigitte's Dolce Vita

Rome was the city of the hour epitomising post-war morals run riot. Reckless, often murderous sex, drink and drug orgies were the pastime of international playboys, impoverished Italian aristocrats, high-class prostitutes and aspiring starlets who congregated in the cafés and hotels of the Via Veneto. This was the *dolce vita* which was rampant long before the film with that title starring the voluptuous Anita Ekberg made it notorious.

Brigitte Bardot, at twenty, would have been insensitive and ignorant of the gossip among the film fraternity had she not felt the vibrations of Rome's highly-charged atmosphere. With a thriving film industry, the Italian capital was also the habitat of the screen's current sex goddesses, Sophia Loren and Gina Lollobrigida. While Hollywood was a distant dream, Rome was easily within reach.

A few feet of celluloid with Brigitte's image were already in the can, a tiny part in *Si Versailles M'Etait Conté* which she had completed before her stunning impact on Cannes. It was just as well that the film was not yet on show because, publicity being the life-blood of the film industry, her pictures in the papers were a better advertisement than her pale performance in a minor movie, albeit one scripted and directed by her venerable compatriot Sacha Guitry who also played the lead as Louis XIV.

It was inevitable that the new glamour girl who had electrified the mediocre film festival should be invited to perform in Europe's sex capital. The Italian film in which Brigitte was cast in a slightly bigger role was *Tradità* and another part was quickly lined up for her. In *Helen of Troy* she was cast not in the title role of the most beautiful woman in antiquity (that went to Rosanna Podesta) but as Helen's slave and companion, Andraste. Warner Brothers who produced and Robert Wise who directed must have caught some of Brigitte's sensuous signals because they seriously considered giving her Rosanna's part, but the groundwork for the project was too advanced to permit the change. Brigitte had to content herself with the compliment that she had almost stolen the show from the star.

Small parts, small rewards. Not for Brigitte the smart and fashionable Excelsior. She could only afford a smaller hotel sharing a room with seventeen-year-old Ursula Andress who had run away from boarding school to be with her lover, Daniel Gélin. From time to time, Vadim managed to join them in Rome where the two couples, Brigitte and Vadim, Ursula and Daniel, indulged in a fringe *dolce vita* of their own although we have Vadim's word for it that it was all harmless fun with both men keeping their hands off each other's girls.

But attractive young women in Rome could not parade in the nude without their sex life coming under close scrutiny. Men with intimate knowledge of Brigitte's preferences – quite a number of them not too discreet – bore out Vadim's contention that there was less to it than met the eye, and this remained basically true for some time. Free as Brigitte came to be with her favours, rapidly as she changed her paramours, her *modus operandi* could be described as 'one at a time.' For all her uninhibited love-making which agitated male minds and incited women's anger and envy, Brigitte had no orgiastic ambitions. Two, even three men may have stimulated her in any one phase, she may have flirted from one to the other the same day or night, but it was always a case of playing one off against the other rather than sharing her bed with more than one man or woman at any one time.

While Brigitte and Ursula sauntered around Rome, Vadim may have had cause for complaint but could console himself with the prospect that, whatever happened behind his back, Brigitte would return to him – at least for a while. She still needed him, his moral support, his advice, his approval. She needed constant reassurance. Vadim watched her scrutinising her face in the mirror, saw her getting more and more distressed. There were tears in her eyes as she examined her features – her mouth with the 'swollen lower lip' was not good, her nose tended to wrinkle up (most attractively, incidentally), nothing was right. Vadim tried to still her tears. His love for her was intense though much of it was infatuation of the artist with his raw material, an actor's love of Shakespeare or a painter's total preoccupation with his colours. His masterpiece was beginning to emerge and prospects for Brigitte, thanks to Cannes, looked better and better.

Having made an impression in her eighth film, *Le Fils de Caroline Chérie*, Brigitte was obviously a star of the future; and it so happened that Vadim was working with Marc Allegret on a script (based on a novel by Vicky Baum of *Grand Hotel* fame) which they proposed to call *Futures Vedettes*. That the principal character was 'Sophie' – the name of the heroine in his early novel which Brigitte had adopted – reflected his thinking. Marc Allegret, regretting his early indifference to Brigitte's appeal, persuaded himself that she had matured in the intervening years and was not only most promising but the best available star for his new picture.

The story with a musical background was set in Vienna, Vicky Baum's home town. Brigitte was with Vadim while he worked. She talked, he listened and wrote with the result that the script profited from Vadim's sensitive ear for her natural mode of expression. Once in the studio, it made her job easier because Vadim's lines were simply an echo of her conversation. Gallantly he gave her generous credit for her help in writing the dialogue. There was the obligatory nude scene with Brigitte taking a bath in a tub filled with goldfish, her body as scintillating as theirs.

Her *joie de vivre* in this scene was infectious but upset some people and earned Vadim angry reproaches. Sharing his wife unwittingly with one or two men was one thing but putting her on view for millions was a different matter. Isabella Pia, in a minor role, was the first girl cast alongside Brigitte in a part which suggested a possible lesbian relationship. A trail laid by Vadim, it was cunningly sustained in subsequent films and, as

Brigitte became identified with her fictional characters, the suspicion rubbed off on her. Since the legend of Brigitte excluded no sexual permutation, people assumed quite wrongly that she was bisexual. At the time it was thought that Vadim's purpose in promoting such exhibitions and contingencies was to impress the American market, but when Hollywood eventually called Brigitte did not want the American machine to turn her into another stereotyped glamour girl.

With her much-noticed recent performance to strengthen his hand, Vadim's publicity drums pounded out the message of her remarkable gifts and natural assets. They could be heard in London and were supported by Brigitte's photographs in French film publications. They impressed Betty Box, the British producer who had been watching Brigitte for some time and failed to get her for one of her films (*A Day to Remember*). Betty was preparing a new film, *Doctor at Sea*, a sequel to *Doctor in the House*, director Ralph Thomas, male lead Dirk Bogarde. She offered the part of a handsome young cabaret singer to the luminous Kay Kendall, forever associated with the delightful *Genevieve*, but Kay declined and Betty decided to make another approach to Brigitte Bardot.

This time she was successful. While still reluctant to cross the Atlantic at any price, Brigitte heeded the call from the other side of the English Channel because Dirk Bogarde appealed to her as an actor and as a man. But would she appeal to him? Since his contract gave him the right to approve or reject the leading lady, he flew to Paris to meet Brigitte, liked what he saw and enthused about 'her superb figure, her long legs, her flowing hair and gazelle-like grace.' Her kind of sex, he thought, unlike that of British girls who projected sex as farce, was 'warm, uninhibited, completely natural,' high praise indeed from a man who was not noted for his interest in women. Brigitte was hired.

The horde of photographers who greeted her in London was bowled over by her *je ne sais quoi* – the mysterious X-factor which set her apart. There was a suggestion that the combination of her perfume and her body's erotic emanations was positively aphrodisiac but the myth was never tested. She was undoubtedly one of those personalities who made people turn their heads when they entered a room but, given her looks, this was not really surprising. In spite of her intelligence, Brigitte loyally obeyed Vadim's instructions to act 'the dumb blonde.' If Marilyn Monroe could make such milage with her answer to the question of what she wore in bed – 'Chanel Number Five' – Brigitte could match her. Asked what kind of clothes she had brought along she replied disingenuously: 'several nightdresses because I hope someone will take me out.' Whatever she said – in basic but passable English – was enhanced by her French accent which sounded highly suggestive to English ears. The total effect was, as the French say, *formidable*.

B and B (Bogarde and Bardot) worked well together; his English manliness (in the part of a ship's doctor) gelled with her French femininity (in the role of the cabaret singer), although she did not quite stay the course with Bogarde who became irritated with her seductive approaches. Years later, in fact, Brigitte said, 'Bogarde hates me;' Bogarde did not hate her, he just did not want her. Every other man at Pinewood Studios appreciated her, however. The men on the set, and there were always twice as many as seemed necessary, followed her every move waiting for her to live up to her reputation. They were rewarded when it came to the scene in which 'Doctor' Bogarde walked in on her as she was taking a shower.

This was the moment the men had been waiting for and Brigitte did not disappoint them. Unlike other stars who would have asked for the set to be cleared of all but a skeleton camera crew when they had to perform in bras and pants, Brigitte made no such request. Since she was to be photographed through a transparent plastic curtain, her wardrobe mistress covered her nipples with plaster and applied an elaborate cover-up for her pubic hair. A protective undergarment was produced but the complicated camouflage threatened to ruin the effect of the scene. While Ralph Thomas and Betty Box were still discussing ways and means of preserving the impression that Brigitte was in the nude, she briskly discarded all the protective covering and presented herself to the camera crew and a dozen or more open-mouthed studio hands in her full natural glory. What a revelation, what a delight! By today's standards, it was still a restrained, almost decorous performance.

The film was greeted with much acclaim by Leonard Mosley ('Look what happened to the little girl I found on the beach!') whose clarion call from Cannes two and a half years earlier still echoed in many memories. Like other critics, he took a poor view of the film but stressed that Brigitte's 'humming-bird personality had scored a triumph of sheer charm over a bad script.' The public agreed and expressed Vadim-inspired sobriquets for Bardot: 'modern Venus de Milo,' 'twentieth-century Juno,' 'gorgeous Pekinese.' Girls compared their measurements with hers which, rendered in inches, were 34–20–34. It was not long before they copied her hair style, affected a pout and moved slinkily in the Bardot manner, until Brigitte said she was fed up seeing Bardots all over the place. In the meantime, her curves were prominently displayed on the covers of English, German, Italian and American magazines. However mediocre the film, it marked a turning point for her. *Doctor at Sea* made her an international star.

Because my ear was close to the journalistic grapevine in London, I was privy to the nudge-nudge whispers about Brigitte's private life after lights out at Pinewood. She was rarely to be found at her local hotel. Each morning envious eyes were scrutinising the male scene to discover who might have spent the night with her. With Vadim tied to Paris by his own business, she may have sought consolation with other partners but I doubt whether her love-life was as hyper-active as it was thought to be – she excited the imagination of non-starters even more than the ardour of the participants in her sex games. According to Peter Evans, diligent chronicler of her exploits, Brigitte asked Betty Box: 'What is the matter with British boys? They don't make love?' Ralph Thomas corrected: 'She said *can't* make love.' It was suggested that Brigitte's preference for garlic-stuffed dishes like rustic omelette was responsible for the low performance of her English partners on whom her garlic breath may not have had the same aphrodisiac effect as it apparently had on French men.

She was still in need of Vadim, if not in bed then as her confidant and adviser. Two or three times the pull was so strong that she flew to Paris to be with him for a few hours. They were together in their home on 18 June 1953, but Vadim and his friends were preoccupied. In the United States, Julius and Ethel Rosenberg, convicted as spies and sentenced to death in 1951, were due to be executed. Left-wingers and liberals all over the world camapaigned to save them from the electric chair, some because they were in sympathy with the Soviets, others because they opposed capital punishment. Vadim and his friends were hotly debating what could be done to save the life of the American couple at the eleventh hour. They wrote fiery articles without any chance of them being published and scribbled slogans – 'Eisenhower assassin!' 'Save the Rosenbergs!' – on pieces of paper.

Brigitte listened avidly, getting emotionally more and more involved. Without examining the political implications, she felt a deep urge to save lives, even the lives of traitors. The Rosenbergs had to be saved! She gathered up the mini-leaflets and put them in her handbag. They were still talking about the Rosenbergs next morning when Vadim drove her to Orly airport to catch her plane to London. Carrying out a plan she had conceived in a sleepless night, Brigitte opened the car window and scattered the slogans along the route, hundreds of bits of paper: had the startled passers-by realised that the ardent campaigner was Brigitte Bardot, the response might have been stronger. She was back in London and on the Pinewood set when the news of the Rosenbergs' execution was announced. Her great humanitarian gesture had proved futile. She gritted her teeth and got on with her job.

Her English enterprise completed, Brigitte returned to Paris and to Vadim who latched on to the rumours that she had been disappointed with English men who had been neither skilled nor potent enough for her requirements and that frustration had only whipped up greater desire. Since she was most effective portraying characters with whom she could identify – playing herself – Vadim arranged for her to be cast in a role which neatly reproduced her experiences in England. The film was *La Lumière D'En Face* in which her part that of an over-sexed girl with an impotent husband. Such was the explosive sexuality of her performance that it could only have been the reflection of a deeply felt experience. To enable Brigitte to identify with her screen part, he named the principal character in their next film, *Cette Sacrée Gamine*, Brigitte.

Such parts were no longer hard to come by. René Clair engaged her for his first colour film, *Les Grandes Manoeuvres.* The impact Brigitte made was best explained by Alan Brien who wrote that she 'glows in the dark like an open stove' and, though now twenty-one, looked like a schoolgirl who had been in too many night clubs. She had oomph before she knew how to spell it and graduated from the sixth form with an X-certificate. The lens of the camera, Brien said, must have been shaped like a keyhole as it observed her standing against the strong light in a nylon nightie, washing her legs under the tap, bending over an ice-bucket in a loose blouse, and bathing naked in the river. In London, the film ran into trouble with a conservative local council. They were behind the times because the candid camera trail which Brigitte blazed led straight to the film of the future.

When producer Jacques Gauthier who had providentially obtained an option on Brigitte for two more films did not live to take it up, Ray Ventura, the astute entertainments entrepreneur, stepped in and, indirectly, influenced the next phase in Brigitte's life and career. Ventura was the link between Vadim and Raoul Lévy, the young producer who made her a superstar.

Brigitte was working non-stop. Without curtailing her busy private life, she flitted from one film to the next but always an hour or two behind the appointed time. She was a compulsive late-comer – it was arduous to rise early after an active night and desperately hard to overcome her chronic inferiority complex which stared back at her from the mirror every morning. Producers and directors coped as best they could with her idiosyncrasies and superstitions. She was demanding like a naughty child, her personality problem and star allure made her difficult to handle, but once she settled down to concentrated work, she was responsive, untiring and the delight of every box-office-conscious associate.

Her natural instinct for titillation was given free rein in such films as *En Effeuillant la Marguérite*. The production was a joint effort by an accomplished, familiar trio – director: Marc Allegret; script writer: Vadim; leading man: Daniel Gélin. Brigitte made 'plucking the daisy' appear like defloration. While affecting girlish innocence, she seemed to offer every man in the audience the '*droit de seigneur*' – the master's right to the first favour of every bride on his estate. The effect was heightened by Brigitte taking part in a strip-tease contest which was the story of her career. 'Offensive, immoral, shameless' were some of the censorious comments in Italy but more sophisticated British critics found the offering tame. Perhaps they were expecting Brigitte to do something really outrageous.

VI

Wiggling Her Way to Damnation

Brigitte's married life was a hotch-potch of contradictions. Vadim was brother, protector, mentor; he never stopped rehearsing her and making her work at her job. His presence was reassuring – being afraid of 'monsters' she would rather wait for him in the car while he was working than spend the evening alone at home. She wanted to hear him say that she was not ugly, that she was an able actress. When the tasks of daily life threatened to defeat her, he talked to her like the proverbial Dutch uncle.

Vadim as a husband, that was a different matter. Although he pretended to himself that his wife was faithful to him – and still insists that he was strictly monogamous – their sexuality drove them in opposite directions and created tensions which stretched their nerves to breaking point. When she railed at him about this, that and the other he withdrew into his shell. On the principle that it takes two to make a quarrel, Vadim, weary of arguing and fighting, let Brigitte's temperamental outbursts sweep over him without putting up a defence. Sometimes, his silence, his phlegm only went to inflame her even more, more often his patience was rewarded when her futile fury spent itself. Abandoning his brief journalistic career, he devoted himself exclusively to his great love, the cinema, which kept them together when he and Brigitte grew apart as lovers. Though as yet not aware of it, they were heading for a grandiose climax.

On a visit to the offices of Ray Ventura, bandleader turned impresario, they met the flamboyant, extravagant Raoul Lévy, a young man with enormous talent and a sad record of failure in the film industry. Enjoying the trappings of wealth – caviar, champagne, villas, yachts – but none of the substance, Levy was an indomitable character whose imagination was not always matched by the ability to translate his projects into something positive. Moving swiftly from an abortive venture to a new idea and impervious to rebuffs, he managed to rouse the interest of financiers again and again only to lose their confidence and go on to peddle his plans elsewhere. His last four projects had ended in disaster but his optimism was undiminished.

For Lévy and Vadim it was love at first sight. Vadim sensed a kindred spirit, detected a spark of genius below the surface and was not put off by Lévy's shaky reputation and lack of achievement. Brigitte embraced him no less enthusiastically. That Ray Ventura thought highly of him was an asset which Vadim proposed to exploit for the good of all three – Raoul, Brigitte and himself.

Lévy responded to Vadim as one ideas merchant to another. Looking from one to the other as they bounced their flashes of inspiration across the table like a couple of Chinese ping-pong players hitting the ball hard and fast, Brigitte was caught up in their game whether they played at home, at Lévy's place, in cafés, restaurants or in Ventura's office where their collaboration took on a more solid shape.

The first tangible result was an extraordinary project – there was not much more to it than Brigitte's body and Vadim's resolve to exploit it to greater effect than ever. An important ingredient was Raoul Lévy's unquenchable confidence that whatever it was that would eventually emerge would be good, very good indeed. The catch-words had not as yet been coined, yet if they had set out to promote a new concept of morality or immorality called 'permissive society' or, say, 'woman's liberation' they could not have gone about it in a more effective fashion. Since both Vadim and Lévy believed that publicity was creative, they announced their new film before they had a title, a script or a story line. All they were able to offer interested parties was Brigitte Bardot. She would be the star of their film although she was by no means an established star.

That even such nebulous exchanges between the two unorthodox talents were bearing fruit became apparent when – as they were still racking their brains for a commercial plot – Raoul Lévy recalled reading a newspaper story about a crime in a remote village involving three brothers and a beautiful girl. That was it! Without bothering to transplant the characters from the newspaper page to a film script, they decided on a plan of action as sweeping as their fertile minds could conceive. Large screen, of course; colour – *ça va sans dire*; novel angles; huge close-ups. It sounded fantastic. They settled on a location before they concerned themselves with more immediate prerequisites. Their choice fell on the fishing village of St Tropez which boasted a small colony of famous artists but none of the social glamour which it later acquired – largely as a result of this flippant decision of a couple of virtually unknown young dreamers.

There was one very obvious flaw: who would invest the considerable funds needed for a film without a plot or a star with marketable box-office appeal? The two comrades-in-arms were not bothered. How they went about obtaining the money, how they proceeded from dream to reality is the subject of several accounts as haphazard as the origins of the whole enterprise. Raoul Lévy (who blew his brains out several years later) is no longer around and Vadim relies on a memory that automatically transforms the most mundane real-life events into sequences worthy of a thriller.

One recent contribution to the saga has come from Curd Jurgens, the superstar of international renown without whom the project might not have materialised at all. Jurgens recalls meeting his French agent, Olga Horstig, for lunch at Fouquets in the Champs Elysées to sign a contract for a film she had negotiated for him. The formality completed between dessert and black coffee, Olga casually mentioned that she was expecting a client of hers, a very handsome young lady.... Acutely aware of his own reputation as an indefatigable ram, Jurgens thought he was being offered an easy lay: 'Thanks, Olga,' he said, 'I'm afraid my needs are catered for....'

As if on cue, at this very moment Brigitte Bardot appeared on the scene to join the tête-à-tête. Jurgens, as I mentioned earlier, was enchanted – Brigitte's walk, her skin, her soft breasts covered by a cashmere sweater which stimulated her nipples. He was still absorbed in contemplation of the lovely creature when Olga continued: 'Ray Ventura is preparing a picture in which she will play the lead. . . .' (Jurgens thinks Olga hinted that Brigitte had not been in a film before.) 'There isn't enough money,' she went on using her considerable powers of persuasion, 'but if you would take a part they could get a guarantee from a German distributor.' Shooting in St Tropez, studio at Nice – she made it sound very attractive.

All it needed was three weeks of Curd's time: 'Young Roger Vadim will direct and write a part specially for you,' she added.

'Send me the script to Bavaria,' Jurgens replied.

'It's here. You can take it with you.'

'And the name of the film?'

Jurgens seems to think he was told the title, *And Always the Woman Lures* (as the film was eventually called in Germany). He told Brigitte: 'You are very beautiful. I can well imagine that God thought of you when he created women' (a reference to the film's original French title).

'*Merci,* Curd,' said Brigitte distorting his German name with her French accent. As a farewell gesture, she brushed Curd's cheek with her lips – Brigitte is credited with having started the fad of theatrical people greeting each other with a kiss (even if they have never met before) which has since spread via the jet set to wider circles of European and American socialites.

Vadim's recollections are vastly different and even more colourful. They seem to suggest that he was unaware of the historic meeting between Curd Jurgens and Brigitte Bardot which is highly unlikely. As Vadim remembers, the telephone woke him in his Paris flat one morning at eight. Raoul Lévy was on the line: 'I'll meet you at ten-thirty at the Gare de l'Est,' Raoul said. They would be going to Munich together. Rubbing the sleep from his eyes, Vadim packed a bag and dashed off to meet his friend. Only when they were in the train did Raoul explain that the purpose of their trip was to book Curd Jurgens for their film: 'Columbia will give us the money to make it in Cinemascope and colour if we have Jurgens. . . .'

At Munich, the two hopefuls took a suite in the expensive Vierjahreszeiten Hotel – legend has since turned the suite into 'a whole floor' – and Lévy managed to get an appointment with Jurgens for the day after the next: 'You have forty-eight hours to write a part for Jurgens,' he told Vadim. To keep his associate at his typewriter, Lévy sent a mountain of caviar and bottles of vodka to his room and supplied a young lady by the name of Maria who made herself useful to Vadim in many ways and also typed his manuscripts. Jurgens was cast as the older man who comes upon the heroine in the very first shot when Brigitte would be seen lying on the beach in the nude. In later scenes she would appear in various stages of undress.

Being not only a first-rate actor but also a shrewd judge of dramatic possibilities, Jurgens was impressed by Vadim and his script. Although the part was small for a star of his calibre, and the script as yet incomplete, he accepted the proposition. He liked the prospect of working in the South of France and with Brigitte and signed the contract there and then.

When it was finally completed, Vadim's story revolved around Juliette, an eighteen-year-old girl, desired by all men in and around the coastal village where she lived. Unburdened by inhibitions – 'limited neither by morals nor social taboos,' as Vadim put it – she dallies with the three sons of a wealthy shipping magnate and their father, one of whose lines – 'That girl can drive men wild' – clung to Brigitte for all time. Vadim's title for the film was *Et Dieu Créa la Femme*, but less adventurous exhibitors in many countries decided to leave God out of the immoral happenings and change the title to *And Woman Was Created.*

Cast and production staff congregated in St Tropez where Jurgens was, rather inappropriately, put up at the hotel L'Ail Au Lit (Garlic in Bed), which has since given way to the fashionable Byblos. He was required for the opening scene on which Vadim gambled heavily like a journalist putting everything into the first paragraph of his story. Putting his faith in the same sequence, Raoul Lévy leaked the information that Brigitte would be basking on the beach in the nude when Jurgens (playing the shipping magnate) arrived. He agreed to let reporters and photographers attend the rehearsal.

They watched Vadim carefully orchestrating each move until Jurgens' shadow fell across Bardot's body, a searchlight intensifying the contrast of light and shade. They heard Brigitte exclaiming: *'Mais qui est cette immense armoire normande?'* – Who is this enormous Norman chest? (chest for cupboard) – which was not in the script but an early example of her gift for improvisation. The reporters roared with laughter. To cast and crew Jurgens was henceforth known as 'the Norman chest.'

The cast included Vadim's old friend Christian Marquand who, as one of the brothers vying for Brigitte's affection, was scheduled to play some torrid love scenes with her; and young Jean-Louis Trintignant, a French James Dean (BB's idol) in whose arms she was destined to end up. According to Vadim, Brigitte was not enamoured with the prospect of playing opposite Trintignant. The first time she met him she screwed up her nose and screamed at Vadim and Lévy: 'How do you expect me to play a love scene with him? He's too small! He's ugly! And he's not my type!'

Vadim's will prevailed. Was it to overcome her resistance, was it in the interest of verisimilititude that he urged her and Trintignant to ever more realistic embraces? 'Vadim is forcing his wife into another man's arms to gratify his own perverse desires,' murmured the camera crew who watched the couple's performance with growing fascination. Their clinches – no other word describes them better – became more passionate with every scene; until, more often than not, they lingered in each other's arms long after the director had signalled: 'Cut!' But Vadim has stoutly denied that he was so determined to depict the real thing that there was actual copulation on the set: 'Vadim played with fire,' Raoul Lévy said.

Grimly, every morning, Vadim resumed where they had left off the previous day. Improving on the script as he went, he urged Brigitte to scrape the depth of her emotions. He swears that while on the set he was immune to jealousy – another few years and he would complain that people failed to understand how he could remain detached when seeing his third wife, Jane Fonda, cavorting with a partner on the bathroom floor. As a script writer and director he did not mind Brigitte's lust taking over and making every scene twice as realistic and convincing as he had dared to hope.

Vadim was not perverse but desperate. He had been preparing himself for almost a year for the day when he would lose her. Realising that she was infatuated with the partner she had originally rejected, he seemed like a condemned man urging the executioner to put him out of his misery. Did he encourage Trintignant to hasten the inevitable break? Others thought that Brigitte was also attracted to Raoul Lévy. What a problem she was, and not only to Vadim! As on previous occasions – and forever after – she was difficult to track down. Jurgens recalls taking breakfast by the harbour before starting work: 'First Brigitte has to be traced,' he recorded. 'The production staff often do not know whether to find her with Vadim or Trintignant or Raoul Lévy. . . .'

For Vadim, the agony of losing the girl who, he said, had wanted to die for him, who had promised to love him always, the body he loved, the secrets they shared, was compounded by Brigitte's behaviour. On the set she did her job conscientiously, as near perfectly as possible, tempting, taunting, exciting, inviting, loving the camera and all who saw her with the camera's relentless, voyeurist eye. As soon as the day's work was done, depression engulfed her. She was despondent and tearful. Vadim thought she was mourning their lost happiness. Perhaps she had a conscience after all, perhaps she was afraid to leave the safe harbour of his love as the storm of passion carried her out into an unknown sea.

When the company moved to Nice, Winston Churchill visited the set, said 'Enchanted' when he met Brigitte but provided no worthwhile copy for the publicity department. Trintignant wanted Brigitte all to himself and pressed her to leave the apartment at the Hotel Negresco she shared with Vadim and to move in with him. She and Vadim had another of those lachrymose farewells, she packed her things and unpacked them again when it occurred to her that it was the thirteenth of the month – unlucky thirteen! Next day in the studio she played out the same scene – leaving her husband because she was in love with another man – which figured prophetically in Vadim's script, except that it was Trintignant who played the husband. That evening she left with her lover.

While totally wrapped up in her affair, Brigitte did not allow her personal problem to interfere with her work. By the time she had to repeat some of her lines in the Paris recording studio in the rue Jean-Giraudoux to synchronise with the background music, she and Vadim worked together as if nothing had happened. One afternoon when she was due at three but late as usual for a session with the band, she hardly noticed the good-looking young guitarist and was certainly not aware of his anger at being kept waiting. Yet he could not take his eyes off her. Like most young men – older ones, too, for that matter – he thought Brigitte looked even more desirable in person than on the screen. He could not have foreseen the time, not too distant, when she would happily gratify his desire.

As if the thought of taking off her clothes for the delectation of one man or the delight of millions had never crossed her mind, and while the worst she had done (in *Et Dieu Créa la Femme*) was still under wraps, Brigitte looked decorous and decent to a fault when I saw her in London a little later that year. Like my colleagues I was professionally (through my work on *Picture Post*) preoccupied with Marilyn Monroe, the acknowledged sex-goddess or sex-bomb, as I called her. Marilyn was in England to make a film with Laurence Olivier, not the most explosive chemistry, I thought; and her own beauty-and-brains love match with Arthur Miller absorbed most of our attention.

Unless my memory deceives me, Marilyn's rampant sexuality obscured lesser stars such as Brigitte Bardot who was popular enough in France but had as yet made no great impact on this side of the Channel. Yet I remember her vividly in her demure white satin dress, her Bébé face angelic rather than wicked, lined up with Marilyn Monroe, Anita Ekberg and other stars to meet the Queen. She looked almost virginal curtseying handsomely, smiling sweetly when shaking hands with Princess Margaret, a romantic figure in her own right. The real Bardot only revealed herself – I was one of the few to notice – when she yawned irrepressibly during the Royal Film Performance of *The Battle of the River Plate*.

Back in her own world where her matrimonial conflict was becoming acrimonious, the promotion of *Et Dieu Créa la Femme* and the public reaction to the film kept her and Vadim and Jean-Louis Trintignant locked in reluctant togetherness. The press published their names side by side but it was Brigitte who scooped the pool. First with his comments, as so often, was my friend Donald Zec, Britain's most popular film critic, who saw the film at a private showing in Paris and described it with characteristic flourish as 'the most flagrant, suggestive, near-the-knuckle picture I have seen.' After the opening scene with Brigitte lying prone naked under a bamboo awning, 'she appeared in and out of clothes, in and out of bed with the rapidity of a mannequin modelling nightdresses' – but without a nightdress.

In her wedding-night scene, her facial expression, semi-strip-teasing and suggestive movements had everyone gasping with amazement. Gary Cooper who was with Donald Zec sighed: 'Ah guess, ah oughta put a sack over my face.'

It was a good augury. So was the French censor's horror at some of the scenes – he called Vadim 'Satan' (a gift to publicity) –but cut only a few feet of celluloid so that *Et Dieu Créa la Femme* and Brigitte were unveiled in their full glory at a gala première in Paris in December 1956. London proved surprisingly broad-minded, the censor contenting himself with a few more snippets, and in the United States various self-appointed apostles of Decency and the Catholic Church led the noisy protests. With an outsize poster of the naked Brigitte dominating

Times Square, *Et Dieu Créa la Femme* opened in New York in October 1957 and became a roaring success, grossing over eight million dollars which, as the French noted, was as much as the proceeds from the export of Renault Dauphines. Brigitte and the Dauphines were hailed as France's chief dollar earners.

In the course of its progress to triumph – or 'damnation', as some suggested – Brigitte's performance collected a few rare accolades. At Lake Placid, New York, where Catholics, Episcopalians and other religious groups had been fighting each other for years, they came together in sweet harmony to oppose the showing of the film. 'Brigitte Bardot,' said the Irish priest in charge of the parish of St Agnes, 'is an actress whose name is synonymous with every outrage to decency and morality.'

He put the cinema out of bounds to his congregation and barred his church to parishioners who went to see Brigitte. At Philadelphia, she was caught up in the campaign for the mayor's re-election. To curry favour with the puritanical matrons of his constituency, Mayor Richardson Dilworth set his attorney-general on the film which, since there was no censorship, was banned under the obscenity laws. The campaign for mayor turned into a contest between pro- and anti-Bardot factions. In Cleveland, Middleton and York, cinema managers were arrested for showing the film. It was all grist to the mill of the cash registers which tinkled merrily along to record takings. Princeton University jumped on the bandwagon and conferred an honorary doctorate for physical culture on Brigitte; and in Britain, Leslie Hale MP suggested she should be sent to the House of Lords to brighten up the proceedings.

Et Dieu Créa la Femme ushered in a wave of sex films far more explicit than Vadim's soft-porn offering. Feminists welcomed it as the first 'Women's Lib' film, which was strange since Bardot offered herself for exploration by every male chauvinist pig. Vadim – and who better qualified than he? – contributed some quasi-philosophical observations to the controversy about Brigitte. She loves nudity, he proclaimed, and hates hypocrisy. She knew people would be shocked seeing her prance around naked (for a total of five of the film's ninety-five minutes). That was hypocrisy, she thought. Besides, she had not been acting – she had, as always, played herself. He cited the real-life Trintignant affair – Brigitte was the character she portrayed. Was there an element of sado-masochism involved? Tony Crawley thought that Vadim had taken his cue from de Sade whose disciple he was.

Loyally, Brigitte told all who wanted to hear that she was indeed as lacking in morals as the film's heroine. Less philosophical in their approach, ordinary people were simply intrigued with her suggestive hip movements, the way she swivelled her bottom and flashed her breasts. As if the clothes she had worn were invisible, some persuaded themselves that she had been nude throughout the film. Vadim, rather than Brigitte, became the butt of the puritans who accused him – as if that was new – of exhibiting his wife to the prurient gaze of the world. That was when Vadim adopted 'Devil' as his other name and Raoul Lévy announced triumphantly that, if God had created woman, it was the Devil who had created Bardot.

Losing no time at all, Vadim set out to capitalise on the infinite possibilities the over-emotional reactions opened up for Bardot projects in the United States. He and Raoul Lévy conceived the idea of pairing Brigitte Bardot and Frank Sinatra in a musical: 'It will be the greatest chemical fusion since nitroglycerine,' Lévy announced. Following the productive Jurgens pattern, the two masterminds flew to America to see Sinatra. Sinatra was said to be willing; it was also said, quite wrongly, that Brigitte was not. There was a good deal of shadow boxing. It was true that Brigitte did not want to work in Hollywood, and would not be parted from Trintignant. Sinatra refused to make the film in Paris.

Visiting Europe, he avoided Paris – and Bardot – although she was still talking about 'the chemistry' in terms which sounded like mating calls. To extract some kudos for her from the abortive attempt, word was put around that Lauren Bacall, who was infatuated with Sinatra, had discouraged him because she did not want him to become exposed to temptation: 'Miss Bacall is no fool,' Brigitte said, 'If I were her, I would do the same.' Failure to put a deal together and produce the potent Sinatra-Bardot potion haunted all concerned for some time. Vadim and Raoul Lévy would not give up and Brigitte made some spicy comments hinting at what might have happened if Sinatra had met her just once: 'Once would have been enough,' she said.

The formal termination of the popular love match – Brigitte v Vadim – was enacted in a Paris court in December 1957 when a judge granted them a divorce on grounds of incompatibility, saying they were both equally to blame and equally guilty of insulting each other. Vadim claimed that Brigitte had said some nasty things about him. She countered that he had expressed some less than flattering views about her. His main complaint was that she was 'capricious'. Turning her back on the past, Brigitte said she wished to marry Trintignant which was impracticable since he was already married and his wife refused to give him a divorce. Less and less was heard of their marriage plans.

Vadim had already found 'another Bardot', a future wife and star, in the delightful Danish model and ex-au pair in London, Annette Stroyberg, whom he proceeded to groom as he had groomed Brigitte and glowingly, approvingly described as – would you believe it? – 'capricious'. The press introduced Annette with the headline: 'After BB – the new Madame Vadim.' As to Brigitte, it was a matter of 'After Vadim – who? And how many?'

A solitary child, Brigitte, aged five, prefers the company of her teddy – this one continued to accompany her for many years. (*John Hillelson*)

Brigitte as a bespectacled schoolgirl gave no hint of the future sex symbol. (*Rex Features*)

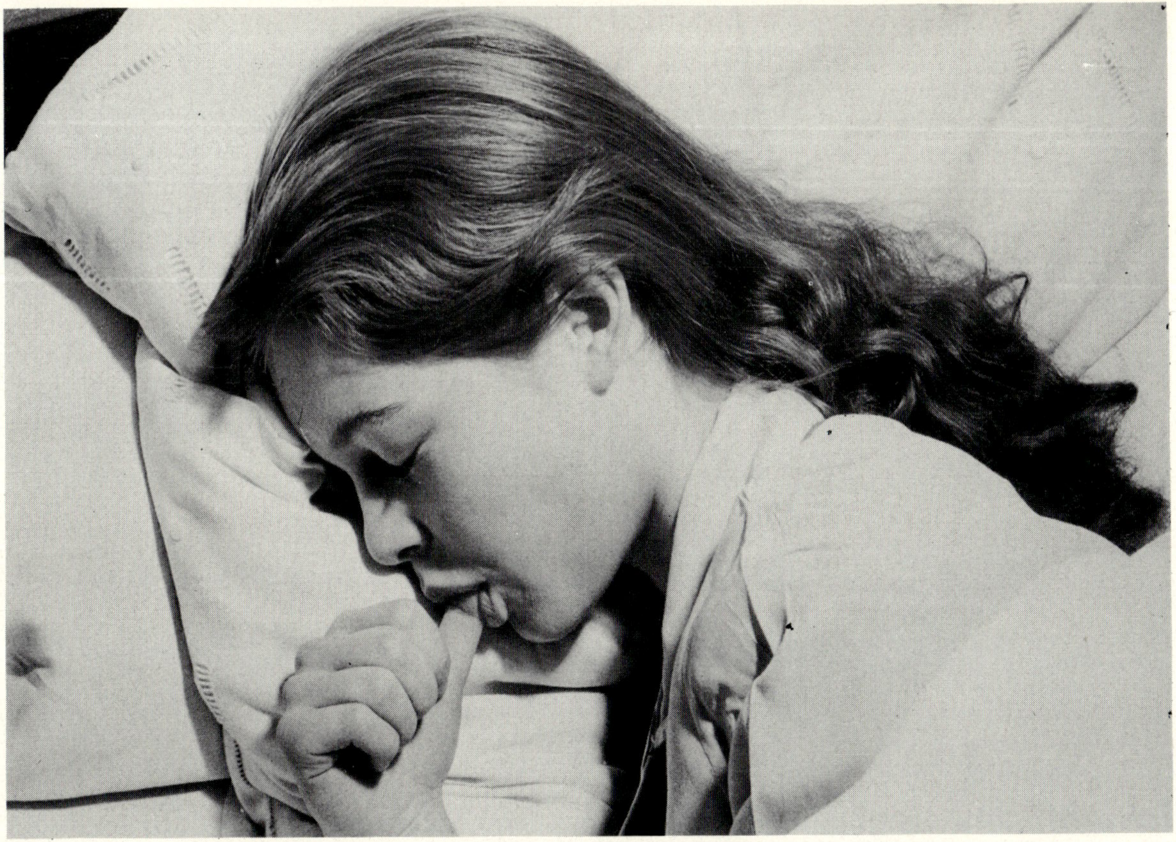

Emerging from the chrysalis – Brigitte in her teens. The baby doll or Lolita pose came naturally. (*Rex Features*)

As a youngster, Brigitte projected her emotions in dancing. Later, the grace and sensuality of her movements owed much to her early training as a dancer. (*Rex Features*)

Brigitte's early ambition was to be a model. Here, still in her teens, she is seen modelling gloves for her mother's boutique. (*Rex Features*)

In *La Fille Sans Voile* Brigitte gives a foretaste of things to come, while her father protested angrily against the film's sexy scenes. (*Kobal*)

Brigitte spent hours before the mirror, though she did not always like what she saw. (*Popperfoto*)

At the 1953 Cannes Film Festival, Bardot, little known starlet, draws the cameramen like a magnet and reduces superstar Kirk Douglas to a supporting role. (*Kobal*)

Four years later, she returns to Cannes as a superstar. (*Popperfoto*)

'Do you love my eyes, my lips, my nose, my bosom?' – a question every one of her pictures posed. (*Kobal*)

Roger Vadim, Brigitte's first husband, to whom she owed much of her success. Vadim came to the rescue whenever Brigitte was in difficulty with a film or lover, and remains her life-long friend.
(Popperfoto; John Hillelson)

Jean-Louis Trintignant's passionate scene from *Et Dieu Créa la Femme* became real life when Brigitte left husband Roger Vadim for Trintignant. (*Kobal*)

While Brigitte was making *Le Mépris* in Rome, Sami Frey flew in to spend weekends with her. She liked wearing the black wig which director Jean-Luc Godard made her wear for her part. (*Camera Press*)

Brigitte and her second husband Jacques Charrier were in love but passion and jealousy nearly destroyed the emotional young actor and military service did the rest. (*Rex Features*)

Above A rare picture of family bliss. Brigitte and Jacques Charrier and thei baby, Nicolas.
(*Rex Features*)

Sacha Distel owed Brigit his fame, but did not want to become 'Monsieu Bardot'.
(*John Hillelson*)

Luigi Rizzi, one of the many young men in Brigitte's life who enjoyed her generous favours and, after a year or two, was discarded to make way for the next. (*Rex Features*)

Mike Sarne, pop star turned film director, took Brigitte to his Chiswick pad; she took him to Paris where he felt a stranger on her home ground. (*Popperfoto*)

Brigitte loves the ski slopes – at Meribel, Haute Savoie, with another of her beaux, Patrick Gilles. (*Rex Features*)

Christian Kalt, part-time barman and ski instructor, saw himself as the next 'Monsieur Bardot' – alas, her love cooled and he fell by the wayside before they reached the altar.. (*Popperfoto*)

A moment when she is without any attachments, and Laurent Vergez is given a part in her film and time off to take her on picnics. (*Camera Press*)

Bob Zaguri took Brigitte to Rio where she caused a sensation and traffic chaos; they toured his native Brazil for many months. (*Rex Features*)

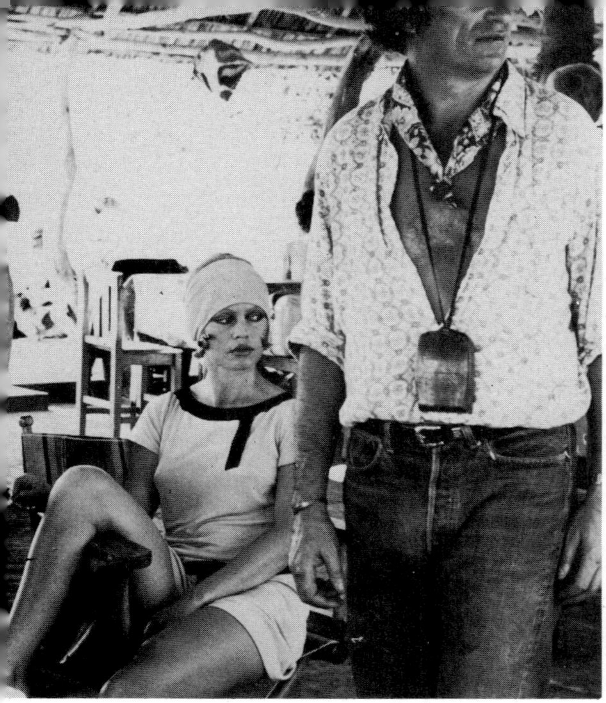

Jicky Dussart, photographer and *amant du coeur,* for whom Brigitte posed more liberally than for any other cameraman. (*Rex Features*)

Brigitte and her third husband, Gunter Sachs (*on the left*) – at a famous Riviera night spot while the fun lasted. They fell in love at first sight and out of love almost as quickly. (*Camera Press*)

Gunter Sachs joined Brigitte and Sean Connery on location, but left abruptly when they were evidently getting on so well together. (*Camera Press*)

VII

Brigitte Alone – But Not For Long

Could it be that Brigitte Bardot protested too much when she repeated over and over again that she was always playing herself? Was it not, perhaps, the other way round – Brigitte, a nice girl at heart, modelling her life on her film characters and turning into an apostle of immorality and promiscuity? It was a bit of both. It so happened that the apotheosis of Bardot as the symbol of *la vie française* or, rather, *la vie parisienne* (and of the Côte d'Azur) coincided with Françoise Sagan's trend-setting novels which exploited the same theme.

Hitched to Vadim's publicity engine – if no longer to the driver – Brigitte talked in quotes ready-made for headline writers and, good actress as she was, made them sound credible. Playing those 'simple, wild, sexy parts,' she claimed to represent the new generation, but this was vehemently denied: the serious and hard-working younger generation in France, it was said, no more saw themselves in Bardot's alley-cat antics than they saw themselves in the spoiled, self-pitying heroines of Françoise Sagan. I wonder. What Brigitte Bardot and Françoise Sagan set in train was the movement of the young for which Françoise Giroud (Jean-Jacques Servan-Schreiber's right hand at *L'Express*) created the expression '*la nouvelle vague.*'

There was no argument about Brigitte's effect on the mature and the lecherous middle-aged who were turned on by the explicit representation of sex which, after the Vadim-Bardot breakthrough – to quote the most telling definition – replaced the ponderous Freudian symbolism of 'the effusive copulation euphemisms of fireworks, waves crashing on to rocks, coupling railway carriages and even Hitchcock's penile train rushing into a vaginal tunnel.' As the release from old sexual taboos percolated down the social scale, Brigitte, blithely, achieved greater effect with her body contortions and her facial expressions. She came closer to orgasm than any performer before her and all but matched the offerings in the popular voyeurs' bordellos where people went to watch rather than do.

It disturbed not only the puritans but all those trying to hang on to old standards which were no longer universally accepted. When Brigitte was denounced as 'a national disgrace,' Raymond Cartier asked: 'Fame and fortune are hers – should one add the word "shame"?' Was she a challenge to morality, an appeal to vice and an insult to decency? Did she deserve blame or praise for feeling in harmony with an age that wanted nothing to do with neckties, stays and make-up? Like ventriloquists' dummies, Vadim's publicists said she did not have a comb because her fingers were the comb God gave her; she did not have a watch because she did not want to know the time; she had no jewellery and almost no wardrobe. That stamped her as a rebel. Cartier thought it would not be surprising if she were to encounter an experience of mysticism one day and thought he could discern behind her caprices and extravagances a search for the absolute.

Removed from Vadim's supervision, Brigitte expressed herself more naturally. Asked why she had parted from her husband, she answered: 'It's simple – I fell in love with another man.' She liked many types of men, she explained, but particularly a man with a big mouth because it showed he was generous. No, she added, her man did not need to be rich. She liked money to spend it – this was not quite true because she did not like spending money and hardly changed her mode of life when it began to roll in. She had just refused 250,000 dollars to go to Hollywood, she said. When asked whether it was ture, as Vadim maintained, that she was interested in philosophy and existentialism, she replied firmly: 'Nonsense.' She was not clever but silly. 'Cleverly silly, I'd say.' She could say that again.

It was not only what she said in interviews that mattered; what she did told as much about her. One reporter, Ronald Payne, now a distinguished author, was admitted to her presence at the studio: 'It was a great experience,' he said with a wink. Brigitte, in her dressing gown, was facing a big mirror: 'In her narcissistic way,' Ronald recalled, 'she was totally absorbed with her own image and watched herself all the time.' Casually, she slipped her hand inside her dressing gown and caressed her breast: 'I was fascinated, lost for words,' Ronald said. He could not take his eyes of her, neither could he think of anything to ask her. If she was infatuated with herself, the feeling was infectious. It was an exciting but wholly unproductive interview.

Brigitte kept up her dancing exercises managing to look sexy in the thick crumpled woollen stockings which covered her celebrated legs. Whatever she did, she looked good. No mystery; on the contrary, total self-revelation. She smiled indulgently when shown one of the more solemn assessments of her impact which claimed that, 'To the people of Paris, Brigitte Bardot is less girl than she is an exciting philosophical attitude, a problem in aesthetics to be closely examined, and a symbol of eternal woman in rebellion who finds that life unfortunately is sometimes sad and frequently futile.' She preferred to be accepted at face and body value or, as one American described her, 'a round and soft honey-voiced girl with a puckered pout and an explosive laugh and a tendency to remove large parts of her clothing and show much more than American audiences were used to see of twenty-three-year-old girls.'

Having made an undistinguished quickie, *La Mariée Est Trop Belle,* with Louis Jourdan who was predictably suspected of continuing his love scenes after the day's shooting, Brigitte was cast in a romantic spectacular – *Une Parisienne* – opposite Charles Boyer, French lover incarnate. Dressed in spectacular gowns, she played a French premier's daughter who flirts outrageously with the consort of a visiting queen. Not too tactfully, newsreel shots of Queen Elizabeth's and Prince Philip's recent visit to Paris were included in the film in which Brigitte was seen curtseying to a queen (played by Nadia Grey) as she had been seen curtseying to the real Queen of England. At fifty-eight, Charles Boyer in the 'Prince Philip' part of consort was too old to arouse

Brigitte's extra-professional interest. The veteran French heart-throb paid her some handsome compliments – she was lively, impulsive and undressed with great amiability but did not run around in the nude. 'She will become a very good actress,' he concluded.

Just when a well-known sculptor, Alain Gourgon, better known as 'Aslan', persuaded Brigitte to bare her bosom and pose for a new bust of Marianne, the symbol of France – he thought the traditional busts with their Greek features were not representative of France – and the Mint prepared an issue of Bardot medals in gold, silver and bronze, Brigitte did not feel very patriotic. The needs of France were the least of her worries and she was angry when it called Jean-Louis Trintignant to the colours. Taking her lover from her – unpardonable. She waxed lyrical about him. What most attracted her to him was his jealousy (for which he had plenty of reason). Hidden in her bouquet for Trintignant was a barb aimed at Vadim to whose notorious lack of jealousy she owed her association with Jean-Louis. Jean-Louis, she said, was much more serious; they never used nicknames for each other. ('Oh yes, they did,' one BB watcher countered, 'she called him Jean-Lou and he called her Bri-Bri.')

She did not take their separation too hard. With Trintignant confined to barracks and unable to visit her at her new apartment, 71 avenue Paul Doumer, only a stone's throw from her parental home, Vadim reappeared on the scene. So did Raoul Lévy. The film for which they recruited Brigitte, *Les Bijoutiers du Clair de Lune*, was a gruesome tale about a murderer and sex-fiend and a young convent girl who make violent love in the mountains of Spain. The unit set up headquarters in the future package-holiday-maker's horrible seaside paradise, Torremolinos. Stephen Boyd, a fine Irish actor, played the pervert Lambert opposite Brigitte's Ursula.

Off-the-set dramatics rivalled anything the camera could hope to catpure. While the film was not much more than a conventional thriller with a dash of unconventional sex, Brigitte's relations with Vadim and Boyd were the stuff of life in the raw.

That Annette Stroyberg was hanging around, several months pregnant awaiting Vadim's child, did not help matters. (Their daughter Nathalie was born the day Vadim's divorce from Brigitte became final.) Annette said she had expected to be jealous of Brigitte but was not. Brigitte, who was not expected to be jealous of Annette, manifestly was. Rehearsals and social gatherings were fraught with tension. That the man she had loved was in love with another woman was more than Brigitte could bear. It hurt her vanity so much, she completely forgot that she had walked out on Vadim in the first place. She was in a foul temper.

Since she was not Stephen Boyd's type, she could not play her old game of involving her partner. More interested in his job than in his legendary leading lady, Boyd was intensely irritated by Brigitte's whimsical behaviour. Even her dedication to her work put him off. He might have understood that, like every star, she would want to put her best side forward, yet he complained bitterly: 'All I can say is that when I'm trying to play serious love scenes with her, she's busy positioning her bottom for the best angle shots.'

Frustrated by every man in sight, Brigitte turned her attention to animals. She picked up a stray dog and called him Guapa, 'to keep Clown company,' she said. She also acquired a donkey to present to the local children, and there was a small bull whom she was to confront in a mock bullfight. It was all too much for her. Her old nervous rash threatened her skin, spots on her chin drove her to distraction. Brigitte said she was on the verge of a nervous breakdown, as was Vadim, and even Raoul Lévy was showing some disturbing symptoms. Their problem was real enough; hers was exaggerated with some judicious play-acting.

'I want a doctor!' she screamed retiring to her room. Two, three, four, five doctors were called in. She managed them adroitly. They agreed that she needed a rest which was what she wanted them to say. She was off to Paris like a shot: 'This picture is dogged by misfortune,' moaned Vadim. Dogged by Bardot. Brigitte tried desperately hard to recover her self-confidence in Jean-Louis Trintignant's arms until he had to disentangle himself from her embrace to return to his military duties. Brigitte could not bear to be without a man.

'I live my whole life around my man, work, play, dreams, everything,' she said. And while most of her pronouncements were strictly for public consumption (and indigestible to her friends), it sounded like a genuine *cri du coeur.* 'When I am alone, I am lost,' she went on. 'I can only find myself with a lover. Some actors say they can only exist when they are playing a role; me, I can only play a role – only exist – when I am loved.'

In the absence of Trintignant, she relied on the company of one Alain Carre who acted as her secretary-companion-factotum or, as he described himself, 'her slave' and, when she got tired of him a few years later, wrote about his life with her, her excessive demands on him and others, some of whom he named – Gustavo Rojo, the Spanish actor, Jean-Noel Grinda, the tennis player, directors, extras: 'She needed physical love as flowers need sunshine,' Carre said. His revelations should be taken with a grain of salt and certainly without the acid with which he flavoured them. But there were complications when Rojo, intoxicated by her heady passion, announced rashly that he and Brigitte planned to marry. It was news to her and shocked Trintignant who would soon turn his back on her, the first man known to have left Bardot and not the other way round. To forget her misfortune, Brigitte gave herself over just as passionately to the Flamenco, the fiery Spanish dance: 'It's like making love,' she declared.

About this time, Simone de Beauvoir was composing a eulogy of Bardot coupled with a savage indictment of women's attitude towards her to counteract the notion of Brigitte possessed by the Devil, the unpleasant heritage of Vadim's clever-clever publicity – there was no touch of Satan in her, she wrote. Because Brigitte was pure at heart women loathed her and felt threatened by her. Not all women, though. Olga Horstig-Primuz doted on her; Betty Box who first introduced her to British films was genuinely fond of her and Brigitte reciprocated with lasting friendship. *La Mariée Est Trop Belle* was produced by a woman, Christine Gouze-Renal (eventually Mitterand's sister-in-law) who was full of praise for her star.

Brigitte was without a man and alone – as far as a superstar and sex idol could ever be alone – when she started her love affair with St Tropez which has outlasted all her sexual affiliations. She bought La Madrague, a handsome ochre house behind a wrought-iron gate in the Bay des Canoubiers, half-hidden in the tall beach-grass. She surrounded it with a high wall to protect her from the tourists who poured into St Tropez in her wake, and, though they could see nothing, revelled in the thought (well founded) that La Bardot was gambolling behind the wall in the nude. Entertaining frequently – men and women – she tended to leave her guests to themselves much of the time. She basked in the sun, swam in the sea which was soon infested with hordes of photographers. The camera which she seduced more effectively than any living performer was forever poised to rape her privacy. Before long she bought a boat which she used to take her to lonely beaches where she could enjoy the air and the water undisturbed.

Ever since *Et Dieu Créa la Femme* Brigitte was making money hand over fist, her pay and share of profits escalating (except for two films for which contracts had been signed earlier), profits coming in year after year. Americans clamoured for every inch of celluloid which showed her face and body and lionised her as they had done Marilyn Monroe before her – Marilyn's decline, while eliminating a rival, worried Brigitte because it showed her how fickle the fans were. It did not matter that she was the biggest box-office draw in the world and was getting richer month by month, a shrewd manager of her new-found wealth. She was still exceedingly, excessively careful with her money – more so even than many of her notoriously tight-fisted prosperous compatriots – because she was desperately afraid of the future, lacked faith in her ability, her career, her appeal – in herself.

Trintignant was with his unit when Brigitte was about to start work on a new film in Paris, *En Cas de Malheur*, directed by Claude Autant-Lara, an aging master of the medium. A day before she was due to report to the studio, she met Gilbert Bécaud, a pop singer, and fell for him. When Trintignant arrived home on leave, Brigitte was not there. It turned out that she had gone in hot pursuit of Becaud who was not anxious to continue the affair. Brigitte would not let go of him and made such a nuisance of herself that Bécaud called a press conference and told flabbergasted reporters that Bardot was pestering him. It was more than Trintignant could bear – he wanted no more of her either. In desolation, she took some tablets; it looked like another suicide attempt but she said it was just a case of food poisoning. Shooting was held up for a fortnight while Brigitte recovered. The great Jean Gabin, her leading man, thought she had stepped back from the edge. Still, the prospect of playing a love scene with Gabin, Marlene Dietrich's idol and friend, terrified her. It was a precarious situation.

Claude Autant-Lara explained: 'I have to go softly with her because she seems so afraid. She has no confidence in herself' – the result of her set-back with Bécaud. Olga Horstig talked about the fears which haunted the poor girl: 'She is constantly worrying about her looks.' Putting it as discreetly as possible, Olga went on: 'She flirts a lot because she needs reassurance that she is still attractive.' Vadim stoked the embers of speculation about his ex-wife: 'She is well on the way to becoming a neurotic,' he said. Coming as near as anyone dared to calling her a nymphomaniac, he added: 'To be happy, Brigitte has to be in a constant state of physical excitement,' then qualified: 'Unless she is physically stimulated, lying in the sun, swimming in the sea, making love or playing with animals, she is unhappy.'

Behind the guise of a sober factual assessment, Vadim deduced from Brigitte's rejection of him as a lover that she rejected mankind: 'Her trouble is that she does not like people,' he said harshly. 'She is like a selfish child, the centre of her own world.

She does not realise that she is part of society.' By force of habit, Vadim was packaging his product as an enigma making it appear infinitely more complicated, unusual and mysterious than it was. His parting shot: 'She is good-hearted and utterly uncalculating but these qualities are spoilt because of her incapacity to live with other people.' Raoul Lévy went further: 'She is a very sick, sick girl.'

Other analysts explored her as ruthlessly. They stripped her psychologically thinking they could see her soul as bare as fans saw her body in nude scenes which only existed in their imagination. Because Brigitte had recently played an immature girl, she was stamped as 'permanently immature,' Nabokov's Lolita come to life. There was a backlash in France but when she was attacked for her 'masculine approach to sex,' liberated women and intellectuals rallied to her defence. François Truffaut praised her: 'More than an actress, she is a person – unique,' he said. Convoluted verbiage pervaded both attack and praise such as Marcel Achard's involved encomium: 'A malicious coquetry serving an ingenious perversity; the mystery of a woman and a child; an irritating gesture, a disarming smile; the only vamp in the world who looks like your childhood sweetheart; the hair of Mélisande, the face of Colombe; almost as much poetry as sex-appeal; dynamite touched off by a golden wick.'

Donald Zec brought us back to earth: 'Take a simple film idea', was his recipe for success, 'put Brigitte in it, then permutate the following: BB taking a shower; slithering between bed-sheets; walking towards the camera; walking away from the camera (that's favourite); teasing, pouting, partially disrobing (she can also be soaking – but it's not strictly necessary). After which it's merely a question of counting the money.' Tony Crawley summed up the effect this formula had on some Americans who vilified her as 'the tramp who keeps mothers of young daughters awake at night . . . the diamond eater . . . the monster . . . just the kind of girl to take home to mother if you want to give her a heart attack.'

All good stuff to fortify her status as a star. And, recovering from her bout of depression, Brigitte behaved like a star. The Cannes Film Festival? Not for La Bardot! What was good enough for the starlet on the make, was below the dignity of the acknowledged Queen of the Cinema. Instead of attending the festival, Brigitte threw her own party at home – that day the only people on view in Cannes were the pathetic few who had not received her invitation.

Though Brigitte played the star with style, she did not trust fate. 'Bardolatry,' she said, 'is a cult which may not last.' She thought she would leave the screen at twenty-five when her beauty would begin to fade, and meant it at the time. Distrusting the future, she often rejected the people who had a vested interest in her success. Vadim regarded her love of animals as one element of her rejection of people, and there was no end of talk about the menagerie she kept although there were only two dogs, a pigeon and a couple of canaries. A secretary and a maid completed her establishment except for the gentlemen who passed through without leaving a trace.

Since none of them commanded Brigitte's exclusive attention, she found time for her younger sister who was in need of help. Nineteen years of age, smaller than Brigitte, with coarser features but still very handsome, Mijanou had been signed up for a film, *Ramuntcho*, to play a woman parachutist in Indo-China. Mixing business with pleasure the two sisters went to Cortina at the high season of wintersports but spent most of the time talking to each other. Brigitte offered professional advice, initiated Mijanou into the mysteries of camera angles and lighting, stressed her good points and ventured a few tactful warnings – she was as anxious as Mijanou was herself to persuade people that ability rather than her name had earned her sister the part. They enjoyed the less energetic seasonal pastimes like après-ski. Brigitte gave Mijanou a spectacular publicity send-off by allowing herself to be photographed with her in sisterly togetherness: *'BB lance BB junior'* was the headline under which the pictures were published.

The next film on Brigitte's own itinerary was *La Femme et*

le Pantin which means *The Woman and the Puppet* and was promptly – there was no getting away from it – retitled *A Woman Like Satan.* I happened to be in Paris while shooting was in progress and, without knowing much about the film, had a glimpse of Brigitte's idiosyncratic attitude towards the press. Taking a leaf out of Garbo's 'I want to be alone,' she refused to see the American reporters who had come over specially to provide copy for the millions of Bardot addicts in the States. 'She's crazy,' one of them fulminated. 'They are queuing five blocks to see her pictures and the dame says she won't see anybody.' They had been cooling their heels for a fortnight.

Among the American contingent queuing to talk to Bardot was Hedda Hopper, Hollywood's supreme purveyor of film gossip, whose syndicated column was devoured by forty million readers. Hedda was steaming with anger which was not cooled by the martinis she consumed in the Bar au Ritz. Someone had just informed her of Brigitte's reaction when told that Miss Hopper demanded an interview: 'Who,' Brigitte had asked, 'is Miss Hopper?'

It soon transpired that veteran director Julien Duvivier did not find Brigitte much easier to handle. Although she had performed well on location in Spain – her blonde mane was the sensation of the Feria de Seville – and had given the Flamenco a new super-sexy dimension, work in the Paris studio went far from smoothly. Only the previous week, Bardot's chin had been hurt – 'dislocated' in the exaggerated movie parlance – when her face was slapped as the script demanded. Poetic justice triumphed, however – when slapping her hard, co-star Antonio Vilar had over-balanced and slipped a disc.

Now they were both back in action in the studio working on a bedroom scene. One solitary outsider who succeeded in penetrating the studio defences observed Brigitte and Antonio wrestling in bed – the eight or ninth take – and heard Duvivier pleading with Bardot: 'Let me show you . . .!' What presumption! Bardot reared up: 'Let me make love my own way! I know how to love.' Nobody disputed her claim but Duvivier explained patiently that they were working for the big screen and it had to be big. Two dozen people around the bed – and one underneath to catch the bed lamp Brigitte was expected to knock over in a fit of passion – kept their eyes on the screen lovers. The handsome Vilar looked fagged out, Brigitte thoroughly fed up: 'Making love is very exhausting,' she sighed after completing the short scene, 'my jaw is sore.'

Meanwhile, since Brigitte would not co-operate with the American reporters, all they could do was to speculate: 'It is difficult not to wonder,' one of them wrote, 'what will become of her. In time she may become a fat, conservative and terrible old lady. . . .' Kept away from the studio, the *paparazzi* made doubly sure of catching her off-duty and were more successful than the writers. The day she refused to be interviewed – actually at two the next morning – she was discovered at the Club d'Etoile in a tête-à-tête with Raf Vallone who seemed to be doing better with her than Antonio Vilar. The flash lights popped and drove Brigitte and her companion to flight. She cursed fate. Why did she have to be a star? Would she not have been better off marrying a stable man? Her capacity for self-delusion was infinite and she never accepted that she was the unstable element contributing to the violently changing fortunes of her diverse relationships.

The arduous days of love-making in the Boulogne studios were nearly over, *La Femme et le Pantin* was almost completed when she went out again after working late. She was with a small party at L'Epi Club near the studio when she saw a face which struck a chord in her memory. Wasn't he the young guitarist with the band which had played the background music for *Et Dieu Créa la Femme*? Wasn't this the boy who had been so angry when she had turned up late for rehearsals? And had she not come across him again in Ray Ventura's office? A good face but, then, she had been so much in love with Jean-Louis Trintignant, she had not taken much notice. They exchanged a few words. Was he still angry with her? Not at all! He even remembered the beige cashmere dress she had been wearing:

'You were speaking your lines beautifully,' he recalled mistily. 'But you did not give me a glance.'

'And your name?'

'Sacha Distel.'

VIII

'. . . *And Brigitte Created Sacha*'

A handsome young man, Sacha Distel. Not tall but well-built with shining eyes and a crop of dark hair. Big flashing teeth, a fine voice. He was two years older than Brigitte and was still playing the guitar. What an 'interesting' boy he was, Brigitte thought – 'interesting' in the sense of the male chauvinist describing a desirable girl as 'talent'. She wanted to know more about him. He was Ray Ventura's nephew; Brigitte liked Ray a lot. And, what a coincidence, his father had been a Tsarist officer who had settled in France after the Russian Revolution, just like Vadim's father. After spending some time in Britain and the United States, he had been Juliette Greco's accompanist for a while, accompanying her during and after the performance; Juliette, like Françoise Sagan, was a woman much after Brigitte's heart. Even more intriguing, he had been around with Annette Stroyberg as well. They talked about his career (the relevant stages of which have since been shuffled around a bit to obscure the fact that he owed his fame not entirely to his winning smile, his guitar and his voice). 'We must meet again,' Brigitte told him.

They met again at St Tropez the following year when Jean-Louis Trintignant was no longer in Brigitte's mind – like so many others, discarded from her memory once the affair was over – and there was room in her empty life waiting to be filled by a new passion. They ran into each other by accident which, Sacha's friends said, was carefully staged by him. When one of his friends threw a birthday party at L'Esquinade, St Tropez's best-known 'cave', Sacha suggested: 'Why not invite Brigitte?' As soon as she arrived, barefoot and in a casual dress, she spied the bronzed, very virile young guitarist across the proverbial crowded room. Her tentacles reached out for him – the inviting eyes, the provocative lips, the suggestive legs and undulating thighs. Within minutes he was in her arms. He was caught, not at all unwillingly, his first experience of the possessive power of Brigitte's embrace. They danced and danced into the small hours until there was no one left in the place but the two of them.

There is, surprisingly, no photographic record of the consuming encounter. For once the *paparazzi* missed out on a significant turn in Brigitte's life. Their revenge was swift. No sooner had word of the evening got around than they rushed in droves to La Madrague where the young lovers were hiding, refusing to answer the telephone which, Sacha said later, rang every five minutes, and oblivious of the crowds who rolled up on foot, bike, scooter, car and barge, their telescopes and cameras competing with those of the professional photographers, as avid for a romantic sensation as the ghouls who collected around the hapless 'ace in the hole' in Billy Wilder's perceptive film. (While the crowds were kept at bay, a burglar sneaked into the villa and got away with a great prize – a pair of Brigitte's panties.)

Behind the ochre walls, we now know, Sacha serenaded Brigitte in his most seductive tones – not that much seduction was required on either side. As soon as the echo of his love songs wafted over the wall, he was, at a stroke, acclaimed as 'the French Sinatra', a little ironic in view of the American Sinatra's snub to the object of his adoration. Never mind! The tom-tom of the media beat out the news of the new romance. Sacha was famous, alas not in his own name but as 'Monsieur Bardot'. With indecent haste, American show-biz promoters pounced on the new celebrity. Ed Sullivan requested the pleasure of Sacha Distel's appearance on his show, the supreme accolade.

For Sacha, the invitation posed a dramatic dilemma. To tear himself away from Brigitte was sheer torture but his pounding heart could not ignore the knock of opportunity. Love or career? Brigitte pleaded with him to stay. Sacha – shape of things to come – decided to try for the best of both worlds. If Brigitte's white-heat destire could not last out a brief separation, it was not worth the sacrifice of a unique chance. If she really loved him he could have success – and her. A tearful parting and he was off.

Had there been any doubt in his mind to what he owed his summons to New York, it would have been quickly dispelled when he reached the television studios. He was billed not as 'singer and guitarist' but as 'the most envied man in the world' who, only the other night, had held Brigitte Bardot in his arms. Pressed to proclaim his love for her in public, he refused but as a compromise agreed to sing *'Parlez-Moi d'Amour'*. It went over big. There would be many more appearances like this, he was told, if he worked hard and produced a balanced programme. That was the only way to make it in his own right.

Back with Brigitte, Sacha lived a good life. Nights of love at La Madrague, days spent boating, swimming, lolling in the sun, strolling around St Tropez. They were so wrapped up in each other they no longer worried about the stares and whispers that followed them. Evenings they slipped into little *boîtes* where Sacha joined the orchestras with his guitar, and Brigitte could not take her eyes off him. Loud enough for others to hear she breathed: 'Marriage is beautiful,' and the implication was clear. Sacha taught her to play the guitar and she adopted the instrument as enthusiastically as she had devoted herself to the Flamenco. The sound excited her and soon she was serenading Sacha. The announcement of their engagement could surely not be delayed much longer. Friends were saying that a great change had come over her – she wanted a baby.

Sacha was not as idle as it seemed. His guitar's haphazard tunes took on a more concrete shape echoing the rhythm of American folk songs which went through his head. He was composing a catchy tune which he called 'Scoubidou'. With words by Maurice Tèze, it became his first big hit.

Before returning to Paris at the end of the summer, Brigitte agreed to show herself at the Venice Film Festival to help publicise *En Cas de Malheur*. When it was announced that she would be attending, Gina Lollobrigida cancelled her visit – few stars would willingly test their popularity in competition with Brigitte Bardot. Raoul Lévy flew into Venice in an aircraft marked 'BB'. Sacha, of course, went with her. The handsome couple were swept along the Grand Canal on a wave of adulation such as few celebrities had ever enjoyed. The only sour note was struck by an Italian deputy who complained in parliament that it had cost the festival twelve million lire to entertain Brigitte and her party.

In autumnal Paris, Brigitte tried to keep her lover to herself with such intensity that the fire of their togetherness threatened to burn into ashes. It was difficult to put a finger on it but Sacha was straining at the leash, missing his work with a band, public appearances, public acclaim.

There was still talk of marriage but it was either for public consumption or a means of reassuring each other. Brigitte said she admired Sacha because he was 'a real man' – she did not want to wear the trousers. He was more of a man than she had bargained for. Almost effortlessly, he cornered the publicity which concentrated on him rather than on Brigitte. It did not matter that she loomed large in everything he said for publication; soon he would say with ill-disguised irony 'I am Brigitte's best publicity agent,' suggesting that every time his name was mentioned, Brigitte could count on hers being coupled with it.

Reporters and, presumably, their readers could not hear enough of 'Bardot's beloved' and asked him his views on every topic under the sun. Anxious to say something new about Brigitte, he contradicted what people had been led to believe about her: 'She's nothing like her screen self,' he pronounced, almost destroying the myth which Vadim and associates had laboriously built up over the years. All this talk about Bardot playing herself – pooh! 'She is a nice, simple girl and not a vamp,' Sacha said. He did not seem so sure when he composed a new song and flew to New York to record it:

Brigitte, Brigitte,
Pouting, smiling,
Angel or Devil –
Which is your face?

Two-faced, perhaps? One evening, Brigitte and Sacha went to the Marignan Cinema to see *Les Tricheurs* whose star was a strangely fragile young man, tall, rather Nordic, the opposite of the Mediterranean types for whom Brigitte had such a penchant. His name was Jacques Charrier. 'What do you think of him?' Sacha asked. 'Not bad,' she replied. From her this was high praise indeed. It sounded ominous.

It was also ominous that Brigitte was ready to make another film, a sure sign that she was no longer absorbed by her love. It was again a Raoul Lévy project, a story entitled *Babette S'En Va-t-En Guerre* and, Brigitte having agreed to star in it, all that was needed was to find a suitable leading man to play opposite her. It was not as easy as might be expected. Rossano Brazzi, the first to be approached, declined rudely: 'I am offered a role in Bardot's next picture,' he said, 'but I do not want to commit professional suicide. Leading men in her pictures spend most of the time just looking at her. So does the audience.' A number of established stars, including David Niven, felt like him.

Raoul Lévy came up with an amusing suggestion: since Brigitte had so often adopted her screen lovers as bedfellows, why not engage her current lover as her screen partner? His choice for Brigitte's new leading man was Sacha Distel. It was not a practical proposition and when it was quickly discarded, Sacha tried to save face by announcing that he had no intention of co-starring with Brigitte. At this point she had already decided to find her own man.

In the wake of her visit to *Les Tricheurs*, she took Alain Carre along to see Jacques Charrier on stage in *The Diary of Anne Frank*: 'Not bad, not bad! Very good!' was her verdict on him. Her mind was made up. She had found the actor she wanted. 'For her it's Charrier and no one else,' Raoul Lévy said with an air of resignation.

A young man from a military family – his father was an artillery colonel – he had grown up in French garrisons in Metz, North Africa, Germany, Montpellier. With two brothers also in the services, he had opted out of the family tradition and come to Paris to study dramatic art. He lived in a simple studio apartment near the Sorbonne, dabbled in ceramics, pressed his own velvet trousers, cooked his own breakfast of semolina and milk, rode a Lambretta and spent his leisure sitting on the balcony with his feet up. He was notoriously shy, so shy he would not attend the opening of *Les Tricheurs* and sent a friend to watch it and report back to him at a café on Montparnasse.

Meeting the great Bardot who was three years older than he, he was completely bowled over. Although a handsome, dimpled youngster he had not come across a woman like her before. Brigitte was all boa constrictor and involved herself with him as fully as only she could. He was cast as Babette-Brigitte's boy-friend in the film and, in the usual Bardot manner, became her boy-friend in real life, too. But the idea that, after the day's shooting, his nights were spent with Brigitte was not entirely correct. Filming in the *Babette* studio all day, he worked on another film, *Les Dragueurs*, in the streets of Paris from eight p.m. to two a.m.

Brigitte squeezed all her emotions into the brief hours they had together and soon told him that she wanted a baby and that he was high on the list of potential fathers. In passing she also informed Vadim of her ambition to become a mother which led him, and others, to believe that she wanted a baby from him – he assumed that Annette Stroyberg's baby was a challenge (although his marriage to Annette was already on the rocks). And Sacha Distel, who was still around, believed that she expected him to father her baby. Who was it going to be? Vadim was the first to be disabused of his hopes – or fears. Distel's prospects receded. Barring an unexpected new contender entering the Bardot baby stakes, this left only Charrier.

Once more it is impossible to separate the strands of truth and publicity in the ensuing events. At a time when only she and

Raoul Lévy knew that their new film would present her, literally, in a new guise, Brigitte sounded off on an entirely novel tag. She did not want to appear in another sex film, she declared solemnly, implying that motherhood and strip-tease did not go together. What? A Brigitte Bardot film without stripping and teasing?

This was precisely how Raoul Lévy saw her as Babette. She would not be required to show her knickers. True, the Babette portrayed by Brigitte was – the only hint of old times – a bordello maid but the script envisaged no unseemly goings-on. With her bordello past behind her, Babette was due to be evacuated from Dunkirk and, enlisting with the Free French, to train as a parachutist and drop into occupied France to kidnap a German general. Stirring stuff leavened with a dash of comedy. Brigitte was made to announce that this would be her first sexless film: 'I want boys under sixteen to be able to see me!' Throughout, she would be wearing khaki – Brigitte in uniform would be a challenge to the fans' imagination opening up all sorts of vistas.

She was flown to England to be acquainted with the rudiments of parachuting or, rather, handling a parachute harness and the mechanics of a machine-gun. At the RAF station at Abingdon, Berkshire, where she underwent instruction, frustrated British servicemen, denied a glimpse of her bare skin, were in a rebellious mood. So were the film journalists, one of whom, when told that Brigitte would not be showing herself in the nude, warned gravely: 'She will have to act well.' This was precisely what she did. With Sacha Distel back from a crooning tour of Portugal watching intently, she performed superbly before the camera and excelled in the scenes which tested her talent as a comedienne. If anything, her performance demonstrated that her unclothed beauty in earlier films had distracted attention from her ability as an actress. Public reaction was significant. Sanctimonious cinema-goers who had looked at her with studied disdain felt released and hailed her achievement. The sensation of the film was summed up in one headline: 'Brigitte Bardot keeps her clothes on.' She attended the première of *Babette* in Moscow and was hailed as the heroine of a film which paid tribute to the French Resistance, and to resistance everywhere.

If she had kept her clothes on as Babette, she was less reticent in private. The clash of arms which the film portrayed had not died down when the battle of Bardot's baby was joined in earnest. The first casualty was Sacha Distel who was peremptorily excluded from the proceedings. To please Jacques Charrier – if she wanted him to marry her, this was what she had to do! – Brigitte instructed her secretary to issue a curt statement: 'Mlle Bardot asks me to announce that she has severed all relations with M. Sacha Distel.' There were suggestions that Sacha had anticipated her and thrown her over, an impression which he has since tried to reinforce: 'I had to make a choice between Brigitte and my work,' he declared. 'Brigitte is a very beautiful person but I must get on with my music. I did not want to become Monsieur Bardot.'

Whoever ended the affair, Sacha Distel had one consolation: since taking up with Brigitte, he had sold 300,000 records and there was no stopping him. In the fast-moving amorous merry-go-round of the Bardot set, he spent some time in harness with Annette Stroyberg but got off in time to marry the attractive French Olympic skiing champion Francine Bréaud, who bore him two children and helped him to live down the playboy image he had acquired while with Brigitte. He kept on singing, very profitably, about his lost love and broken heart but still saw her now and then, and, by 1973, was, to quote him, 'confident enough' to make a record with Brigitte, 'The Sunshine of My Life'. When last seen, he was still going strong although he could not escape the sneers of his rivals who said that Sacha Distel was a minor player when he climbed into Bardot's bed and a star when he climbed out of it.

Having given Sacha his marching orders – or, as the case may be, having seen him decamp to pursue his career – barely six months after their rapturous encounter in St Tropez, Brigitte lost no time coaxing her new partner into a more solid relationship. Nudging and pushing Jacques Charrier in the direction of marriage, she was nonplussed by his reticence. Though besotted by her, Jacques held back. Why? There was his lingering fear that Distel might come back but the chief obstacle, though Brigitte was unaware of it, was Colonel and Madame Charrier's reservations. An unbending military man, Jacques' father was not happy about the prospect of his son marrying the lady every Frenchman and a few million foreigners worshipped as a sex goddess and seduced every night, albeit only in their dreams. This, in Colonel Charrier's book, made her the world's most profligate woman. He felt more strongly about Jacques marrying Brigitte than Pilou had felt about Brigitte marrying Vadim. Madame Charrier said bluntly: 'Brigitte Bardot is not a right wife for my son.'

For the first time in his life Jacques Charrier summoned up enough courage to defy his father which was like disobeying military orders. Pleas to stop and think out the implications of such a marriage fell on deaf ears. For reasons not difficult to guess, Brigitte was in a hurry and would not allow Jacques to listen to his parents. Arrangements were made for the wedding to take place on 19 June 1959 at Louveciennes, the Bardots' weekend village. They decided to keep their plans secret but underestimated the determination of the press to cover the romantic sensation of the year. Anyway, someone at the town hall yieleded to temptation and gave the secret away.

Brigitte went to Louveciennes with her parents, Mijanou and her double, Maguy Mortini; Jacques was accompanied by his reluctant parents. When they arrived at the town hall they were hostled by a small army of photographers, newsreel cameramen and reporters and engulfed in a huge crowd. The wedding party had the greatest difficulty fighting its way to the door. The lone policeman on duty grabbed the first man he could lay his hands on, who issued a strangulated cry: 'But I am the bridegroom!' Inside there was pandemonium. Brigitte burst into tears. The irate papa Bardot attacked the mayor: 'I wanted this wedding in the strictest secrecy,' he shouted, inferring that the mayor was responsible for the leak. Brigitte threatened to call the whole thing off. The mayor turned on Pilou: 'You are beginning to annoy me,' he hissed and made to withdraw from the ceremony.

Brigitte switched on her charm and pacified the mayor who motioned his officials to go ahead. 'Let's get it over quickly!' Brigitte said. Seven minutes later it was all over. By the time Brigitte and Jacques reached their little car, a truckload of police reinforcements arrived. Outside the Bardot chalet, workmen were ripping up the road, the noise of their drills adding to the general turmoil. Nothing mattered now that Brigitte and Jacques were at last man and wife. Recovering his composure, the groom was almost delirious: 'I am the happiest man in the world – what makes millions of men's mouth water belongs to me,' he said at the wedding lunch in the garden of the chalet – words that would turn as bitter as poison in his mouth before many months.

The couple returned to Paris and spent their wedding night at the avenue Paul Doumer before taking the Blue Train to the Côte d'Azur where they retreated to La Madrague. Within days, Jacques collapsed and was taken to hospital with appendicitis. A week later he was back with his bride. 'Before the honeymoon was over,' wrote Peter Evans, 'Brigitte was pregnant.' Or had she been pregnant well before it started? If Evans was correct, the little boy who came into the world the following January was a seven-months' baby. But the speed with which Brigitte had got rid of Sacha and married Jacques gave rise to the suspicion that she was anxious to legitimise the child she was already carrying. When little Nicolas was born, he looked anything but premature. At St Tropez the honeymoon fever rose. La Madrague was besieged by press and well-wishers who clamoured for a glimpse of Bardot: 'Not since the legendary Lady Godiva stripped to ride through Coventry has one girl thrown a town in such a tizzy,' said one of the few visitors to be admitted.

The honeymoon was still in full swing when it was spoiled again, this time by the army which had previously ruined Brigitte's affair with Jean-Louis Trintignant and now called up

Jacques Charrier for national service. It was a blow to Jacques; for Brigitte it was a disaster. To have a lover rudely snatched from her was bad enough; to be left alone in her delicate condition was shattering.

It is difficult to reconcile the popular view of Brigitte with her state of mind and body, a recurring problem for an independent observer. The contrast could not have been more striking. Not many months earlier, a French magazine had totted up some imposing statistics of Brigitte's fame: a million words devoted to her in French newspapers, twice as many in magazines; her photograph published more than 29,000 times; forty-seven per cent of all French conversation devoted to her (as against forty-one per cent concerned with politics). Professional analysts were sounding off with their involved conclusions describing her success as 'a liberation of eroticism, a defection from the moral code, a retreat from the metaphysical'; and the process of her artistic development as 'bringing back regressively to contemporary feelings the first mother-child relationship.' Whatever this was intended to convey, it did not refer to Brigitte's attitude towards the baby she was expecting. Sociologists saw her as an imitation Madonna, Freudians as a reincarnation of the orgiastic deities of Greece and the East.

Some of them conceded that it must be hard for her to be treated as a goddess and not to believe that she was one; they recalled her answer to the question of what she thought of de Gaulle – 'He's much bigger than I in every way' – and interpreted it as a subtle hint that a comparison was possible. In fact, she did treat him as an equal, as one star to another, when she wrote to him demanding a fairer treatment from the tax authorities. She was earning millions of dollars for the country; if she was not shown greater consideration, she would stop making films. The President did not reply. *Vogue*, a little more realistically, called her 'the sensuous idol, with a seething milky bosom below a childish pout.' Neither *Vogue* nor the psychologists and sociologists – ordinary people even less so – had the slightest idea of how she looked and felt at this time.

Brigitte was hiding away in her apartment and giving herself over to total despair. Whether she was in the second or fourth month of her pregnancy, the effect on her superb figure was less evident than she imagined but every additional millimetre around the waist felt like a giant step towards abysmal ugliness. The mirror told her that her features did not glow like those of some expectant mothers but were coarsening and showing signs of strain. The view of herself made her choke and there was nobody this time to reassure her that she was still beautiful and desirable. In her heart, she blamed Jacques for putting her in this condition, as if she had not told everyone in the first place that she wanted a baby. 'Ah,' one of her friends told me, 'there was some deliberate obfuscation – she only said it when she was already pregnant.' A measure of her suicidal mood was her purchase of a burial place and a tombstone (inscribed Brigitte Bardot-Muscel) at St Tropez cemetery.

Although her parents were embarrassed by her reputation and could not adjust to the limelight which reflected on them, Totty was as solicitous and comforting as she could be with a daughter who wanted to be comforted by a man. Brigitte was in a bad way, 'the worst time in her life,' it was said, although she had not as yet reached rock bottom.

She pined for Jacques, not as the father of her child but as the man who could give her love. She quarrelled with God and with fate, and blamed the growing embryo inside her body for her predicament, not the most auspicious mental condition in which to approach motherhood. Jacques, alas, was in no happier frame of mind. Joining his fellow recruits with the 11th Lancers in barracks at Orange, in the Department of Drome, he was taken aback when photographs of his wife in various stages of undress or completely unclothed stared at him from the wall over every bunk. Brigitte was the soldiers' favourite, their unrivalled pin-up.

As soon as they became aware that their new comrade was the husband of their sex idol, they let off a barrage of questions such as come easily to the mind of a bunch of sex-starved young men in the forces. What was it like to make love to Bébé? When? How? How often? A sensitive, insecure young man floundering at the deep end of emotion and confused by his precipitate marriage to every man's 'mistress', Charrier was completely unsettled by the constant battering with crude, indelicate suggestions and bawdy jokes. He, too, was in a state of deep depression. The medical officer diagnosed a nervous breakdown and sent him to hospital for observation. The army did not take kindly to such a namby-pamby recruit. He was treated as if he were a madman.

Relief was in sight. It was not his but his wife's condition which saved him – for the time being. Brigitte's doctors sent an urgent request to his superior officers to grant him compassionate leave to visit his wife whose health gave them cause for concern. There was nothing unusual about such a request and leave was granted – only to put Charrier in double jeopardy. The reunion of the harassed couple did not solve their problems. They were at such a low ebb and in such a state of agitation that, rather than easing their burdens by sharing them, their combined troubles became too heavy to bear. It dawned on them that they had become man and wife before getting to know each other properly. As Brigitte felt diminished by her condition and Charrier felt inadequate, they quarrelled and got on each other's nerves.

Returning to barracks more despondent than ever, Charrier broke down again and was sent to Val de Grâce Hospital where Brigitte could visit him. Then it was his turn to be called to his wife's side once more – another compassionate leave. When he was observed visiting a film studio in Paris to complete work on his latest film and was seen with Brigitte at a fashion house, there was a public outcry.

Private Charrier's comrades were getting angry. Their grudging admiration for the man Bardot loved gave way to indignation about his 'preferential treatment' – his frequent leaves to see his wife while they were separated from their women adding fuel to the general resentment. They complained to their members of parliament, one of whom put down a biting, satirical question in the National Assembly: 'What measures does the government intend to take to ensure equal treatment for all recruits even when they come from the arms of a great actress?' The press called Charrier a shirker and compared him unfavourably with his gallant father and two brothers who were serving officers. His nineteen-year-old youngest brother Philippe volunteered for service with a parachute unit in Algiers 'to redeem the family honour.'

Brigitte was in two minds. She did not think Jacques was manly enough, at least not as manly as she liked her men to be; perhaps the army would make a man of him! She promptly jumped to Jacques' defence: 'My husband is really sick,' she wrote in a letter to *Paris Jour*. 'He has only one desire – which I share with him – and that is that, as soon as he is well, he can go back and carry on his military service. The public should consider him an ordinary soldier and stop making cracks at his expense.' Poor Jacques dragged himself back to his regiment but was soon back home on another forty-eight hours' leave. This time Brigitte did not live up to her indignant statement and would not let him go back: 'Forty-eight hours – baah!' Thoroughly fed up with the reluctant, emotional, useless recruit, the army had the choice of punishing him severely or getting rid of him. They decided to bring the curtain down on the farce. After twelve inglorious weeks under colours, Private Jacques Charrier was told to go home and come back in a year.

IX

Bébé's Baby

If it was difficult for Brigitte not to think of herself as a goddess, it was even harder for the national Bébé to reconcile herself to becoming the mother of a *bébé*. She did not find the prospect 'much of a joy,' was as frightened of childbirth as of advancing years, losing her figure and her looks, of the future and a hundred imaginary threats. Anxious to put her relations with the men in her life in perspective, she defined the place the four principal characters occupied in her emotions: 'Vadim – he discovered me; Trintignant – he understood me; Distel – he annoyed me; Charrier – he loves me.' In another interview she elaborated, varied some aspects and extended the range of her review: 'Vadim revealed me to myself,' she said. 'Trintignant seduced me; Rojo fired my passion; Sacha gave me tenderness with every word, every kiss; but Jacques stole my heart.' At least Charrier did not try to domesticate her: 'Today,' she said, 'I'd rather starve than cook.' But her habits remained bourgeois and frugal for a rich woman, and she was not above arguing with her greengrocer about the price of potatoes.

A little Left Bank dressmaker – Brigitte rarely frequented *haute couture* houses – made her a couple of maternity dresses; on the rare occasions when she went out, she wore a simple cloth coat to disguise her growing protrusions – since she vehemently disapproved of the killing of animals, she did not wear furs gladly. While she looked fuller, Jacques, who had lost nearly forty pounds in the army, was pitiably thin. The fear of losing Brigitte, which had tortured him throughout his brief army service, still oppressed him. He suffered from claustrophobia, a legacy of the iron bars across the windows of his room in the military hospital. Brigitte, too, felt the world closing in on her. Since she had let it be known that she intended to have the baby at home, where two rooms had been converted into a maternity ward, photographers and reporters camped outside the house day and night. Returning home from a walk and hurrying upstairs to dodge the cameras, she slipped and fell. Alerted by her cries, Jacques rose from his sick bed and rushed out on to the landing in his pyjamas. It made an even better picture.

'Mother-to-be fine; father-to-be might just survive,' was the word. Not until early January was Jacques prepared to show his face in public. With two bodyguards in close attendance, he accompanied Brigitte on a brief stroll. Brigitte managed to look radiant and gave the photographers a sweet smile but deep inside, as her time approached, she was not as happy as she looked. Ten days later the great moment was at hand. On the morning of 11 January 1960, 'Monsieur Bardot', as everybody called Charrier, presented himself to the press at the Café Royale, next door to 71 avenue Paul Doumer, and told them that, at two-thirty-one, Brigitte had been delivered of a healthy boy weighing just over seven pounds. They had decided on a name for him – Nicolas.

The reaction was frenetic. Reporters and photographers fell over each other to get close to the father. Some fainted in the crush, one was carried out with a broken ankle. As people surged in from the street, women were trampled underfoot. In the pandemonium, Jacques struggled to cope. Coyly he revealed that his son had inherited his dimples; he and Brigitte were already calling him '*Fossettes*'. He was pouring champagne all round when reporters came up with a baby they had discovered outside: 'Give him a kiss,' they told Jacques. 'His name is also Nicolas.' It was not true. They fell over each other to photograph the touching scene and some of the café's glass tables were shattered in the commotion.

When the press announced the birth, France forgot about the sensational new oil strikes, the atom test in the Sahara, the Algerian troubles and the bickerings of politicians. Telegrams, bouquets and presents, toy railways and cowboy outfits among them, arrived by the thousands. The local post office started a special service to deal with the avalanche of Bardot mail. Hysteria was not confined to France. The University of Iowa offered the new-born babe a place in the class of 1988. The Germans referred to Nicolas as 'Child of France.' Foreign astrologers sent horoscopes and artists created 'impressions' of BB's boy as he would look when he grew up.

Within days, baby Nicolas was installed in a nursery apartment next door, the youngest citizen to occupy a flat of his own. It was a heaven on earth in blue and white – blue walls, white wool carpet, blue and white curtains. The baby cot on wheels was covered with a frilly canopy. There was a white high-chair, a play-pen and an ornate white birdcage in Second Empire style filled with Brigitte's toy animals and stuffed birds she had collected since childhood. A chest of drawers was brimful with a baby's dream wardrobe – tiny duffle coats, hooded bathrobes in white towelling. Brigitte sent fifty sets of similar outfits to babies born around the same time. She asked her friend Christine Gouze-Renal who had produced *La Femme et le Pantin* to be Nicolas' godmother; the two remained close for many years to come.

Since a Bardot had only truly arrived when his picture was in the paper, Brigitte posed with her son for the cameras within forty-eight hours. Once this formality was completed, the mother-and-baby idyll did not last long. Less than two weeks after giving birth, Brigitte was on her way to St Maurice film studio to start work on her next film. She barely acknowledged congratulations and brushed questions about the infant aside as if it was a subject that did not fit in with her work or her life. It looked like a deliberate detachment from motherhood.

The new film was *La Vérité*, director Henri-Georges Clouzot, producer Raoul Lévy. It was another made-to-measure Bardot theme about a Quartier Latin harlot without morals who ends up or, rather, starts as a murderess because the story is largely told in flash-backs.

The manner in which Brigitte went about her first chore in the studio was a measure of the distance she had put between herself, her baby and the baby's father. When the question of a male star was raised, she shocked everyone, not least Jacques Charrier, by asking very categorically for Jean-Louis Trintignant. The thought of his wife's former lover playing torrid love scenes with her drove the jealous husband into a frenzy. Luckily, for him, Trintignant was laid up recovering from a skiing accident: 'Let's wait for him,' Brigitte pleaded. There was no time.

As the tests went ahead without Trintignant, the cameras were trained on a four-poster bed in which Brigitte, snuggling under the blankets in jeans and T-shirt, awaited her conquerer. Henri Clouzot lined up a succession of candidates who assumed that the one who would perform the explicit scenes most realistically – and to Brigitte's satisfaction – would get the part. First to be put through the hoop were Jean-Paul Belmondo and Laurent Terzieff, both friends of Charrier who appeared with him in *Les Tricheurs*.

Although neither of them was really suitable, Brigitte received them with open arms on her bed of love. They went through the most intense 'tests' to which actors had ever been subjected. Brigitte teased – in the sense of strip-teased – them mercilessly and joyfully. As they were followed by half a dozen others, Brigitte's sense of duty never flagged: 'However exhausted,' Clouzot recalled, 'she would resume tests whenever a new potential partner was produced.' What drove her on? 'She loves to excite men,' Clouzot said. And herself. A decision could not be delayed much longer when Clouzot brought in his own favourite, Sami Frey. The pattern of Bardot's reaction in such a situation had not changed with the years. Frey, handsome, dark-haired, was a popular French pin-up but Brigitte objected: 'I don't like him!' Was she playing for time, still hoping for a reunion with Trintignant? Clouzot implored her to give Frey a chance.

In the end she allowed herself to be persuaded. Once Sami slipped under the blanket with her, he did not need the director's exhortations – Clouzot encouraged Brigitte and her partner as recklessly as Vadim had ever done – and responded so magnificently to the leading lady's practised technique of seduction that, in the best Bardot tradition, the test looked as good as the real thing. Brigitte was quickly converted.

The studio staff suspected that she was not only testing a partner for *La Vérité*. In truth, they thought, she was testing a lover and Jacques Charrier was sure their guess was not far out. Tormented by jealousy, he fled from the studio and tried to hang himself but survived. He cut his wrists, not too deeply, and was saved again. Weirdly, as he sought death, Brigitte 'slashed her wrists' in a crudely authentic scene on the set, an experience that unsettled her deeply. Jacques went to hospital to recover from his injuries and his depression but his ordeal was by no means over.

Brigitte's affairs were becoming impossible to unravel. She took time off, not to look after her husband but to travel to Geneva. It was said she had gone to consult a lawyer about a divorce from Jacques, which was not true. When it was suggested that she was having an assignation with a young actor, Philippe Leroy, there was a weak denial on her behalf. The real purpose of her trip, it was announced, was to register a company for the commercial exploitation of her initials, 'BB', which had been patented as a trade name (for use with perfume, cosmetics, toothpaste and the like). The Trade Marks Journal described her as 'a merchant.'

With each detail of Brigitte's hectic life more or less accurately but always prominently reported in the press, public bewilderment grew and her popularity slumped again. People were clearly angry with her. When she went for a walk with her father a stranger confronted her in the street: 'You bitch,' he shouted in her face. 'It has not taken you long to find another man!' Tears streaming down her cheeks, she ran home. The whole repertoire of her trouble was regurgitated: she was too immature to be a mother, only juveniles suffered from skin trouble. Had Brigitte not been too upset to read the papers, she would have been aware of the full extent of the anti-Bardot campaign, the reverse side to Bardolatry. Whenever a youngster was in trouble with the police, there was an outcry – 'Bar all Bardot films! Protect our youth against the influence of Brigitte Bardot!' In Rome the Vatican commissioned an outsize poster of her as 'a symbol of evil' but had it taken down quickly when it became a popular attraction.

Out of hospital, Jacques tried to resume married life with her. He drove Brigitte to the studio every morning and stayed on the set all day watching her 'making love' to Sami Frey, who played the part of Gilbert Tellier whom Dominique Marceau (Brigitte Bardot) lures away from her sister and murders. There was murder in Jacques Charrier's heart, too. Pacing the studio floor like a wounded lion, his roars of fury and agony destroyed the mood of the performers until Raoul Lévy barred him from the set and engaged a guard to keep him out. For a week or so, Charrier spent his days in the studio canteen waiting for his wife to finish work but it was an uneasy compromise. By mid-May, the unhealthy situation exploded in a fearful row. According to Brigitte, Jacques had threatened to disfigure her and take his own life. 'Another nervous breakdown,' said his doctor.

They could not very well continue to live together; it is a moot point whether Brigitte threw him out or whether Jacques went of his own accord. He was in poor shape. Unshaven ('growing a beard,' his friends said), he trundled his misery around the *boîtes* of the Left Bank. A mutual acquaintance who came across him described him as 'a man utterly destroyed.' Totty Bardot said his trouble was excessive jealousy, and Colonel Charrier complained bitterly that his son was in no condition to work – there was no work for him – and did not have a sou: 'He has to come to me for the money if he wants to buy a packet of cigarettes.' The Colonel was scathing about Brigitte: 'No woman has the right to ruin a man in this way,' he thundered. 'My son has committed no crime!'

Little Nicolas, out of the firing line, was being cared for by a nurse in Brigitte's rambling new country house at Bazoches, some thirty miles from Paris. The farm land around it was protected by a twelve foot high wall. She saw little of the boy: 'He's all right, I suppose,' she said. 'He's looked after well enough. I'm no mother – and won't be one!' She had never intended to let her baby change her life or stand in the way of her career, she added.

Such sentiments freely expressed only went to inflame public opinion still further. 'Don't rely on the people,' says an old proverb, 'those who shout "Hosanna!" today, shout "Crucify!" tomorrow.' Brigitte was called 'the witch of the century.' New rumours were thought up every day to denigrate her. The latest was that she and Clouzot were in love although, at fifty-one, he fell into the category of 'RFC,' Brigitte's private code for all but the youngest men, those who, in her view, were 'Ready For Chrysanthemums.' It was suggested that the break-up with Charrier had been deliberately provoked to enable her and Clouzot to be together. That Vera Clouzot, the director's wife, distressed about her husband's association with Brigitte, retired to a clinic was meaty news for the reporters. 'She has cut her wrist,' it was said – not true.

Clouzot protested: 'My interest in Brigitte is purely aesthetic,' but she did not hide her feelings and snuggled up to him suggestively whenever he came within reach. A second version of the near-fatal love tangle soon contradicted the first. Brigitte, it was said, refused to work with Clouzot who was jealous of Sami Frey; or was she once more playing a triangular game, this time with Clouzot, Charrier and Frey? Frey seemed to be the front runner. When he and Brigitte arrived at La Rhumière, a Left Bank night club, they came face to face with Charrier who, mad with jealousy, pounced on Sami with his fists. Sami gave as good as he got. Brigitte screamed. Photographers were conveniently present to snap the fight round by round. The only redeeming factor of the ugly incident was the suspicion, not too remote either, that it had been staged by Raoul Lévy whose sense of the outrageous failed him in his search for headlines. The pot was stirred by Pascal Audret, Sami Frey's girl friend who whined that Brigitte had bewitched her fiancé.

With the press in full cry after her, Brigitte issued a statement which sounded genuine enough: 'I am a woman like any other,' she pleaded. 'I have two ears, two eyes, a nose and a mouth. I have feelings and thoughts and I am a wife and a mother. . . . My life is becoming impossible. My soul is not my own anymore. . . . I cannot live like I want to.' She complained that she could not get fresh air because she did not dare to open the windows while photographers with telescopic lenses kept her under observation from the roof opposite. If all this continued, she said, she would give up films.

On the set, Clouzot was still flogging her mercilessly, squeezing every drop of sexuality from her versatile body and weary mind. He was asking too much. Once in exasperation he slapped her hand, and she slapped him back. 'It did not affect our friendship,' she said later. Kept in a state of high tension, Brigitte was taking tranquillisers and sedatives by the dozen. 'Under Clouzot's lash,' one of her colleagues said, 'she was depersonalised completely into a robot, a sleepwalker.' On the verge of hysteria, she could no longer distinguish between acting and real life. When asked to point a (toy) pistol at Sami Frey, as the script demanded, she refused, protesting that she would not kill the man she loved.

Understanding her better than most, Raoul Lévy seemed for once to serve the truth rather than his vivid imagination when he said that she was heading for a crack-up. Yet she sounded in full control of herself when she showed herself on television in another frantic attempt to refute all the rumours about her but only fed speculation with her language of poetic despair. 'I must kill the monster that is in me,' she declaimed, 'I must chase away from my hall the intruder who has the name of BB. I want to say: BB is no more. Long live Brigitte!'

At that moment, Brigitte did not seem destined for a long life. She cancelled a film in which she would have co-starred with Jacques Charrier. Then, as if running away from herself and the traumas that pursued her, she flew to the South of France but, rather than go to St Tropez, went into hiding with her friends Jean-Claude Simon and his wife Mercedes, Sophia Loren's former secretary, at their villa at Carbolles, a few miles from Menton. For Brigitte there was no hiding place. She was discovered by a pack of persistent reporters and photographers who settled down at the house, cameras and pencils at the ready, waiting for an incident, any incident. While husband Jacques was motoring somewhere near the Spanish border, and baby Nicolas was in her country house near Paris, Brigitte emerged from her seclusion to celebrate her twenty-sixth birthday at a restaurant at Cap Martin; the host was Henri Clouzot. The photographers were hard on her heels: 'Leave me alone,' she implored them, 'I'm going to die anyway.'

She was in a melancholy mood but not visibly distressed when the lunch ended, drove back to Carbolles and locked herself in her room. Nobody saw her leaving the house but as night fell, the Simons' neighbour, Antoine Valetta, heard a strange noise from the well at the bottom of the sloping garden. He called his wife, alerted Mercedes Simon and the three went to investigate. They found Brigitte lying face down in the grass with blood all over her. Her hair was picturesquely draped over the well. There were deep cuts in both her wrists and a razor blade was found nearby. It looked as if she had slashed her wrists in the house and dragged herself over the ground until consciousness left her. An ambulance was called and she was rushed to the St François clinic in Nice where doctors established that she had also swallowed a large dose of drugs – a whole bottle of sleeping pills. Another twenty minutes and she would have been dead.

In the villa, the Simons found a confused suicide note: '*Je déborde de cafard, je suis désesperée et malheureuse, je pars me changer les idées de toute façon. J'ai mal alors autant avoir mal pour quelquechose. A tout à l'heure, B.*' Roughly translated it meant: 'I am fed up, I am desperate and unhappy, I am changing my ideas. I am suffering and I might as well suffer for something. So long, B.'

As doctors fought for her life, Totty Bardot arrived in Nice. She met reporters at the Hotel Negresco and pleaded with them to let her daughter live. Yes, Brigitte owed a lot to the public and the press but it was not her career that was at stake, it was her life.

France flared up in a welter of inquests, recriminations and accusations. Some of the guilty parties joined in the hue and cry for 'the culprits' who had driven Brigitte to despair. 'The journalists!' Henri Clouzot cried in a broadcast, and singled out

France Dimanche whose reporters had been lying in wait for her in Menton; even *Paris Match*, Europe's most respected picture magazine, did not escape reproach. Bardot was the victim of the rat-race which was fought out as ruthlessly in the small showbiz bars and cafés of Paris as in London and Los Angeles! Of course, Brigitte was familiar with the scene, it was said, but, whether through conceit or silliness or, more likely, inadequacy, she was overwhelmed in the long run and suddenly could not cope with the strain. *France Dimanche* hit back at Clouzot who, the paper contended, had tyrannised the actress into giving a performance worthy of her talent. There were others who, even in these tragic days, denied her sympathy. Interviewed in a bar near the Arc de Triomphe, another actor dismissed the incident contemptuously: 'If all the stupid ones would hurry up and cut their wrists, things would be a lot better for serious actresses.'

One rather pretentious comment was that Brigitte's crack-up was a grave national embarrassment with ominous repercussions. The number of young people who took a lead from her was legion; might they not be tempted to emulate her and give up in despair? The girls were all Bardots now – typically, the chemist who had sold Brigitte the sleeping pills told the police that he had not recognised her: 'How could I know it was her? In my shop I serve hundreds of Bardots every day.' The film industry was said to be feeling 'criminally' guilty, and one French film producer delivered himself of a grandiloquent judgment: 'This may be the crash of the epoch.'

Theories abounded. The attempt to kill herself, it was suggested, had more to do with her public persona than with her private life; she wanted to do away with BB – had she not said so herself? – not with Bri-Bri. She could not bear the limelight any more. At least one perceptive observer disagreed: 'Film stars do not kill themselves for receiving too much publicity,' wrote Leslie Mallory of the *News Chronicle*.

Brigitte's own explanation was as confused as her farewell note. She had been at the end of her tether, she said, and had thought she would have to die some time, so why not now? The sceptics had a different explanation. With the suicide scene in *La Vérité* in mind, they wondered whether the whole thing had not been a stunt to advertise the film. Raoul Lévy was capable of anything: 'They have a million pounds invested in that film,' the doubters whispered. 'They must try something to get it back!'

The dividing line between screen and life (or death) became further blurred when one of Brigitte's visitors at the St François clinic turned out to be Francis Cosne, the producer of the next picture on her schedule, *Le Bride sur le Cou*. Inspecting the damage to his most valuable asset? Cosne was close to her when she was discharged and left the clinic after three days, looking chic in a pair of spotted narrow trousers, loose black pullover and head scarf. Her wrists were heavily bandaged and she carried a single red rose. In her car was one of the cuddly toy animals that had kept her company throughout her ordeal. Protected by a posse of policemen, the Bardot entourage, including her parents, moved off.

That Vadim was closely associated with the Cosne project strengthened the suspicion that the sad interlude was an attempt to win back public support for Brigitte. If so, the ploy was successful. Overnight, she was back in public favour; she was also back with Vadim – 'My best friend; everything I am, I owe to Vadim' – but, no, there was no question of a remarriage.

With Brigitte back at La Madrague, the good citizens of St Tropez discreetly looked the other way when she left the house and strolled through the town with Totty never far away. Roger Vadim was at hand to cheer her up – it was just like old times. Mercedes Simon helped to deal with her affairs and Sami Frey who, not wanting to be left out of the drama, had also spent a few days in hospital, soon turned up – he and Brigitte cuddling and kissing behind a hedge made a valuable picture for the photographers. But the peaceful *dolce-far-niente* atmosphere at La Madrague was deceptive. Things were stirring below the surface. Within a week or so, Brigitte was ready for new action.

So, incidentally, was Jacques Charrier who tried desperately hard to stop loving Bardot and pick up the thread of his career.

Although totally innocent of scandal, he soon enjoyed a kind of *succès de scandale* with agents and managers knocking urgently at his door. One offered him a splendid part – the role of a man who is ruined because his wife is a great star. No, thank you! Before he could consider other parts, the army intervened and recalled him. He was quietly flown to Algiers to join his old regiment. His comrades were not too pleased to see him as his arrival at camp was preceded by an order that 'photographs of Brigitte Bardot will no longer be tolerated in barracks, stores, guardrooms, halls and offices. . . .' It did not do Jacques much good. Hard as he tried to be a good soldier, he was again in a sorry state and promptly transferred to Maillot Hospital (psychiatric wing). He never put on uniform again. This time he was discharged for good as unfit for service.

Work was waiting for him when he returned to Paris. He accepted a part in a film which was being made in Munich. When German reporters pressed him to talk about his wife, he managed to sound philosophical: 'My marriage was a mistake,' he admitted adding quickly, 'but a mistake I'd like to make again.' He would gladly marry Brigitte all over again. He explained his predicament, none too delicately: 'One can't have to oneself what titivates a whole nation – whether it's Bardot or Camembert.' Switching to a new metaphor, he said that the crown of the prince consort had become a crown of thorns. Divorce was only a matter of time but, like most of Brigitte's ex-amours, he remained a friend: 'We are on quite good terms,' he said in the event, 'which does not mean that I have breakfast with her and Sami Frey.' He saw his son regularly, he said: 'I slip up the back stairs.'

Jacques took an apartment in the rue de la Faisanderie and resumed his old life. The wound Brigitte had struck him was deep but not, as some had predicted, a mortal one. Ironically, if Brigitte had failed to make a man and the army a soldier out of him, he still looked the perfect choice for the part of a soldier. His next big success was in the role of a Fascist officer dedicated to Mussolini who realises his mistake and exchanges the Fascist uniform for the ragged clothes of a Partisan.

Brigitte's involvement in the film business grew apace with the progress of the plans for *La Bride sur le Cou*, a comedy rather than a sex-epic. Although her wish – plus a little huffing and puffing and sulking – had been command to producers and directors in most of her films, it was an oblique form of influence which no longer satisfied her. Wanting direct, cast-ion authority, she appointed herself co-producer of the film with Jacques Roitfield and Francis Cosne. Thinking lofty thoughts and spouting some post-*nouvelle vague* ideas, she engaged an up-and-coming young scriptwriter, Jean Aurel, to put them into shape. When he would not do as he was told, she sacked him – causing another rumpus in the press – and ran for help to Vadim who took over as artistic director and scriptwriter.

Pretending to defer to Brigitte, Vadim operated a system of extempore shooting which made his carefully prepared plans look like spur-of-the-moment stuff. Their co-operation was smooth. The film's most startling scene featured Brigitte's appearance in total frontal nudity but this time it was a sham. She was wearing a skin-tight transparent body-stocking. As a symbol of their enduring relationship, Vadim called the character Brigitte portrayed Sophie. It almost looked as if she and Vadim were back at square one.

X

Brigitte Won't Play

Brigitte Bardot reminds me of a shapely, tasty concoction of all sorts of exquisite flavours and ingredients. Unorthodox to a degree, conventional in some ways, she either buries her head in the sand or soars to great heights. Although she does not like to submit her ideas to argument, she talks in poignant, well-modulated phrases but is often monosyllabic or stubbornly silent. She writes well and has put a great deal of what she would not say to a man's face into subtly erotic love letters which would make a stimulating contribution to literature if she did not adamantly object to their release. Casual meetings with her are mostly unproductive, leading frustrated acquaintances to assume that she has not a thought in her mind except for her lover or his successor standing in the wings and waiting for his cue.

Her reaction to the fate of the Rosenbergs was put down to Vadim's intellectual influence on an impressionable eighteen year old. But, though Vadim was back in the picture in the early sixties – had never really stepped outside the frame – the new causes Brigitte espoused were entirely her own. From passionate love of her pets she went on to take up the cudgles on behalf of all animals. The merest hint of cruelty and she reacted with a fury love of her pets she went on to take up the cudgels on behalf of the harsh and insensitive procedures in abattoirs roused her to angry protest. She insisted on appearing on television to appeal for more humane methods of slaughtering. With her name behind them, the advocates of the protection of animals against the inhumanity of man were able to bully the cabinet into action and obtain substantial improvements.

Brigitte showed a lion's courage when, like other people in the public eye, she received a peremptory demand for a contribution from the extreme right-wing OAS (Organisation of the Secret Army), an ugly sore on the body of the Algerian problem. They had the gall to stipulate the amount – 50,000 new francs (approximately £3,700) – and threatened reprisals if she refused to pay up. Hundreds of prominent personalities had submitted to the blackmail. Not Brigitte. She sent the threatening letter to *L'Express* together with her reply which said: '*Moi, je ne marche pas, parce que je n'ai envie de vivre dans un pays Nazi.*' (I won't play, because I have no wish to live in a Nazi country.) She added that she was taking legal action against 'X' for extortion and blackmail, and asked the public to rally in defiance of the extremists. Her brave reaction threw light on the extent of the rackets, some political, some plain criminal, which harassed leading French men and women. To guard Brigitte against OAS revenge, a policeman was posted outside her house. At the studio, her beloved mongrel Guapa was kept 'in protective custody' while she joined film workers at a protest rally and, her fist raised high, swore to fight fascism to the death. Threats continued and there was a vague but disturbing hint that OAS gangsters were planning to abduct little Nicolas and hold him to ransom. Brigitte dropped everything and took the boy to Switzerland until matters had cooled down. But she did not compromise.

And, while on the subject of Brigitte's causes, it ought to be explained why she did not join the eminent French women – Françoise Sagan, Simone de Beauvoir, Catherine Deneuve, Jeanne Moreau among them – who campaigned for a repeal of the law against abortion. They challenged authority and defied the law by publicly admitting that their pregnancies had been deliberately terminated: 'A million women have abortions in France every year,' read a statement they signed and published, 'I am one of them.' Their public confession made them liable to a big fine and a prison sentence. The absence of Brigitte's signature was noted with some astonishment. Was she opting out of the campaign? She was not. She did not make a public confession for the simple reason that, not having had an abortion, she had nothing to confess. She sent a large donation instead.

In spite of Brigitte's interests, views and life style being diametrically opposed to those of her parents, she remained a – how shall we say? – dutiful daughter. The older Bardots took turns with Jacques Charrier's parents looking after their grandchild, and it was touching to see Pilou spoon-feeding Nicolas ('Petit Pilou'). Brigitte forgave her father his frequent outbursts about her behaviour and the adverse reactions she provoked. She sensed his deep affection beneath the futile outrage and suspected that in spite of himself he was really proud of her fame. In the early sixties he presented her with a slim volume of poems of which she was the principal subject: 'I have been writing for her since she was a baby,' he said. They were stilted and gooey and made her wince but she accepted the tribute with a white lie: 'Most enjoyable,' was her public comment. Pilou could not deny himself a little sting – well, a mild rebuke – in at least one of the verses:

> Pretty, light shepherdess, I think you exaggerate
> Lover, husband, children are not enough for you,
> You need yet another lover, a respectable one, you say
> And still you run around the night clubs
> Oh! Shepherdess, you darling daredevil.

Was Brigitte looking for another beau? Beau was the operative word, and there was one around at St Tropez just then, Jicky Dussart, a young Left Bank sculptor and photographer, who moved into La Madrague with his big alsatian. Twenty-seven, dark-haired, broad-shouldered, Jicky might have passed as a bodyguard had he not so perfectly fitted Brigitte's specifications – 'I adore good-looking young men' – and soon been followed by others cast in a similar mould. Dussart's photographic studies of the nude Bardot glowed with the inspiration derived from the special, very personal facilities he enjoyed while taking them. Fully preoccupied with love, Brigitte decided once more to give up films and said so on several occasions, but it was always a matter of fulfilling her contract for 'three more films.'

She was always definite about what she wanted to do instead of acting although her predilections changed: this time she wanted to devote herself to interior decorating. No need for her to go out looking for assignments; she was her own best employer. First she commissioned an extension, a new wing, for La Madrague and outlined her plans for the decorations. She told the builder she wanted the brick walls white-washed. 'Cement is smoother,' the man protested. 'Exactly,' was her reply, 'I want a rough surface!' The craftsman could not help himself and smoothed the walls down. Brigitte followed him step by step roughing up his work: 'He was furious,' she giggled when she told the story. Even greater effort went into the house at Bazoches where Nicolas spent much of his time. 'It's nest-building,' her friends explained this intense preoccupation with hearth and home.

However prolific her ideas, the emphasis was on simplicity with a good deal of do-it-yourself techniques. The style was rustic rather than elegant – ginghams, checks, coarse fabrics. Thoughts came to her at odd times. She was lying in bed looking at a wall when she decided it needed a picture. There was no question of going out and buying one: 'When I want something, I want it at once!' She got out of bed, sat down and painted the picture she had in mind, a flower arrangement which turned into a collage when she adorned it with artificial flowers. She was mad about fireplaces. No room without a fireplace! She designed them herself and they looked very stylish. The same with lamp-stands. One she fashioned herself was made of a big flower-pot and a parasol mounted on a wrought-iron base. Flowers, real and artificial, everywhere, some in baskets fixed to the walls; and mirrors, mirrors galore, velvet cushions by the dozen. And beams along the ceilings. She went to the Haute Provence, picked out three magnificent trees, bought them on the spot and had them cut up for beams.

She did not take kindly to official interference. When the local authority ordered her to take down an eight foot fence around the grounds of her country house 'because it spoilt the natural beauty of the area,' she appealed to M. André Malraux, the Minister of

Culture: 'If it is your duty to protect natural beauty, you are obliged to protect me, too,' she wrote with incontrovertible logic.

Out of the blue, she decided to find a new apartment. It may have been, as her friends suggested, the need to break away from the recent past and from memories of her abortive marriage – the urge to invest everything Brigitte did with some oblique significance was irresistible; it was more likely the desire to get away from all those photographers on the roof opposite who made her life unbearable. While visiting a friend, the Comtesse de Diesbach, at her eighth-floor apartment in the rue du Bac (boulevard St-Germain) she fell in love with the place; it so happened that the Comtesse wanted to sell. For Brigitte, the chief attraction was an enormous terrace, big enough for a helicopter to land and ideal for a sun-worshipper wanting privacy in the heart of Paris. The view of Paris was superb ('Paris at my feet') and while she could see she could not be seen.

The deal was quickly struck. Brigitte paid half a million Swiss francs (about £36,000 at the time) for the splendid flat consisting of one major bedroom, a guest room, three living rooms, two elaborate bathrooms, an exquisite boudoir. Although the price covered the furniture, Brigitte got rid of it and introduced her own style – no chi-chi, no dust-gathering carpets, a black-and white design for the bathrooms, big settees and couches covered with a multitude of cushions. Typically, after all this, she changed her mind and decided to stay on at the avenue Paul Doumer. She let the new apartment, the first of several she acquired and rented out to wealthy tenants, drawing a handsome regular income as a landlord.

Her taste for mountain air and snow was rekindled by a stint at Villard-de-Lams in the French Alps for the winter sports scenes in *La Bride sur le Cou*, although for the dangerous bob-sleigh ride, the insurance company insisted on Brigitte being replaced by a male double dressed *à la* Bardot. She bought a chalet, Le Chouan, at Meribel, where she has since spent most of her winter holidays.

By the time *La Bride sur le Cou* was completed, the script

of her next picture was on her table. *Les Amours Célèbres* was set in Bavaria which, five years later, was the backdrop to one of her great romances – and her third marriage. Hers was the part of a village maiden who secretly marries a prince of the ruling house of Wittelsbach, played by Alan Delon who could best be described as a male Brigitte Bardot – as handsome, as notorious for his love affairs, providing as much, if not more, gossip for press and public.

Michel Boisrond was directing Bardot for the third time – their previous films were *Cette Sacrée Gamine* and *Voulez-Vous Danser Avec Moi?* – and the prospect of a Bardot-Delon match generated the obligatory in-talk of 'ideal chemistry,' the trade code for a crowd-pulling sex combination. But although Brigitte had her nude fling, a back view of her bathing in a lake, the two stars did not achieve a sensational amalgam. Instead of fusing, their egos clashed. It was each for him or herself. Delon was generous with praise for Brigitte as a woman but for once nobody suggested that she reciprocated.

If a French heart-throb did not set Brigitte Bardot ablaze, perhaps an Italian sex hero would do the trick. This was the thinking behind the plan to mount a Franco-Italian production for her next film and engage the magnificent Marcello Mastroianni of *La Dolce Vita* fame to play opposite her. The film was *Vie Privée* to be made at the St Maurice Studios in Paris, and on location in the Italian cathedral city of Spoleto, in Rome and Geneva. The producer was Brigitte's close friend Christine Gouze-Renal, the director Louis Malle, a young *nouvelle vague* disciple.

After the lack-lustre *Les Amours Célèbres*, it was essential to revive interest in Brigitte and give the public something to talk about. Reports of her imminent retirement were played up – 'positively her last appearance' sort of talk – and she aided and abetted the campaign by talking in the familiar vein about her own private life, complaining bitterly about the gossips who, whenever she put an arm around a man, said she was trying to break up another home.' *'Alors c'est final,'* she sounded off, 'this is my last film.' Her fingers crossed behind her back, she offered an after-thought: 'Maybe one more with Vadim, that's all!' She might have added that the contract for this one was already signed and sealed.

This time the ploy almost misfired. Ten years after first setting eyes on her in Cannes, Leonard Mosley, persuading himself that he had actually discovered Brigitte rather than giving her a publicity leg-up, was on hand to do the obsequies. 'Bardot will retire,' he wrote, 'and as the man who found her I'm glad.' He thought that, whereas she used to look like a precocious school-girl, she now resembled an aging Juliet: 'Brigitte Bardot is beginning to look horribly, pathetically old-fashioned. It is time she retired.' False news, journalists know, is as eagerly followed up and developed as a true story, and the report that Brigitte Bardot was about to hang up her mini-bikini sent cameramen chasing after her as she waded in to the sea; they photographed her so as to suggest that she was putting on a lot of weight, another nail in her empty coffin.

Although the reports of her retirement were, as the saying goes, greatly exaggerated or rather premature by some twenty-five films, her professional obituaries rolled glibly from dozens of inventive typewriters. She was mourned – or dismissed – as 'the first of the beatniks' who had ushered in the era of the great unkempt, unpowdered, unwashed, the latter being particularly wildly off the mark considering she spent more time bathing in the sea than all female Hollywood superstars between them immersed in their tubs. The fervour with which Bardot dedicated herself to her work – like a cook grinding her fingers to the bone to create the lightest of soufflés – should have warned the prophets of her doom.

To the sound of decorous denials that *Vie Privée* – about a star persecuted by the media and driven to suicide – was a thinly disguised account of her private life, Brigitte threw herself with abandon in the very scenes which echoed her personal experiences. Once more she 'committed suicide' with such an impressive display of despair (taking an overdose of sleeping tablets in her lover's bathroom) that it looked as dramatic as her real attempt; another sequence depicted a confrontation with a stranger (a charlady) who denounced her as 'an evil, immoral woman' – shades of her unpleasant encounter in a Paris street. Ingeniously orchestrated off-set noises included Mastroianni playing the old record about Bardot being two women under one skin, one eating men for breakfast, the other a simple, ordinary girl. For good measure he added that she sometimes did not know the difference between the two: 'She has these two personalities,' he mused, 'and one lives in fear of the other.'

'The sex-kitten is trying to claw her way out of her legend, the cage in which she is incarcerated,' was another comment. What nonsense! She was drawing on her legend to strengthen the plot of her film, and was, in any case, not the only one who got her legend mixed up with life. As the scriptwriter drew on reality to make make-believe believable, so make-believe became confused with reality during the scene in which she played a film star and was being mobbed by the fans. Bit-actors as the fans put such enthusiasm and vigour into their performance that they nearly crushed her: Brigitte fainted and police had to extricate her from the crowd. She was carried from the studio unconscious, a frightening experience, but she could at least congratulate herself on being the only actress ever to rouse her colleagues into such uncontrolled frenzy.

Her brave stand against the OAS having helped to restore her popularity, she completed her rehabilitation and reconciliation with the public with a fifteen-minute appearance on French television to see in the New Year (1963). Before going on the air, she tidied up another little private matter, announcing that her friendship with her TV co-star Olivier Despax was over. They had been keeping close company in recent weeks and had been expected to spend the rest of New Year's Eve after the show together but Olivier had committed the familiar sin of exploiting their liaison for personal publicity.

The little contretemps did not affect Brigitte's performance. She appeared – shades of Marlene Dietrich – in trousers and a man's morning coat with a camellia in her buttonhole, a diamond pin in her cravat and with a top hat perched on her locks. Piquantly biting her lip like a shy schoolgirl giving a recital, she strummed a mandolin and sang 'On the sunny side of the street . . .', then joined the famous Frères Jacques act in a comic routine. Presenting her *alter ego* in the next act, she wore a strip-tease costume – what there was of it – and a black wig and sang a few *risqué* chansons with such refrains as 'I invite you to be immoral' and 'I give myself to the one I like.' Altogether she changed costumes eight times in a quarter of an hour. Then she wished all and sundry a happy New Year. Viewers seemed to like what they saw but the press was critical of her singing voice.

Reaction to *Vie Privée* was not very good either, the critics obviously failing to discover the deeper meaning of this fictionalised account of Brigitte's life at the top which ends in unhappiness. Louis Malle's attempt to turn Bardot into a tragedienne had not come off. Did it matter? Again, the future blotted out the past. Before the printer's ink was dry on the poor reviews, Brigitte was already in the throes of her thirtieth picture, *Le Repos du Guerrier* which, by the way, brought her total earnings, even without the appreciation of her investments, to beyond one million pounds. With a Vadim script based on a successful novel, *Le Repos du Guerrier* was a sordid tale of a neurotic caveman whom Brigitte saves from suicide, falls in love with and marries.

Astutely guided by Vadim who inspired her lines on and off the set – no need for him to be present at her interviews with reporters – she talked his language to perfection: 'I am different from the conventional kind of woman,' she was heard to say above the sound of scratching pens, 'I refuse to control the feelings and emotions that nature gave me. This is how I am made – I cannot help it.' She ended up with another polished gem which was pure Vadim: 'I may wear mink but I think blue jeans.' It sounded fine except that she did not wear mink.

Discarding the Bardot dummy and speaking with his own

voice, Vadim gave a definition of the new Brigitte, oh so different from old times: 'Her reactions to future catastrophies, tragedies, sensations will be more tranquil,' he said as if it was a foregone conclusion that all these would recur in future. 'She is like a stone washed for years by the sea. All the rough edges have gone and she rolls with the tide.' Surveying the tangled love-life on the beaches around her, 'rolling stone' Brigitte saw her new leading man, Robert Hossein, entwined in the arms of a girl who was all of fourteen years old; Roger Vadim, divorced from Annette Stroyberg, with his new love, Catherine Deneuve, aged seventeen; Annette Stroyberg seeking consolation with Italian star Vittorio Gassman; and Jacques Charrier, all but forgotten, only waiting for his divorce before choosing a second wife.

Brigitte herself spent most of her free time with yesterday's man, Sami Frey, restored to her favour. She talked freely about their on-off relationship: 'It is true,' she said, 'that it is painful to live with me. I am expansive, I laugh, I play, I dance. Sami is the opposite. He is afraid, he suffers, he is hyper-sensitive.' But it was not true, as one report had it, that she was about to convert to Judaism for Sami's sake or, for that matter, that she would marry him. When one Paris paper reported that Sami was terrorising Brigitte, he sued and she gave evidence supporting him. 'It's all untrue,' she sighed. So were reports that she was keeping a ferocious watchdog and had aimed a shot at a photographer: 'I have no gun,' she said.

As to Vadim, the little flame burning for him inside her was not easily extinguished. Much as she liked working with him, she turned down his next *sujet*, a film in which he wanted to cast her alongside Catherine Deneuve. Was she jealous? There could be no other reason for as soon as Vadim came up with a project which did not include Catherine, Brigitte readily accepted.

Although her morale was high again (and her morals still exuberantly low), she was genuinely pleased when her 'beatnik performance' in Clouzot's *La Vérité* was rewarded with a European *grand prix* and when the Belgians, acclaiming her as the most popular star of the last three years, presented her with a cluster of suitably undraped statuettes. Work on *Le Repos du Guerrier* went ahead smoothly except for a few extraneous incidents, one of which could have been, and probably was, staged for publicity. It happened when Brigitte came storming out of her hotel room in Florence in her nightgown complaining about the man next door who was keeping her awake. He was identified as the Italian poet Domenico Buono who was loudly reciting his ode to Bardot. He was still singing her praises in ringing tones when police led him away: 'You are my shell, my pearl . . . I love you . . . I love you, Brigitte, Brigitte.'

Back in France, Brigitte ran head-on into an angry anti-Bardot campaign. Visiting Dijon to film a scene in *Le Repos du Guerrier* she was officially received by the mayor who had already provoked a public outburst two years earlier when he gave a civic reception to Khrushchev. The opposition was just as vocal this time and the mayor was told in no uncertain terms that Brigitte Bardot was the subject of scandal and not worthy of a public honour.

A week before her twenty-eighth birthday, Brigitte attended the film's première in Paris. The critics' reaction at the preview and the thunderous applause of the opening night audience added up to a triumph for her: 'Bardot's best bedtime story to date!' was the verdict. The Vadim-Bardot magic worked as well as ever. It was Sami Frey, though, not Vadim with whom she nuzzled the night away in a fashionable club.

A less romantic occasion was her brief reunion with Jacques Charrier who flew in from Rome where he was working and living with his Italian girl-friend Stefania Sandrelli. Jacques and Brigitte came together in the chambers of a divorce judge who made the obligatory attempt to bring about a reconciliation. Nothing doing! The couple reaffirmed their decision to divorce. The only point which remained to be settled – the future of Nicolas – created no problem. Brigitte was prepared to give up her son and agreed to Charrier being given formal custody. 'She just does not have a maternal instinct,' one of her friends told me. A few weeks later, the divorce was finalised, the marriage of 'the witch with the lion's mane' – her latest sobriquet – was at an end. A banner headline in a Swiss journal announced: 'BB once more available.'

In the professional sphere, Brigitte's availability generated a host of new projects to emulate the success of her latest effort but she was still talking of retiring: 'After the Warrior's rest comes Bardot's rest,' she quipped. Her decision, she said with apparent conviction, was irrevocable. Those who knew their Brigitte paid little heed. What she said today was not necessarily what she would do tomorrow. Perhaps they guessed that, even before she had properly retired, she was already planning a come-back.

XI

A Monument, A Statue

The man who halted Bardot's headlong flight into premature retirement in 1963 was Jean-Luc Godard, a highly idiosyncratic, practically untried film maker who had tempted her before without much luck. Like Vadim, Godard believed in improvisation and had the courage of his convictions. Catching up with Brigitte in the nick of time, he told her that he had the outline – no more than the outline – of a film which only Bardot could bring to life. Based on a novel by Alberto Moravia, *Il Deprezzo*, his project was backed by the astute American super-promoter Joe E. Levine and his co-producers Georges de Beauregard and Carlo Ponti, Sophia Loren's future husband, who hoped to marry Godard's experimental *nouvelle vague* concept with commercial techniques. Godard's enthusiasm was infectious, his imagination exciting. Brigitte was unperturbed by warnings that he was difficult to work with, intolerant, and dictatorial in his pursuit of perfection. Later she said that she had felt his vibrations – vibrations meant a great deal to her – which augured well for their collaboration.

Vadim was appalled by the prospect of Brigitte falling into the hands of a man he regarded as a charlatan. Better for her to retire than stake her prestige on Godard's experiments. They would never hit it off when it came to the hard grind of film making, he predicted. Brigitte was not deterred. She told Vadim she would throw in her lot with Godard. 'The film will never be made!' was Vadim's acid parting shot. His doubts were echoed by the French trade press which gave voice to the alarm of film experts that Bardot was gambling with her career and putting her talent at the disposal of a far-out novice director. 'A wild decision,' howled the anti-Godard brigade.

As Sami Frey flew off to film in Madrid, there were colourful reports that Brigitte had got rid of him for good. They made the front pages in a dozen newspapers which displayed pictures of Brigitte in fond embrace with Jicky Dussart – the photographer photographed. The pictures of them kissing 'surreptitiously' behind some trees – she could never resist these semi-public, semi-secret displays of affection – were indistinguishable from similar ones of her with previous boy-friends. Jicky joined her staff as her 'private photographer' and was in her party when she flew to Rome to start work on *Le Mépris*, but those who thought that they, or Bigitte, had seen the last of Sami soon knew better. Brigitte had not been in Rome long before she dispensed with Jicky's private – but not professional – services and called Sami back – 'the only man who makes me vibrate.' Sami's producers agreed to a new clause in his contract which permitted him to leave Madrid every Friday evening so he could spend the weekend with Brigitte in Rome.

Work on *Le Mépris* started under poor auspices. Brigitte's last two films having made no great impact, an opinion poll revealed that only five per cent of the men questioned and only two per cent of the women found her *'sympathique'*. Sixteen per cent of the men and twenty-nine per cent of the women said they did not like her at all. *Il Messaggero*'s welcome was cruel: 'The truth is,' the Italian newspaper wrote, 'that the ingenious and perverse adolescent, both innocent and naughty . . . has given way to a girl-woman almost thirty years old without the freshness of a girl . . . She is among the least sexy women we have seen. Greek sculptors would have used her as a model for a discus thrower.'

With several million dollars invested in the Godard-Bardot gamble the producers could take comfort from other indicators. Confounding the poll and the paper, *paparazzi* – and the magazines for which they worked – were interested enough to hire a helicopter which hovered almost permanently at the window level of Brigitte's well-guarded apartment. Their assignment was to catch her in her full blonde beauty which gave the lie to suggestions that she was wearing a black wig for her part in *Le Mépris* because the fans were tired of her famous fair tresses. From farther afield came news that American universities were collecting material about the Bardot phenomenon and that a Soviet diplomat had been punished for smuggling three thousand photographs of the scantily dressed Brigitte into his anti-sexist country.

Although her guide – Godard – had no record of big-time film making, Brigitte advanced courageously into *terra incognita.* With the formidable Levine-Ponti combination behind her, the risk she took was not as fearful as it looked. She was thrilled to hear that Ponti had abandoned plans to cast the two main parts with Kim Novak and Frank Sinatra – or, alternatively, with Sophia Loren and Marcello Mastroianni – and had opted instead for her and Jack Palance, Hollywood's archetypal tough guy. Reactions to early soundings on the other side of the Atlantic had persuaded the producers that the cash registers of American movie houses would tinkle as merrily for Bardot, preferably for Bardot without clothes on.

Apart from putting himself on the screen in the minor part of an assistant director, one of Godard's clever unorthodox ideas was to recruit Fritz Lang, the German-American genius, to play himself as a film director working on his screen version of *The Odyssey* which is being rewritten by one Paul Javal (Michel Piccoli). A hack more at home with cheap thrillers and in dire trouble with his sultry, sullen wife Camilla (Brigitte Bardot) Javal does not feel equal to the assignment which he has undertaken for her sake to pay for their apartment. Palance plays Prokosch, the ruthless American producer.

Le Mépris starts – a scene added in deference to American audiences demanding more than a pound of Bardot's flesh – with Brigitte naked in bed with her husband, exacting from him a detailed declaration of love for all her charms: 'Do you love my feet?' she asks, 'my ankles, my thighs, my breasts, my eyes, my hair?' 'I love you totally!' the husband professes rapturously as the camera inquisitively explores every inch of her body. The foreplay is carried far enough for the audience to believe that it is seeing the logical climax.

There is not much more love and happiness in *Le Mépris* which goes on to show the gradual disintegration of Paul Javal whose self-confidence evaporates. Floundering in the studio and in the bedroom he can see his wife's desire turning into contempt. The action, the better part of it played out against the background of sun-drenched Capri and the Javals' apartment, is agonisingly slow, the dialogue desultory. Nothing is spelled out yet Brigitte projects her thoughts sharply as she paces the apartment in the rhythm of Godard's skilful choreography for her dance around the grave of a marriage. Circling her husband like a wild animal, threatening to jump at his throat one moment, turning away in disgust the next (and, at one point, coming to rest on the lavatory seat), she spits out angry half-sentences and crushes him with cruelly eloquent silences. The atmosphere of desolation and foreboding becomes unbearably oppressive as the undefinable climax looms ahead. Brigitte monopolises the eye so compulsively that the ear struggles to keep up with the conversation to which Godard attaches as much importance as to the visual effect, if not more.

Prokosch-Palance, a gangster of the mind, makes a ruthless play for Brigitte. Paul Javal sees the hunky American kissing his wife but has no stomach to fight for her. Faced with a dilemma of losing her or his job, he throws in the towel and loses both. Going off with the Prokosch character, Brigitte is killed when their car crashes. The final shot shows her blood-stained, lifeless face which haunts the mind long after the lights have come on.

The surprise of *Le Mépris* is that Godard, having sacrificed principle for the sake of commercial success, yet produced a memorable film. He took the view that the nude scene was not alien to the subject and shot it in such a way as to make Brigitte more unreal, more profound, more serious than simply BB on a bed. There was controversy around the half-hour sequence of the quarrel between wife and husband. Some critics thought it could all have been said in three minutes, others loved every second of it. Such criticism as there was focussed on Moravia and his novel. The *New York Times* complained that the film did not make it clear why the wife becomes so contemptuous of her husband: 'Maybe he should be contemptuous of her!' Brigitte's performance left little to be desired.

During her stay in Italy, Jicky Dussart and the *paparazzi* commandos were not the only ones who trained their cameras on her. While Godard was making his film about a film in the making, another crew was filming the *paparazzi* who were laying siege to Brigitte. The guiding spirit and director of this parallel film – *Paparazzi* – was Jacques Rozier who owed the success of his minor opus to Brigitte who gave him *carte blanche* to depict her and her tormentors, the free-booting Italian gigolos of the camera. Almost simultaneously a second subsidiary film, *Tentazioni Proibite* came into being. It aimed to show how Bardot lived. . . .

Paparazzi and *Tentazioni Proibite* went some way towards illustrating Brigitte's reason for going back on her promise or, rather, threat, to retire. She had found, she said, that she would have no privacy even if she gave up work because the fans, the curious and the press would not leave her alone; she was in fact better protected in a studio or on location than in her Paris apartment or at La Madrague.

How Bardot lived could be observed – without being too intrusive – in Cannes where she honoured the 1963 film festival with her presence. In the sketchy diary she had kept for years, impressions of the festival's artistic offerings figured only briefly because the big event of her visit was her meeting with yet another 'man of destiny', a very personable young Moroccan-born Brazilian by the name of Bob Zaguri, a typical *homo brigittis* (dark-haired, boyish, of medium height). It was one of those 'love at first sight' experiences which were a recurrent feature of Brigitte's life: BB statisticians worked out that this was her nineteenth lover in sixteen years, eleven less than if she had fallen in love with the leading men in all her thirty films (as was often suggested) or, to vary the equation, had had one lover for every year of her life, another frequent contention.

Describing himself as a wealthy motor-car dealer – others suspected him of being 'a professional boyfriend' – Bob was a man of the world and far more intelligent than most of the dummies whom Brigitte had hitherto favoured because of their physical attraction; nor did he seem to hang on to her coat-tails to catch a ray of the limelight. He was discretion personified when he accompanied her to London, so much so that I was unaware of his existence when she flew in at the end of October 1963 creating an ever greater upheaval than usual.

A small army of bodyguards could not keep the fans and the press at bay when she arrived at the Westbury Hotel off Bond Street. Brigitte felt threatened and looked distressed. Silent and almost dazed she pushed through the crowd, went straight to her apartment, threw off her clothes and sank into a hot bath. Emerging an hour and a half later, she was greeted by boos from reporters and cameramen whom she had kept waiting. There were tears in her eyes: 'Why are they doing this to me?' she cried. She took to her heels and, all other routes being barred, sought refuge in the hotel's kitchen.

Once things had settled down, she met Anthony Perkins, her co-star in the film she had come to make, a Franco-Italian production of *Une Ravissante Idiote*, in which she was cast as Penelope Lightfeather, a feather-brained dressmaker, with whose help a Russian spy, a male 'Ninotchka', tries to get his hands on the secret files of a British admiralty chief. Brigitte and Anthony made an attractive pair but with Bob Zaguri hovering in the background there was little likelihood of Anthony emulating her previous leading men and continuing the partnership after working hours.

The only coherent conversation Brigitte had with a British film writer was with Donald Zec to whom she responded better than to most. She kissed the tip of her finger and placed it on his cheek, her latest signal of affection (with some others she made the gesture more erotic by moving the finger from her lips to the man's mouth). She said she was sick of being looked at but not listened to – Donald tells me he was looking and listening in equal parts – but would still not have changed a thing in life including the heart-aches and the catastrophes: 'A person like myself cannot buy experience cheaply,' she mused. That day she stepped out behind a pair of big dark glasses to visit a few shops; nothing untoward happened. It was the calm before the storm.

Work on the half-million-pound *Une Ravissante Idiote* had barely begun when. . . . Let me retrace the few short steps to débâcle. As the French film crew set up cameras and props in Flask Walk, Hampstead, for a key scene – Brigitte 'Lightfeather' walking in the direction of an armoured car – a crowd gathered, naturally, and when it became known that Bardot was expected, swelled to hundreds of star-struck maniacs. When she came into view, they surged towards her car. Unable to control them, police ordered the car to drive on but it was once more engulfed when it returned a quarter of an hour later. Order was restored only just long enough for Brigitte – looking gorgeous in a big rough sweater, tight dark trousers and big Russian boots – to pose for a few publicity shots before the crowd again became over-enthusiastic and unmanageable. There was no hope of any real work being done. Even if the police had not told the crew to pack up and go, Brigitte would have been forced to give up.

'Will I ever be able to make a film in London?' she sighed when she had reached the comparative safety of her hotel. She was despondent. Venturing out of doors, she caused a new commotion. It was hopeless. Defeated by her own popularity, she surrendered – one of the rare occasions when fans prevented work on a film. 'We shall have to go back to Paris and build sets and start all over again,' producer Michel Ardan said. 'Thousands of pounds have been wasted.' Brigitte was not sorry to return to Paris.

She was totally wrapped up in Bob Zaguri: 'This will last,' she declared extolling her new lover's South American vitality and humour. Not surprisingly she developed an appetite for more of the same and decided to go with him to Brazil. She was flippant about a big offer to appear in cabaret in Florida which reached her just before they set out for South America: 'Offer me a million dollars and I'll think,' she cabled the American promoter. 'For a million dollars you'll have to do a good deal more than think,' was his rejoinder.

Rio de Janeiro prepared flags and a big red carpet for Brigitte. Rumours that the incomparable Bébé was coming to Brazil to marry a Brazilian stirred volatile South American emotions to fever pitch. So many people were at the airport when the couple arrived that Brigitte refused to leave the aircraft but police could not prevent people climbing on to the wings and pressing their noses against the plane's windows. From several thousand throats the cry went up: 'Brigitte! Brigitte!' Only when Bob's brothers and a group of Rio's *jeunesse dorée* formed a protective cordon did she step straight into a car to be whisked away at great speed. Chaos followed her to her hotel in the Copocabana where the scene became so turbulent that Rio's police chief, an expert in quelling political riots, admitted defeat and called in the military to restore a semblance of order. Bob's friends mounted guard at the doors of Brigitte's apartment.

Bardot fever was not confined to Brazil's *hoi polloi.* The cabinet in session at the presidential palace opposite the hotel broke off and ministers tried to catch a glimpse of Brigitte. I depend on a Brazilian observer – perhaps not too reliable – as a source of the information that, for the following three days, the wife of President Goulard stood at her window armed with a telescope in the hope of seeing *'la grande Bébé'*. There were, literally, no two ways about the traffic chaos in the Copocabana as motorists stopped and stared. Fifty armed soldiers guarded the hotel against invasion.

With her lukewarm French followers in mind, Brigitte felt invigorated, as if new-born, she said, by these ovations, and spent hours peering from behind the curtains at the crowd below. It took four days for the furore to die down and this only after Brigitte had agreed to see the press. With Bob Zaguri by her side – BB and B holding hands throughout – Brigitte said obligingly that 'Brazilian men are wonderful' and that she intended to visit Brazilia and Amazonia. No, she would not be marrying Bob, not here and now, anyway.

Relations between France and Brazil being less than cordial, the press hinted at another possible, nay likely, reason for Brigitte's visit. She had, they revealed confidently, been charged by President de Gaulle with the important mission of improving the climate between the two countries. Brazilians hoped she would at the very least allow herself to be crowned Queen of the Rio Carnival. No, thank you! Brigitte did join in the jollifications but was masked and disguised as 'a King's slave', the king being Bob Zaguri attended by his brothers, Marc and Jojo.

The next time the couple were spotted, they were cruising in a yacht off the shore of Rio, Brigitte sitting on Bob's lap. The news from her camp was that she might be staying in Brazil for six months. That was her intention but, in the event, four months proved long enough for her. Blowing hot and cold – complaining about intrusive Brazilian admirers one day, coming out to thank them for their homage the next – she risked going out in a dark wig, the obligatory huge glasses and a Tyrolean hat and with a cigarette dangling from her mouth, a camouflage which was not very effective but suited her well. Her appearance seems to have inspired a German film lexicon's description of her as 'representative of a pubertal-erotic-coloured style of acting'. Pubertal? She was fast approaching her thirtieth birthday.

As public and press excitement abated, Brigitte and Bob managed to get away for a real holiday at the fishing village of Buzios, a hundred miles from Rio, where the Jesuits had first landed in Brazil some four hundred years earlier and proclaimed that 'for the sake of these beaches alone, one must believe in God.' The couple moved into the converted pigeon loft of a fisherman's house, rode on horseback along the beaches, walked hand in hand into the sea, went skin-diving and made forays into the jungle in search of the brightly-plumed cockatoos. The turmoil of Rio was forgotten: 'I have never been so happy as I am in this country,' Brigitte said with her eye on Bob. To show how well the simple life became Bardot, she agreed to be photographed for *Paris Match*, an indication that, while abandoning herself to such an unsophisticated existence some six thousand miles from her roots, she had not forgotten her career and would be resuming it before long.

With scores of 'special correspondents' cabling thousands of words about Brazil's Bardot hysteria, French readers began to take new pride in their old favourite. That Bob Zaguri's motor-car show-rooms were said to be besieged by customers anxious to buy a car from BB's boyfriend, recalled her achievements as her country's top export. So spectacular was her ressurection that civic officials were scouring the streets of Paris for a suitable square or intersection to be adorned by a statue of Bardot (as God created her).

XII

Via Popocatepetl to Manhattan

Since she had talked freely about the subject, it was no secret that Brigitte's maternal instinct was not as highly developed as her other feminine characteristics. But the popular notion that she had completely washed her hands of little Nicolas was mistaken. She made a substantial contribution to the cost of his upbringing and saw the boy regularly if not too frequently. One of the first things she did after returning from her four-months' unmarried honeymoon in Brazil was to have a day with her son at her country house.

A sturdy four year old with his mother's snub nose and his father's dark hair, 'Petit Pilou' arrived with his nurse and flew into his mother's arms. Her hug was long and warm and her face lit up as he planted a wet kiss on her legendary lips. Bob Zaguri, the man of the house, presented Nicolas with a toy pistol and Brigitte gave a good imitation of a mother worried lest the thing went off in the boy's hand. The three had high tea together and the nurse had to wait long beyond the appointed time to take BB's son back to his father.

Brigitte was soon involved with another youngster, a freckled ten-year-old American boy by the name of Billy Muny. Their meeting in a Paris film studio was the outcome of much correspondence and intensive negotiations. It started with an approach from Henry Koster, the German-born American director who asked Brigitte to come to Hollywood for two days and play herself in a film comedy, *Dear Brigitte* (with James Stewart), the story of a young Bardot fan who writes dozens of fan letters to her and ultimately manages to meet his idol. Her scene would not take more than four minutes, Koster wrote. 'Hollywood will be delighted to see you!' The fee was substantial – ten thousand pounds was the figure suggested.

Brigitte replied that she would be happy to play herself but coming to Hollywood was out of the question. Having haughtily disregarded Brigitte's repeated rejections, Hollywood was stunned. No other European star would have declined – 'dared to decline.' Brigitte would not budge and Henry Koster, being heavily committed to his project, had no choice but to arrange for the scene to be shot in Paris. Young Billy Muny and Jimmy Stewart were packed off to Paris accompanied by Henry Koster and a complete American camera crew. Brigitte allowed a room of her country house to be reconstructed in the studio only on condition that no still photographer be admitted; if people wanted to see her living room they would have to wait for the film. She was carefully coached in the few English sentences she was required to address to the boy such as 'How nice to meet you!' and 'I love your letters.' In a low-cut, sleeveless dress which would have appealed to older fans, among whom Jimmy Stewart counted himself, Brigitte acted out a rather staid version of herself. An unimportant episode? Hardly. It was a classic case of the mountain coming to Mohammed. Her long fight with Hollywood was over. She'd won.

Souvenirs which Brigitte had brought back from Brazil were installed at La Madrague giving the house a distinct South American flavour. A guitar hung above the seven foot high fireplace with the thick double-beam top which Brigitte had had installed at the same time as she had had the attic converted into a veranda with a magnificent view of the bay. Colourful masks and rugs and poncho coats were among her new acquisitions. Only the cosy corner in the sitting-room with the three piece suite and the Roman amphora – an ancient double-handled vessel – and the huge double bed with the check cover and oval mirror overhead were untouched by the Brazilian craze. Bob Zaguri was constantly with her. They talked shop: Bob planned to go into film production and Brigitte promised to star in the first film he could set up and to help with other ventures.

The last of Brigitte's favourites – to date. Miroslav Brozek, inseparable from her for three years, is a French artist of Czech extraction. (*Rex Features*)

BB and 'Pilou', a wealthy industrialist, who was at once embarrassed by his daughter's fame as a sex symbol and proud of her success. (*Rex Features*)

Testing suitable partners, Brigitte worked tirelessly on her couch. Here she is with Charles Belmont, one of the hopefuls. (*Camera Press*)

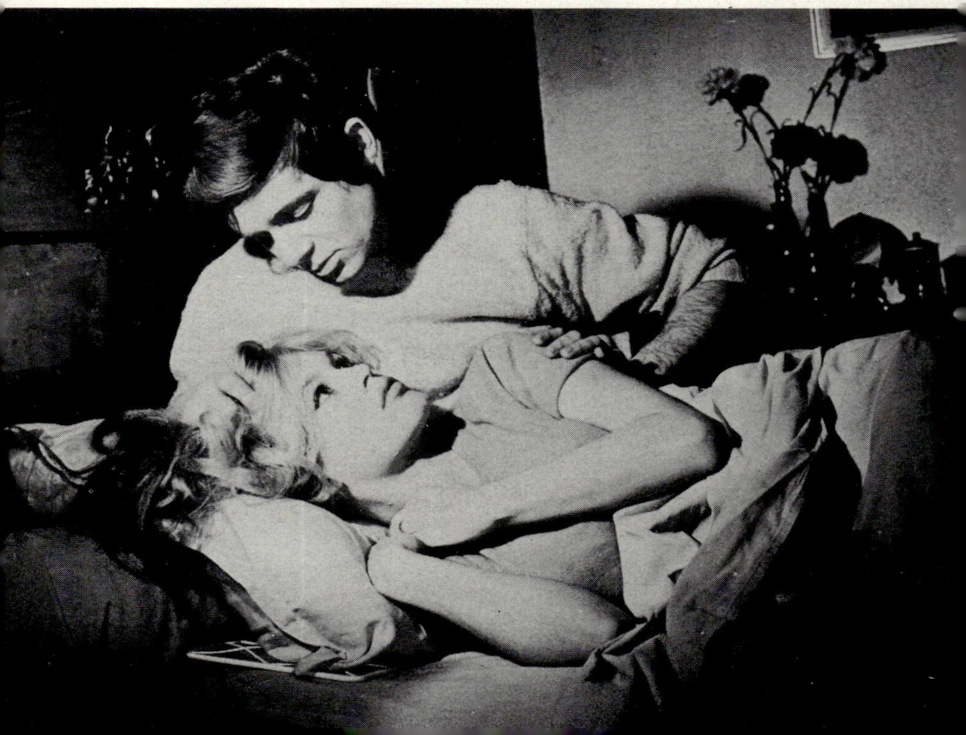

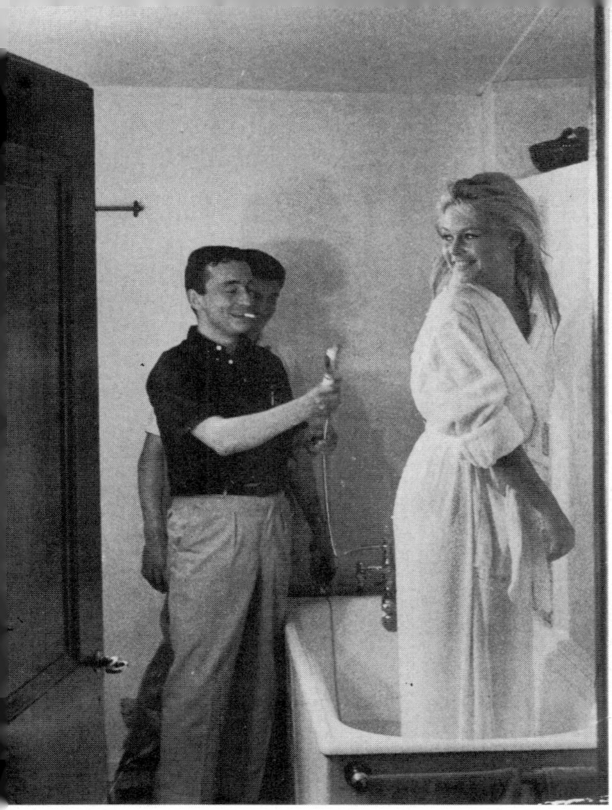

Apart from Roger Vadim, no director coaxed better performances from Bardot than Louis Malle with whom she worked in perfect harmony. (*Kobal*)

Brigitte has few inhibitions, and reveals herself with pride and joy. If she does cover up, it is usually to mollify the censor. (*Kobal*)

An inveterate campaigner, Brigitte joined workers at Billancourt Studios in Paris when they came out on strike. She vowed to fight fascism to the death. (*Popperfoto*)

Quick to despair, Brigitte has made several suicide attempts. Here she is leaving a Nice clinic in 1960, a week after taking an overdose and slashing her wrists, accompanied by director Francis Cosne. (*Popperfoto*)

Having resisted invitations to Hollywood, Brigitte was mobbed when she went to the United States in 1965 to promote her latest picture. (*John Hillelson*)

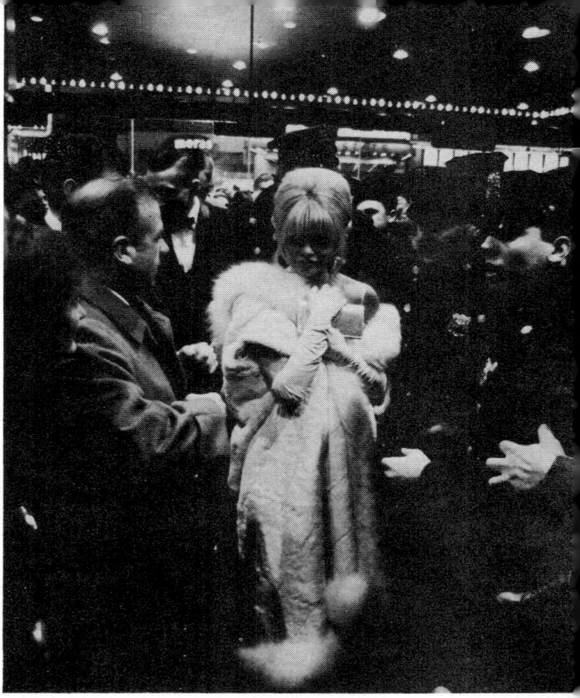

As a bride in this film, Brigitte wore white, naturally, but revealed rather more than is customary. (*Camera Press*)

A nun's habit in *Les Novices* was Brigitte's most unexpected screen outfit – soon to be shed. (*John Hillelson*)

Above Pictured with Serge Gainsbourg who appeared with her on television and partnered her for a record that her husband stopped as too suggestive. (*Rex Features*)

Below 'The Don Juan of 1973 is a woman', said Roger Vadim, whose film included this scene of Brigitte and Jane Birkin in bed together. (*John Hillelson*)

Cast with 'real actress', Jeanne Moreau, in *Viva Maria!*, Brigitte more than held her own and the two got on famously. (*Rex Features*)

While filming *Shalako* Sean Connery as leading man and the film crew were treated to a fuller view of her than the script dictated. (*Kobal*)

Brigitte in her bath stimulates a scenic designer's imagination, though the bath in her home is hardly less decorative than the stage prop. (*Camera Press*)

'Her boots are like two chalices . . .' Brigitte, as seen in a French television spectacular, inspired Serge Gainsbourg to write these lines. (*Rex Features*)

A popular subject for artists, Brigitte has been painted many times, and poses with a life-size portrait by Vincent Roux. (*Rex Features*)

Baby seals became an obsession with Brigitte but, more emotional than practical, her campaign did not stop their systematic slaughter. (*John Hillelson*)

Stray dogs are equally close to Brigitte's heart, and she gave these fifteen doomed animals a home and a new lease of life on her farm. *(John Hillelson)*

Brigitte and her mother leaving the Paris clinic where M. Louis Bardot lay gravely ill. (*Rex Features*)

Having retired from the screen – for the time being – Brigitte involved herself in several enterprises, including a couture house named La Madrague after her villa. (*John Hillelson*)

The sea comes right to the door of La Madrague at St Tropez, and she loves to play the guitar on her doorstep. (*Rex Features*)

An American tourist agency offered tours of St Tropez 'with the possibility of seeing Brigitte Bardot bathing in the nude'. The possibility existed long after she had turned forty, even if the view was no longer as perfect. (*Rex Features*)

Most of the time, though, they lounged on the edge of the Mediterranean, gazing silently at the sea roses and the wild flowers in outsize vases; settled with cool drinks in the heavy white garden chairs hidden in the tall beach grass. They played with Brigitte's favourite pet, the ferocious looking alsatian Jicky Dussart had left behind. Bob felt thoroughly at home in the well-organised wilderness of Brigitte's retreat (which was now well enough shielded from the outside world to frustrate the American tourist agency which offered Riviera tours with 'the possibility' of seeing Bardot bathing in the nude).

Seeing her in her private world it was difficult to recognise some of the features which Marguerite Duras, the French lady of letters (who wrote the script for the trend-setting film *Hiroshima, Mon Amour*) traced in Brigitte's photographs taken on the eve of her thirtieth birthday: '. . . in her face something has frozen, a slight painful puckering of the mouth and the eyes. . . . Yesterday this face was majestically carefree. Today she keeps a close watch on it. That is the difference – her pose. In other words, fear.'

In a similar vein, Marguerite Duras accused Brigitte of atrocious behaviour towards the men who loved her, adding that she had left many corpses in her wake but had remained unharmed and had never been forsaken (neither of which was true). Almost despairingly, the merciless critic admitted that, while all men had been warned of the danger of loving Brigitte, none had as yet recoiled (again incorrect). The long catalogue of her failings contrasted her wish to be alone and independent with her need for someone to lull her to sleep – 'the sleep of her lover is her sleep' and each lover to some degree 'a night-watchman.' The highly literary but often self-contradictory analysis of 'Bardot at thirty' went over the old ground of her relationship with her child, and claimed that she did not behave like a mother because she no longer loved the man who had fathered her child and because the child threatened to become her rival.

Among the raging torrent of words pouring forth in the wake of the anniversary, few well-informed, few very nice (in contrast to the accolades Sophia Loren received on her thirtieth birthday around the same time), was Gregor von Rezzori's nasty post-script, published three months later, which described Brigitte as 'cold and bad-tempered' and as 'a horrible little prig.' Half goddess, half animal, she would be happiest, Rezzori assumed, 'running around in an animal reservation playing with the deer and strumming her guitar....' Brigitte's own comment on this particular birthday came via Anthony Perkins whom she told: 'The ideal age is my age. At my age one is old enough to know what one is doing and young enough to do it all the same.' With a furtive glance at the tiny scars on her tanned wrists, she also said: 'I am thirty but there are things about me that are still fifteen. I have gone through much in my life and yet do not feel that I have suffered great tragedies. I love to love and I hate to leave but I love freely and I leave freely.' She said she could not imagine herself at sixty.

Brigitte celebrated the day amid rumours that she was expecting a baby from Bob Zaguri. They started when someone saw a well-known gynaecologist entering her home and when she took the train rather than a car from Paris to St Tropez. If she was still afraid of growing old, she showed no signs of it. With Bob by her side – she called him her body-and-soul guard – she blew out the thirty candles on the big coffee-cream birthday cake and shrieked with joy as she accepted her first present, a sturdy, obstreperous donkey she immediately named 'Saint Trop'. Mijanou represented the family in the party of twelve, all bearing little gifts – perfume, jewellery, a camera, a radio. Bob Zaguri who sported a delicately-shaped beard and moustache produced his country's birthday present, the Saci Prize, a Brazilian oscar, for the year's best performance (in *Vie Privée*).

Brigitte treated her friends to a display of underwater acrobatics and took some of them on short, sharp rides in her high-powered motorboat which attracted an appreciative audience, including sixteen-year-old Alexander Onassis who had come over from Monte Carlo to pay homage to his favourite film star. It was a happy occasion perfectly in tune with Balzac's view of the age

Brigitte had reached as 'the summit of feminine existence.'

One small benefit deriving from the exploration of Brigitte's psyche by journalists was a pleasant afternoon she spent with Françoise Sagan, the 'Brigitte Bardot among French novelists,' who was thrown in at the deep end of literary acclaim at the age of eighteen with her first novel, *Bonjour Tristesse*, whose characters belonged to the school of life and love of which Bardot was a disciple. About a year younger than Brigitte, Françoise had also been married and divorced twice and, like Brigitte, had a little boy. They were brought together in Sagan's flat by a reporter, Richard Grenier, who hoped to observe and record a sensational clash of minds. It was a damp squib. Françoise, shy and introvert, and Brigitte, outgoing, almost aggressive, exchanged no startling thoughts and rose not far above mundane small talk. Only a brief reference to jealousy generated a little heat when Brigitte refused to believe that Françoise was not jealous and had never had occasion to be. Brigitte countered that she was madly jealous, to the extent that if she ever found out that she had been deceived she would reach for a revolver: 'POW, POW, POW!' Talking about love, Françoise told her about an exchange with an American reporter who asked her what she thought of love. Françoise said she had referred him to Madame de La Fayette, the seventeenth-century novelist, one of whose characters replied to the same question with: '*Moi? L'amour? Je fais beaucoup mais je n'y pense jamais.*' (Me? Love? I make it a lot but I never think about it). Brigitte Bardot and Françoise Sagan found more common ground in less contrived situations than during this stage-managed meeting.

Only a few weeks had elapsed since the relaxed, pleasurable birthday junketing when Louis Malle, director of *Vie Privée,* arrived at La Madrague with the script of a film provisionally – and finally – entitled *Viva Maria!* which was based on Preston Sturges' *The Beautiful Blonde from Bashful Bend,* and sizzled with the revolutionary fervour. Every page rattled with quick-fire dialogue and busts of machine-gun bullets. It was a turn-of-the-century tale of a Mexican circus becoming involved in a popular uprising in Central America. Two vaudeville soubrettes, Maria I and Maria II, are in love with a young revolutionary and when he is killed inherit his mission to keep the flame of revolt alive. Continuing the fight for the liberation of the peasants, they advance through the tropical country aided by a sharp-shooter and a conjuror, 'invent' the strip-tease and get entangled in a series of half-comical, half-significant adventures. Without a proper male lead, the script relied on the effect of the two Marias in juxtaposition.

The theme appealed to Brigitte who read the script in one session. Bob Zaguri loved it, probably because Mexico was near enough in spirit and geography to his Brazilian base. Subject to a satisfactory contract, a matter for Olga Horstig, Brigitte was quite prepared to take the part of one of the Marias. The snag was that it confronted her with a formidable competitor. Whom did Malle have in mind for the other Maria? 'Jeanne Moreau,' he told her a little apprehensively – Jeanne Moreau, the beautiful and accomplished actress with whom Malle had not only been personally involved but also made the highly regarded film, *Les Amants*, which had advanced their careers. Visualising a sensational impact from the clash of the child-woman and the sophisticated *femme fatale*, Malle had persuaded Jeanne to take the part. Would Bardot risk a contest with 'a real actress'? It has been said that Brigitte would never have invited comparison with La Moreau had she not been so desperately anxious to prop up her waning career. The theory did her less than justice. Malle had not underestimated her professional courage for, whoever doubted whether she could hold her own against Jeanne Moreau, Brigitte herself had no such qualms. She did not think she would be overshadowed by Moreau's histrionic talent; besides, Jeanne being seven years older, it was she who would have her work cut out to match Brigitte's sex appeal. The two met for dinner and spent a convivial evening together. Both were on their best behaviour and seemed to respect each other genuinely. Malle convinced them that their individual approaches were so different, each advancing along her own route, each using her own weapon from a woman's armoury, that there was no risk of collision. The contrast was indeed starkly evident – here Brigitte's aggressive, acquisitive sexuality, there Jeanne's more reticent, subtly seductive femininity, one pouncing purposefully on her target, the other spinning a web to catch her prey.

Jeanne Moreau was scathing about the popular belief that two women thrown together by circumstances would be at each other's throats and their relationship essentially different from that which would exist between a man and a woman. She was talking about the two Marias but what she said was intended to apply equally to Jeanne Moreau and Brigitte Bardot, which was fair enough except that, when it came to contracts, Jeanne Moreau received 150,000 dollars while Brigitte's fee was 350,000 (to bring her fortune up to over five million dollars).

With production in the hands of the respected Brothers Danziger, and Louis Malle applying his intuition and youthful zest to the task, the outlook was rosy. The story line had strength and guts, humour and good characterisations. Both girls end up as heroines. That the significance of two women revolutionaries fighting for the freedom was not lost became evident years later when the photograph of Bardot and Moreau behind the machine-gun came into vogue, perhaps a little fancifully, to symbolise the German women terrorists of the Baader-Meinhof Group and associated anarchist gangs.

Under Malle's supervision, the groundwork for *Viva Maria*! went ahead at Cuernavaca, a blasé Mexican resort, where long before the arrival of the two divas, the production staff selected locations and went in search of suitable and, most important, equal accommodation for Bardot and Moreau. Both needed places where their privacy could be protected; standards, comfort and facilities had to be the same for both.

In the event a splendid colonial-style villa was found for Jeanne Moreau (whose boy-friend, fashion tsar Pierre Cardin, was expected to join her) while Brigitte, in spite of rumours that she had turned down three haciendas, settled readily for a self-contained wing in Louis Malle's palatial house. Malle was bringing his fiancée and Brigitte Bob Zaguri: 'A woman needs a man wherever she is,' Malle conceded. When Brigitte arrived only a week or so late – to be received by the French cultural attaché who put a Cadillac at her disposal – her entourage, apart from Bob who was put on the pay-roll as assistant producer, included a secretary, a hairdresser, two photographers and her alsatian; that is before she acquired two ducks, a chicken, two St Bernard puppies, two horses, a donkey and a rabbit which, much to Bob Zaguri's chagrin, misbehaved, rabbit-fashion, in the bed he shared with Brigitte.

Brigitte and Jeanne were soon compared with Mexico's two tallest mountains, Popocatepetl and Ixtaccihuatl, whose solemn peaks could be seen from the windows of their respective residences. The altitude, some two thousand three hundred metres above sea level, and the thin air shortened breath and tempers but when Brigitte and Jeanne reported sick immediately after their arrival, it was tactfully attributed not to nerves and last-minute stage fright but to laryngitis (in Bardot's case) and to the local pineapples, the sun and the water which caused attacks of what the crew described as 'The Aztec Trots' or 'The Curse of Montezuma.' Once filming started there were no hold-ups or complications; satisfied with their parts, the two stars worked well together and, after the day's shooting, went their separate ways.

The cast included Hollywood's 'pretty boy' George Hamilton who made a pass at Brigitte but was shunted off in the direction of Jeanne, and Gregor von Rezzori who moonlighted as a reporter for a German magazine. Malle had a knack of putting his actors at ease and, drawing on his previous experience with Bardot and Moreau, managed them with skill and sensitivity. There was no evidence of 'ferocity' to justify the publicity hand-outs referring to them as 'the tigresses.' With the Mexicans calling her '*La Flaca*' (the skinny one) behind her back, Brigitte concentrated on her acting rather than on her sex appeal, although the script required her to consume three men and to appear in a bikini the size of three postage stamps. While competing for the love of the revolutionary (George Hamilton) – a comparatively brief interlude – the two Marias were not at loggerheads. They were a double-act with well-defined roles and fell into them easily. They giggled like schoolgirls when Brigitte fluffed her lines but went patiently through their routine over and over again. Away from their base, as they moved from location to location, they occupied their own trailers which became homes from home.

Towards the end of the seventeen weeks allotted to location work, time began to drag and the altitude became more difficult to bear. Brigitte was showing the strain. At the end of the day, the adrenalin ceased to flow and the lines around her mouth cut deep into her skin. She was not only tired but bored with the work and looked forward to the evenings when she often snuggled up with her favourite authors – Hemingway, Faulkner, Camus and Gide. She still had her moments. Her colleagues – fellow artistes, production staff, camera crew, stage handlers – were wildly enthusiastic about her splendid impersonation of Charlie Chaplin. Emerging from her trailer complete with little moustache, bowler hat, cane and outsize boots, she shuffled and swivelled on her heels and looked endearingly pathetic. Considering Brigitte did not remember seeing a Chaplin film, the act came off remarkably well.

For a day or so, her little gag relieved the boredom which Bob Zaguri could no longer banish. As their friendship began to wear thin, he became the butt of Brigitte's irritation. When she 'entertained' all the hungry dogs of a Mexican village to a special meal, Bob protested; Malle did not think it was such a good idea either because the food she provided for the animals was better than the locals could afford for their Sunday dinner. Brigitte adopted one of the dogs and it was too much for her loyal friend: 'It's either the dog or me,' Bob cried. 'The dog!' Brigitte replied. For a day, her lover hid away sulking. The following night he was back.

A letter from Vadim arrived signed as usual, 'Your old Russian who loves you.' Brigitte sighed. 'I'm glad he married Jane Fonda,' she said unconvincingly, 'it should work out well.' (It did not.)

The daily chore was so arduous that Brigitte was again, for the umpteenth time, flirting with retirement: 'When I sign a contract,' she moaned, 'It's like getting pregnant. It takes nine months and it's miserable. Freedom is over.' Not even sex could compensate her for the misery. Yet, in front of the camera, she performed brilliantly. Even without recourse to her breasts and her bottom, she more than held her own against France's finest actress, and, just by being Bardot, ran away with the honours. She had counted upon her Mexican adventure to bolster her career and the result proved her right. *Viva Maria*! was very much her film.

Among Brigitte's photographs circulated by the *Viva Maria*! publicists was a spoofy one of her pretty face disguised behind a huge moustache and a full, flowing beard. It amused her greatly. She was less amused by another photograph which magazine editors all over the world found much more appealing. It was a picture showing her on her balcony wearing nothing but the tiniest pair of panties. Her reaction was so violent it confounded those who thought of the world's most photographed female as a creation of the media, who owed her success, her fame, her wealth to her photographs – and should be duly grateful. Brigitte did not see it that way. She went to law demanding protection against intrusive cameramen.

Press photographers staged a demonstration outside her house carrying banners inscribed 'BB – Remember Your Beginnings!' and 'Brigitte – You Exaggerate!' A Paris court came gallantly to her rescue with an order forbidding photographers to focus on their favourite subject without obtaining her permission. Editors who had published the offending panties picture were ordered to pay nominal damages of one franc. The verdict caused an uproar. The French press declared that Brigitte had committed professional suicide. Brigitte herself had second thoughts. Her indignation subsided and normal relations with photographers were quietly resumed.

The brief interruption in the supply of Bardot photos owing to the court case enabled a crop of Bardot copies to fill the empty spaces in newspapers and magazines. This harvest of fake Bardots yielded such ripe fruit as Michèle Mercier, a short-lived celebrity; Brigitte's old friend Ursula Andress who made it to the court of James Bond; Catherine Spaak who could not boast the same measurements; and Mylène Demongeot who eventually reached the top on her own merit. With variations, the fashion of skilfully coiffed untidy hair which Bardot created has, of course, survived to this day.

Brigitte was presently obliged to gird herself for a reluctant foray into 'enemy territory' – the United States of America. She was apprehensive and unhappy when she realised that her contract required her to publicise *Viva Maria!* in the States and to attend the openings in New York and Hollywood. When she pleaded with Joe Levine and implored Carlo Ponti to spare her the trial, even threatened to rebel, she was pointedly reminded that she owned, as Americans put it, 'a piece of the action' – a share in the profits the size of which would largely depend on the film's reception in the States. Very well then, she would do what had to be done.

At first she went about the preparations a little morosely but once she had reconciled herself to the inevitable, set out to show the Americans a new dimension of glamour. The next few weeks were spent in fashion houses arguing with designers and seamstresses working on the fifty outfits and six fur coats she was taking with her. She was also taking Bob Zaguri whose job as assistant producer earned him a place on the promotion team, as good an excuse for his presence as anyone could think of.

Arriving in New York on a very cold day (17 December 1965) Brigitte made her grand entrance on American soil in a white coat with white fox lining, collar and trimming: 'Bardot discovers America,' was the key-note of her reception; 'America discovers Bardot' would have been more apt. Not since the heyday of Marilyn Monroe was such homage paid to a movie star. Since publicity was the sole purpose of the enterprise, press reaction was the only barometer that mattered. The dozen or so French newsmen who accompanied her were promptly submerged by some two hundred American reporters assigned to 'cover Bardot.' Whereas the arrival of the Beatles at their peak merited seven seconds of television time, Brigitte's occupied the little screen for fully two minutes.

A strong squad of tough American cops shepherded her through the menacing throng of people who gave off a roar which, it was said, 'would have deafened a bull moose in mating season.' Hundreds of flash-bulbs exploded and in the fearful crush even the guards pinched her bottom. She had a brief bantering confrontation with the press for whose benefit she opened her coat to reveal a sexy, body-clinging white dress, surprisingly without *décolleté*: 'Those who had come to see the famous bust were cheated,' one commentator remarked.

Escorted by a cavalcade of police cars, Brigitte reached the Plaza Hotel where she stayed hidden for the next forty-eight hours. From then on she did all the right things, inspected Times Square and trotted around Central Park in tight pants and sweater. The photographers had a bean-feast. Her face concealed behind white-rimmed dark glasses and a thick scarf, she 'did a Garbo'; if she was left alone, she said, she would love to tour Harlem and Brooklyn. Half obscured by a dozen microphones, she presented herself to the press and, to quote an old hand at the game, 'led hundreds of photographers and reporters by the nose.' Questions, mostly silly ones, were thrown at her hard and fast. Her answers came as quickly.

'What do you think of the American press?' she was asked.

'*Formidable*!' was her ambiguous reply.

'Do you intend to send your good wishes to General de Gaulle?'

'I have already wished him well by voting for him.'

'Do you think it is necessary for a woman to be a mother to be fulfilled?'

'You should try everything once.'

'How old are you?'

'Thirty-one – and you?'

'Do you feel a sex symbol?'

'I am myself!'

'Well, who are you?'

'Look!' she replied and waltzed past her questioner gyrating and swinging her hips.

'What do you think about free love?'

'I don't think when I make love,' Brigitte answered, adapting the Françoise Sagan-Madame de La Fayette reply to a similar question.

She turned the tables on a tiresome reporter who returned to the same subject: 'Have you tried it since yesterday?' she asked him.

'Yes, I did . . . but what do I do now?'

'Keep trying!' Brigitte said amid general uproar.

Sophisticates described the Bardot tour as 'a pseudo-event' but Levine and associates were well pleased with the press coverage although newsmen did not handle the 'gorgeous non-news' (*Newsweek*) too adroitly and produced some quaint copy. The *Daily News* which had their Paris correspondent and six local reporters and photographers on the job came out with a loud wolf-whistle: '*Mon Dieu!* Hoo boy! She's here! In person!' The *World Telegram and Sun* went completely overboard: 'She is Miss World, Miss Universe, Miss Gemini 6 and 7. She is the Rose Bowl Queen, the Sugar Bowl Queen. She is Miss Everything.' Not to be outdone, *Paris Jour* saw her as 'Lafayette in skirts.'

Withal Brigitte was not comfortable in the American milieu. She was upset – bound to be – when a flashbulb exploded so close to her face as she arrived for the New York première that she was briefly blinded. Two doctors attended her and, delighted to get their hands on the ravishing patient, refused to accept payment. Next she complained bitterly when columnist Earl Wilson sneaked into her apartment dressed in overalls as a maintenance engineer 'to fix the lights' (emulating his recent exploit of gate-crashing a party for Princess Margaret dressed as a pantry-man). But she had a sensible half-hour interview with veteran broadcaster Howard K. Smith which was shown at prime time on New Year's Day.

The press received her as rapturously in Los Angeles but

Brigitte seemed inhibited – 'embarrassed' would have been the word had she been capable of embarrassment – by her old often-ventilated anti-Hollywood sentiments. She went listlessly through a routine of sightseeing and parties with Paul Newman and other stars she had previously met. While trying to make it clear that she did not aspire to the mantle of Marilyn Monroe, she was pursued by the name and could not escape comparison with America's much-lamented sex idol.

Brigitte's American tour was not only a uniquely successful public relations exercise to boost her product. It established her before her biggest press audience to date as an intelligent young woman with a sense of humour and a quick wit. Still, she heaved a sigh of relief when it was all over, and, hidden behind a pseudonym, slipped quietly away. Back in Paris, she took to her bed. It was as if she had made love to America – she was exhausted but content.

XIII

Sex and Sachs (1)

Shortly after their return from America, Brigitte and Bob visited a night club in Paris. A mutual friend who saw them thought they behaved like an old married couple with little to say to each other. Brigitte looked bored, Bob uneasy. He had good reason to be. A table nearby was occupied by Paul Albou, Brigitte's middle-aged dentist, a man about-town with a lucrative society and show-business clientele. Brigitte asked him over, they danced and, while Bob was looking the other way, went off together. Bob did not see Brigitte again that week.

Was it a flare-up of desire? Was it love? With interviewers harping on the subject, Brigitte was talking so much about love, she gave the impression that she spent more than the national average of 2,920 hours per year in bed – if not always asleep. The relay of her lovers commanded more statistical and voyeurist interest than a season of her films. Nor could many of her 'night-watchmen' hope to hide under the blanket – few of them, anyway, would have wished to remain anonymous – but I do not think she actually slept with every one of the gentlemen whose names the press suggestively 'linked' with hers. Many were called but not all of them were chosen.

While the good Albou was soon discarded – as a lover but not as a dentist and friend – there were other similar incidents. As Bob Zaguri's time was running out Brigitte seemed in need of a new emotional stimulus. The odds were that his successor would be another *homo brigittis*, a good-looking nonentity prepared to dance to her tune. That did not mean that it was up to any hopeful, however well endowed with the necessary qualifications, to take the initiative. Her intimates assumed as a matter of course that she would, as she had always done, reverse the traditional role of the sexes, pick her man, set the pace. They knew she had been the dominant partner in all her sexual relationships: trust Vadim to describe her as 'a female Don Juan.' Every man was her poodle. Would the pattern be repeated this time?

Only because it was Jean-Luc Godard who put up another proposition did Brigitte agree to make a film based on two of Guy de Maupassant's short stories – 'a concerto on youth' was how he described it. Hers was a tiny part which did not really interest her, nor did the picture go down well with cinema audiences. After the brief interruption, she went back to La Madrague where Bob was still hanging on for dear life. Avoiding strangers, Brigitte did not stray far outside her circle of regulars who visited each other's houses, celebrated weddings, birthdays and other anniversaries, and met in discos and restaurants. She seemed dissatisfied with her luxurious humdrum existence; something was stirring behind her frozen expression and her languid gestures. Her friends were waiting for things to happen. They sensed that Brigitte was heading for a fall. Something did happen but when it did professional Bardot watchers were thin on the ground and accounts of how it happened differ. Even the man most intimately concerned sounded a little uncertain when I talked to him exactly ten years after the event.

Gunter Sachs was six months short of his thirty-fourth year when he entered Brigitte's life in the summer of 1966, the memory of which lights up his lively and surprisingly kindly eyes with the glint of a practised seducer recalling his finest conquest. We met in his house in Chelsea, one of his half-dozen or so homes including a Munich *pied-à-terre*, a grand-seigneurial estate in Upper Bavaria, an apartment in Paris, a house in Lausanne – his legal residence – a chalet in Gstaad and a villa in St Tropez (not the one he occupied in 1966) where he also ran a boutique, Micmac, which has since become a trademark and sprouted many branches.

The Chelsea house, like all his homes, is crammed with works of art – he owns an exquisite art collection; the lounge strewn with cameras, tripods, lights, screens, the implements of his hobby, photographing beautiful women, which he does with consummate skill; the mantlepiece decorated with embossed invitations from duchesses. Then, with valet, secretary and assistant dancing attendance, the man himself, handsome with strong features in which a crowded life has left few lines, his full mouth curled in an amused smile which suggests that there is not much he take seriously. He is every inch one of nature's playboys with great charm and good manners, linguistic dexterity and the self-assurance which often goes with wealth – in his case a personal fortune of some forty million pounds.

Pacing the room with the slight swagger of a winner – European bobsleigh champion, 1958 – he rehearses a story which, even without the Bardot connection, is worth telling as an account of life at the top in the tumultuous and permissive fifties and sixties although it needs to be supplemented with some aspects on which he does not dwell. Gunter Fritz Sachs is – to use a phrase in his native German – *kein unbeschriebenes Blatt* (no blank sheet). Born into an immensely rich German family, he and his brother, Ernst Wilhelm, owe their fortune to grandfather Sachs who invented the free-wheel bicycle and built up his business, Fichtel & Sachs, into a huge industrial empire (ball-bearings and motor-car accessories). Maternal great-grandfather Adam Opel founded the motor-car firm which hears his name, and was elevated to the minor German aristocracy – over-glamorising the glamorous Gunter, the French press, uncritically copied elsewhere, refers to him quite falsely as Count Gunter Sachs von Opel.

As even the most casual German magazine reader knows, the Sachs family was torn asunder when Gunter's father, Consul Willy Sachs, and his wife, the former Elinor von Opel, separated in the mid-thirties, their elder son staying with father while Gunter went with his mother who sold her Opel shares to General Motors and settled in Switzerland. Switzerland became Gunter's home but it was not until the seventies that he took Swiss nationality. He studied art history and mathematics excelling in both, married fellow-student Anne-Marie Faure, daughter of a French-Algerian politician, and set up home at Ouchy, near

Lausanne, where their son Rolf was born. Gunter did a little work as the family firm's foreign representative, although with an annual income of £250,000 he did not have to try very hard. The idyll was rudely disturbed by two tragic blows of fate, the death of his father by his own hand, and the loss of his wife who died while undergoing a small operation. Leaving the conduct of day-to-day business to his brother, Gunter sought consolation in the traditional playgrounds of the super-rich whooping it up with the rest, challenging death in fast cars, motorboats and bobsleighs.

Had Brigitte Bardot read the newspapers – which she did not – she would have known about Gunter's sleek yachts at sea, his wild parties ashore, the long-limbed beauties with whom he whiled away his time. She would have seen his name mentioned in harness with those of such notorious womanisers as the Aga Khan's son, Prince Aly Khan, and the South American heart-throb Porfirio Rubirosa with whom Gunter collaborated on a text book on the art of seduction: 'Gunter is a nice fellow,' Rubirosa would say, 'but he works too hard' – anathema in these circles. When first Aly Khan, then Rubirosa died in motor-car crashes, Gunter naturally assumed their mantle as King of the Playboys. At Rubirosa's funeral, he met Pat Lawford and Jean Smith, the late President John F. Kennedy's sisters, who invited him to their estate at Hyannisport, Massachusetts, where he made friends with their brother, Senator Edward Kennedy: 'If there is anything I can do for you,' Teddy Kennedy told him, 'don't hesitate to let me know.' For Brigitte Bardot's sake, we shall soon see, Gunter took the Senator up on his offer before long.

In the meantime, while they did not know that their paths would cross, Gunter almost matched Brigitte word for word with the copy he provided for gossip columnists and magazine writers in a dozen languages. Almost every photograph of Brigitte with a new boy-friend had a counterpart in one of Gunter's with his latest girl-friend. While every girl who rubbed shoulders with him was publicised as 'his fiancée' – not infrequently echoing his good intentions – reports about his sexual exploits read like a reverse carbon-copy of Brigitte Bardot's love life.

Following in the footsteps of the 'beautiful people,' as I was obliged to do for some years, I observed Gunter Sachs in Monte Carlo and St Moritz, in Munich, Paris, London, always in the company of a ravishing model girl or jet-set lady, a different one for every place and every season. He had a brief flirtation with the delectable Tina Onassis soon after she lost her peregrinating husband, Greek shipping tycoon Aristotle Onassis, to Maria Callas – Gunter promptly turned up at a fancy-dress ball costumed and bewigged as Maria Callas, a brilliant impersonation but not a joke in the best taste. As Tina turned to the Marquess of Blandford (and married him), Gunter relaxed with Marina Doria, the nubile world waterski champion who eventually married the son and heir of Italy's ex-King Umberto. She was still in the picture – being photographed with Gunter – when he was entangled with Mara Lane, the starlet; then came – the sequence is difficult to determine – Paule Rizzo, the Chanel model, followed by Anka Hahn, an architect's daughter, whom he fitted out with five thousand pounds' worth of *haute couture* and adopted as 'constant companion.' True to form she also married another man, Serge Marquand, one of Brigitte Bardot's closest friends.

In the highly competitive world of rich-boy-meets-beautiful-girl, Gunter was bound to run into the occasional spot of trouble. In a fight over a woman in the bar of the Palace Hotel in St Moritz where the world's most prosperous skiers thaw out with Mimosas and Bellinis after a day on the slopes, he was sent sprawling with a black eye and a cut which needed several stitches but, characteristically for a man who assimilates misfortune easily, turned up later in the evening with an intriguing eye-patch to receive a hero's welcome.

He cut a less admirable figure with his next *armante du coeur,* Persia's ex-Queen Soraya, daughter of a Persian father and a German mother, whom the Shah had reluctantly divorced when she failed to give him an heir. The highly-publicised love match came to an abrupt end when Gunter announced their impending wedding. The result was another black eye – after the Shah's angry intervention, the lawyers of Gunter's intended bride issued a statement saying that she had no intention of marrying him. The indomitable Casanova consoled himself with Brigitte – no, not yet Brigitte Bardot but Brigitte Laaf, another beautiful model girl. Ears were cocked for the sound of marriage bells when poor Miss Laaf went down with a tumour which was thought to be incurable. Disregarding defeatist medical advice that he ought to let the girl die quietly somewhere in the sun, the disconsolate Gunter travelled far and wide with her in search of doctors and remedies, even took her to Lourdes to pray for salvation, until he found a specialist in Heidelberg prepared to risk a life-and-death operation. Surgery was successful, Brigitte Laaf recovered almost miraculously but the year-long battle to save her had drained both and, once she was on her feet, they parted.

Like Brigitte Bardot – *mutatis mutandum* – Gunter Sachs hated being without a partner. As she needed a man around at all times, he was not happy without a girl by his side. The one I saw him with next was a stunning German mannequin, Heidi Balzer. For eighteen months she and Gunter were inseparable flitting around the South of France, sailing in the Mediterranean, winter-sporting in Switzerland, doing the season in London and the night clubs in Paris. In June 1966, they motored from La Capilla, Gunter's villa in St Tropez, to Monte Carlo for the Century Ball, highlight of the year's Riviera social round. They had a good time, and a day later Gunter put Heidi on a plane for New York where she was due to model clothes, while he returned to St Tropez.

At a loose end – 'unattached' was the word he used – he scouted around for company and ended up dining at the fashionable Vieille Fontaine restaurant near St Tropez with some *copains*, his old friend Roger Vadim among them. The atmosphere was vibrant with the presence of Brigitte Bardot who was being wined and dined by Bob Zaguri and a number of acolytes at the next table. Gunter did not know any of them. He told me he had not met Brigitte before – he had, in fact, shaken hands with her in Geneva in 1960 when a friend took him to watch her on location while she was making *Vie Privée*; oh yes, he also had a brief encounter with her while renting a house next door to hers when she solemnly presented him with a rose from her garden which he planted, named 'Brigitte Bardot' and nursed conscientiously. He had also been standing close to her a few days earlier at a wedding party but they had never had a real conversation.

That evening at the Vieille Fontaine Gunter Sachs, like most people in Brigitte's presence, felt the magnetism of her personality. He did not bother – could not have if he had tried – to hide his fascination, and was thrilled when she did not evade his stare: 'It was as if two wafts of fog were meeting and merging,' he said. He paid no attention to the men with Brigitte, and she behaved as if Bob Zaguri was not there. Gunter assumed she was, like him, 'unattached.' Vadim and Brigitte called out to each other from table to table, Gunter was drawn into the bantering conversation, the two parties joined up and Vadim introduced Gunter to Brigitte: 'Surprising that we have not talked before,' Gunter said kissing her fingers. He held on to her hand an instant longer than is customary and she did not pull it away. Wafts of fog merging? It was more like an electric current running from one to the other.

According to one account, Gunter wooed Brigitte for seven days; seven minutes was a more accurate estimate. Tactfully, he left Bob Zaguri out of the version he gave me. Bob was also left out when Brigitte and Gunter rose with one thought that needed no words and walked out of the restaurant together. Vadim knew what was happening; it would be surprising if Bob Zaguri did not. But neither Vadim nor Zaguri was aware that significantly it was not Brigitte who made the running – one reason why she does not look back on the evening with undiluted joy – but Gunter who carried her away with him. That night while Bob Zaguri waited in vain for her to come home she was with Gunter at La Capilla.

Brigitte in the throes of a new affair was a joy to behold. She sparkled, she hummed with pleasure like her guitar when the right note was struck. Messengers arrived bearing huge bouquets of roses – where generous admirers ordered two dozen, Gunter sent a hundred. They talked easily. An ideal couple, it seemed, physically complementary, their totally different backgrounds fusing in an invigorating meeting of minds. But there was no question of Bardot dominating this man intellectually or emotionally.

His life style was more grandiose than hers. His yacht, *Dracula,* was bigger than her boat *Jannique*, his half dozen cars more opulent than her old Rolls-Royce though, while he preferred to drive himself, Brigitte employed a rather imposing ex-actor from the Ivory Coast as her chauffeur and kitted him out with expensive white uniforms from a top Paris tailor. Like her, Gunter had his entourage: he was, of course, at least ten times as rich as Brigitte who, for the first time, savoured the aphrodisiac effect of great wealth.

The impression she made on 'Sachsy', as she called him – he referred to her as 'Bardot' throughout our conversation – was strangely at odds with her popular image: 'She was quite different from what people thought of her and I was led to believe by the things said and written about her,' he told me. 'She is a woman of high intelligence, a superb writer who conveys the intensity of her feelings in beautiful, erotic language. . . .' Gunter keeps a big bundle of Brigitte's love letters in a locked steel box in Munich. 'Amazingly shrewd judgment . . . a quick grasp of a situation. . . . Her decisions are based on judgment – judgment and intuition,' Gunter said, but quickly added: 'She is often right but she is also lazy, and other influences tend to impair or supersede her judgment. Then she can be quite wrong.'

While Bob Zaguri cooled his heels at La Madrague, Brigitte and Gunter swanned all over the Riviera, sailed in *Dracula*. They listened to the famous guitar player at Le Pirate, near Menton, haunt of the wealthy, where a gipsy girl read Gunter's hand and told him: 'This is your lucky day!' He and Brigitte went on to gamble in Monte Carlo, Brigitte's first visit to a casino. Open-mouthed she watched her notoriously lucky new friend backing numbers 14, 13, 15 at roulette and saw each number coming up, netting him several thousand pounds which he, in the manner of an old-fashioned cavalier, presented to her.

Two days later they went to a fancy dress ball as 'Monsieur and Madame Dracula' from which it was but a short step to the idea of *Monsieur et Madame* – or rather *Herr und Frau* – Sachs. It was four in the morning when Gunter told Brigitte: 'I am going to marry you!' She accepted his forceful proposal; her views on marriage had mellowed since Mijanou's wedding the previous year to Patrice Bauchau, an actor, with whom she seemed happy enough.

Next morning Gunter asked his secretary to order a wedding present for Brigitte at Cartier's – three bracelets, one of diamonds, one of rubies, one of sapphires, the colour of the tricolour. It was not as simple to organise the wedding which would galvanise millions of Bardot fans and rouse the media to new paroxysms. Vadim was the first to be told. Brigitte and Gunter consulted him about the best way to stage an elopement and organise a secret wedding. Was there a place in the world where they would be safe from crowds and reporters? Each of them came up with suggestions, shouting out countries and cities as in a game of international monopoly. Paris was out – impossible to keep a secret in Brigitte's own backyard. Not Munich either where the whole of Bavaria was liable to cheer Gunter to the altar, or rather to the register office. 'How about Las Vegas?' Vadim asked – that's where he and Jane Fonda were married the previous year. Las Vegas appealed to Brigitte and Gunter agreed. Neither wanted their families involved.

With people of huge property, the road to happiness must be paved by lawyers and accountants. Brigitte and Gunter contacted their legal and financial advisers in Paris and Lausanne and instructed them to draw up a marriage contract providing for a strict division of property. In this love match there would be no marriage of personal fortunes. Both wanted to get away from St Tropez. Gunter suggested a brief visit to the Sachs estate and hunting lodge in Rechenau, near Oberaudorf, in the mountains of Upper Bavaria. 'Hunting lodge?!' Brigitte shuddered. She wanted nothing to do with a place associated with the killing of animals. Gunter reassured her; he had never killed an animal and had no intention of ever doing so. Brigitte allowed herself to be persuaded. She sent a message to Bob Zaguri that she was going to Paris to do some shopping.

They set off for the alpine retreat accompanied by Serge and Anka Marquand – Serge an old friend of Brigitte's from Vadim's time, German-born Anka a 'Bardot double' and old flame of Gunter's. For Brigitte it was a journey into a new world. While they lost themselves in the thick woods and defied the pouring rain to spend a day on top of the mountain, a local seamstress ran up a bright-red *Dirndl*, the Bavarian girls' national costume, for Brigitte, shortening it at her request until there was hardly any skirt left. Brigitte ordered three more *Dirndl* but the seamstress still did not know who she was working for: 'You look damn like Brigitte Bardot,' she said.

The Rechenau police chief called out his entire force to patrol the estate and gave Brigitte a police whistle which she tried out with ear-splitting fervour. Privacy or no privacy, Gunter could not resist illuminating the landscape with a giant fireworks display which attracted people from far and near. Brigitte watched enthralled as some three thousand pounds' worth of huge crackers exploded and painted fiery patterns in the night sky: 'Bravo! Bravo!' she clapped her hands excitedly. She was beginning to feel like the chatelaine of a fairy castle in Ruritania (but shocked some Germans when she washed down a sizeable portion of sauerkraut with champagne).

Much of Gunter's time was taken up with preparations for the wedding and the honeymoon. He called Teddy Kennedy in Washington and asked him to help with the arrangements. Teddy promised to organise transport and reservations and recommended a Las Vegas lawyer and a judge with the authority to solemnise a marriage. Somewhat rashly he also undertook to keep the press at arm's length.

First stop on the journey into matrimony – by private jet and car – was Paris where the couple put up at Gunter's apartment at 32 avenue Foch (one floor above the Rainiers of Monaco). Brigitte visited her own apartment only long enough to pack two trunk-loads of clothes. They signed the marriage contract and Gunter dropped in at Cartier's to collect the wedding present for his bride. Travelling as Madame Bordat and Monsieur Scar, the couple boarded the plane for Los Angeles with the Marquands, Philippe d'Exea, Brigitte's current 'court' photographer, and two other friends, Peter Notz and Gerard Le Clery. They were still undetected, or so they thought. At Los Angeles airport they were met by a hundred reporters – someone must have given the game away: 'Not me!' Gunter protested when it was suspected that his love of publicity had got the better of him.

Photographers charged Brigitte as if they were storming the Bastille; a radio reporter thrust a microphone in her mouth leaving two of her teeth wobbling. Extricating themselves, Brigitte, Gunter and their party reached two tiny jets hired for them by Senator Kennedy for the half-hour flight to Las Vegas. They went straight from the airport to collect their licence, then on to the lawyer's office which was fragrant with lilac, courtesy of Teddy Kennedy, and were joined by Judge John Mowbray. Brigitte was wearing a provocatively brief deep-red mini-shift and carried a single red rose; Gunter was dressed in a blazer, white trousers, open-neck, nay: open-navel, shirt, white moccasins, no socks – 'He had no time to put them on,' Brigitte apologised for him (but when I talked to Gunter he was not wearing socks either). Thus, on Bastille Day, 14 July – 'Most appropriately,' Brigitte commented – the ceremony was performed in eight minutes flat: 'May the road rise to meet you and may the wind be ever at your back!' was the judge's quaint blessing. Brigitte looked up to her new husband and trilled: 'He's *formidable*, the last of *les princes de charme* – I adore him.' One of the poetic sentiments attributed to her was that she had given herself in marriage to Gunter because 'what else can you give a man who has everything – it is the most beautiful gift?'

With Brigitte's photographer snapping away, the lawyer cheered, there were toasts in champagne and kisses all round, the judge claiming two from Brigitte. Gunter showed off his big wedding ring and looked as smug as if Germany had conquered

France for the second time in a quarter of a century. Brigitte was said to have been frightened because she did not understand the marriage vows she had to repeat in English which may have been owing to the judge's Irish-American accent. It is more likely that she was frightened because she had entered into marriage so precipitately. 'Marriage,' she said before long, 'must be a stroke of madness,' a more characteristic remark. The wedding party celebrated with a breakfast at the Tropicana.

In St Tropez, Bob Zaguri was stunned by the report from Las Vegas: 'It's a big joke,' he said. Shaking his head incredulously, he added: 'I thought she was shopping in Paris.' He packed his bags and moved out of La Madrague. Whispers circulating freely at the time suggested that Gunter had paid off Zaguri with a quarter of a million marks – some fifty thousand pounds sterling. Not Gunter Sachs! If money passed hands, it was between Brigitte and Bob and went under the heading of 'compensation' in respect of film business they had planned together. In any case, Brigitte undertook to make a film in which Zaguri had an interest, the first she would be making when she resumed work.

'It's bound to be stormy,' Vadim predicted. An open letter (by Father Bouyer) in *Vie Catholique Illustrée* flayed Brigitte uncharitably: 'Whether you believe in him or not, Brigitte,' it said, 'may God forgive you for the harm you are doing us. In eight minutes you are married again. You no longer belong to M. Vadim not to M. Charrier, nor to M. Zaguri; you belong to M. Sachs. In eight minutes you have sworn faithfulness for life. If someone else turns up tomorrow whom you do not know today, will you get married again? Will M. Sachs, in turn, use the words of your last boy-friend, M. Zaguri – "Its a big joke"?' A jubilant German headline announced: 'Brigitte Bardot is now Frau Sachs!' The French press retaliated with editorials which sounded as if a German had stolen a French national treasure.

After two days in Los Angeles at the Beverly Hills Hotel's number one bungalow, Brigitte and her third husband were off on their honeymoon in Tahiti. She in a tiny bikini and Gunter in a sarong hopped from South Sea island to South Sea island in a jet, swam and strolled in the sand until Brigitte stepped on a coral or sea urchin and cut her foot. The wound needed two stitches and blighted the honeymoon. Pursued by mosquitos, snap-happy tourists and French cameramen who had caught up with them and dogged her every step, Brigitte was getting irritable. She, too, seemed to blame Gunter for the publicity: 'We are never alone,' she was heard screaming at him, the first crack in the façade of their wedded bliss. Gunter angrily denied a suggestion that he had sold the rights in the photographic coverage of the honeymoon to a French agency for £25,000 – what Philippe d'Exea's arrangement might have been was a different matter. Whoever was the guilty party, long before the honeymoon was over extensive kiss-by-kiss and blow-by-blow accounts appeared in the French press.

Brigitte's injured foot troubled her on the second stage of the honeymoon which she and Gunter spent in Acapulco as guests of hotelier Teddy Stauffer, one of Hedy Lamarr's ex-husbands. While swimming in his pool, her wound broke open requiring more medical attention; her only consolation was that no doctor would accept a fee for treating her dainty foot. She was anxious because she was due to report for her new film almost immediately. If the wound was healing slowly, she was making a rapid recovery from her 'stroke of madness'. A few more days removed from reality, and it was back to business as usual.

XIV

Sex and Sachs (2)

Brigitte and Gunter had not been married six weeks when their friends were already running a private sweepstake, top prize going to the one who guessed accurately how long the 'petite-bourgeoise gone wild' (Henri-Georges Clouzot's sobriquet) and the 'King of the Playboys' would stay together. The most optimistic estimates varied between six and twelve months but those who gave them no more than three months were confident they were holding the winning ticket. They watched like hawks for signs of trouble such as Gunter trying to cope with Brigitte's exaggerated demands on his time: 'She wants a man to be around always,' he said as if he had only just found out. But he tried to mollify her: 'I stopped going to the office and worked from home,' he told me. 'I took to conducting my affairs by telephone and have done so ever since.'

They decided to make Paris their base, keeping their own apartments. As with the apartments, so with their respective interests – they kept them apart. Gunter did not concern himself with her business: 'Very occasionally, Brigitte consulted my financial advisers as well as her own,' he explained. He had a healthy respect for her acumen: 'She is richer than most actresses and has invested wisely,' he said with a tinge of admiration. 'Our communion was mental and spiritual rather than practical; we communed intellectually rather than in our activities. Our view of life, our philosophy, our ethics were the same. We were in total agreement about the things that should or should not be done.'

His respect for Bardot is still as great as it was ten years ago, so is his bewilderment with her: 'Bardot could be full of tenderness and love one moment, he recalled. 'The next minute she was low-key, apathetic, useless. Then again, as rapidly, she switched to wild enthusiasms. She has tremendous resources, can do anything she wants to do.' The difficulty was that basically they had nothing in common but themselves, had their own circles of friends, their own preoccupations, their own predilections which complicated life. For example: 'We both like to eat well but. . . .' A creature of luxury, Gunter loved luxury restaurants; Brigitte liked little bistros and formed an emotional attachment to this one and that one. 'The same with dogs,' Gunter sighed. She preferred simple things rather than cutting a big swathe.

Gunter Sachs has talked freely about the minutiae of his marriage saying a great deal with which Brigitte would not agree. He thought, for instance, that it was useful for a married couple to be apart at times but for no more than three weeks; for Brigitte, three weeks alone were an eternity, such a long time that anything might happen as, in the end, it did. He felt it did not matter if they lived in separate apartments as long as they were no farther than a hundred metres apart: 'Come the night, though,' he said, 'we must be together. In bed – nil metres apart.'

Having been separated for a while, Gunter never asked Brigitte whether she had been faithful and whether she still loved him. To the first question he did not expect an honest answer, anyway. 'The second question was smothered in kisses,' he said. If it was a choice between a good conversation and a good bed, his answer was that good conversation in a bad bed was preferable to a good bed and no conversation. He liked to be alone with his wife – but not at home; he would rather go out with her *à deux*. They hardly ever went to parties. He never expected her to wear models from his boutique – 'She was not my publicity girl!' – but he did not mind people staring at her – it was a compliment. Should she wear trousers? 'Trousers suit her very well,' he quipped. What about pets, boy-friends and slippers? 'Nothing against pets. Brigitte kept – let me see – eight cats and fourteen dogs . . . one can't be sure because there were always new kittens and puppies. But boy-friends – ceertainly not! Slippers – they did not have any, Brigitte and he both went barefoot. Brigitte's favourite food? Potato purée. Her favourite game? Unprintable!

In their halcyon days Gunter was asked what would happen if he met another woman and was smitten: 'That's what happened when I met Brigitte,' he replied. 'It could happen again.' And if he suddenly received a telegram from her: 'Forgive me – but I cannot help it . . .'? 'I would sit down and think and work out a strategy,' was his answer. But he was not going to reveal his battle plan. There was less time to prepare for such a contingency than he thought. The next few months became a strenuous exercise in marriage, a constant struggle against temptations, an uphill effort to keep in step and reconcile differences. A few steps forward hand in hand, followed by retreat into their own shells. To take his own metaphor to the logical conclusion – fog clouds may merge but they soon evaporate.

On the surface all seemed well when they remembered their families whom they had left behind panting and bewildered in their headlong rush into marriage. There was Gunter's mother (Frau Elinor Kirchner, after remarriage), his eleven-year-old son Rolf, brother Ernst Wilhelm who had as yet not exchanged more than a few dozen words with his sister-in-law. Rolf was most eager to meet his step-mother – or, rather, Brigitte Bardot: 'Will she give me a signed photograph?' asked the young Bardot fan. Brigitte tried to be pleasant, none too successfully. She did not enjoy the mammoth party for two hundred and fifty guests which was her introduction to German society. Gunter noticed how impatient she was. It was time to take her back to St Tropez for the reverse process, Brigitte introducing her husband belatedly to her parents. Totty and Pilou were a little wary of their darling's husbands. No good getting too closely involved – one never knew how long it would last.

There were a few cracks in the young marriage which were as yet hair-thin and invisible to the naked eye but it needed only a little knock for the damage to show. It showed when Brigitte embarked on her new film, *A Coeur Joie*, an Anglo-French venture in which Bob Zaguri was involved. The English producer was Kenneth Harper, his French co-producer Francis Cosne who had been much in evidence at the time of Brigitte's famous suicide attempt. Brigitte's contract gave her the right to choose story, director (she picked Serge Bourguignon) and co-star. When she insisted that the male lead should go to Laurent Terzieff, one of her sparring partners during the tests for *La Vérité*, everybody (including Gunter) thought she was more interested in Terzieff's virility than his star quality. They were wrong. Again, everybody (including Gunter) suspected some wicked possibilities because Bob Zaguri was associated with the production and would be present during most of the shooting in Paris, London and Scotland (with James Robertson Justice representing the Scottish element). The problem did not arise because Brigitte rarely revived old love affairs and never worried about meeting an ex-lover; if Zaguri was embarrassed that was his look out.

The subject of *A Coeur Joie* was a typical Bardot story – French model girl goes to England while her lover stays behind. It looked like another case of Bardot's life inspiring a Bardot film, when Brigitte's independent husband refused to accompany her to Scotland. Unlike her film character she did not want to go on her own. 'I'll come and visit you,' Gunter promised. 'Come with me now – or not at all!' she hissed angrily, but this was one husband who would not take orders. Dejectedly, Brigitte went off alone. She was diffident when she arrived in London on the way to Scotland – in the shortest of kilts, sandals and no stockings – looking like a girl no husband would gladly send out into the world alone. Reporters badgered her: 'Why is your husband not with you?' 'I will talk about my new film, not about my marriage!' she retorted sharply. Recovering her composure, she hitched up her kilt even higher for the benefit of the photographers and said: 'It is a very beautiful love story.' The film or the marriage? No further comment.

After a night's rest, Brigitte travelled north in her Rolls. At her destination – Dirleton, East Lothian – she put up, appropriately enough, at a hotel called The Open Arms. Almost a week elapsed before she could fling her open arms around Gunter who arrived carrying a big golf bag. They made up their quarrel at dinner in their apartment but Gunter seemed more interested in his golf than in her work. Next morning, Brigitte rose early for her outdoor scenes at an old castle and on the beach; two hours later, Gunter was on his way to the golf course grimly determined to improve his handicap. That was the routine for a few days with Gunter paying brief visits to the set. Whenever he turned up Bob Zaguri made himself scarce. Brigitte was unperturbed but it was not a situation that appealed to Gunter who turned the tables on her. For once it was not she who walked off but Gunter; when she returned to the hotel he told her that he was off to Bavaria. She pleaded with him to stay but could not change his mind.

Disappointment, a touch of melancholy showed through when she was yet again challenged on the subject of LOVE. Her response was epigrammatic, erudite – the purpose of the exercise – good publicity for the film: 'Love,' she said, 'is the greatest illusion. At the instant when you seem to share the whole world with someone else, you are in fact completely alone. . . . Love is the supreme expression of egotism.' She quoted Graham Greene: '. . . wildly in love, one sees in the eyes of the other person nothing but the reflection, enormously magnified, of oneself.' This emotion, *un coup de foudre* (flash of lightning), was ecstatic, painful and hopeless. . . . It was one of the supreme human experiences but it had nothing to do with marriage, children or washing the dishes.

'That's the subject of our film,' she said coming to the point that mattered. 'I chose it myself. I am a cover girl living in Paris with my lover . . . the affair becomes banal . . . then I meet someone . . . I go to London to model a dress . . . he is there, we fall in love and run away to Scotland. . . .' There was a scene in which her wedding dress is torn off – 'very symbolic,' she said. She was quick to come up with another literary allusion to drive her argument home. She was reading Scott Fitzgerald's *Tender is the Night* but did not like it because it described a man who goes to the ultimate in love but succumbs to self-pity when it turns out badly: 'The point is to dare,' was her own philosophy, 'and not to be sorry whatever happens!' It sounded like a message addressed to Gunter Sachs.

Once the unit moved to London she felt deserted and lonely. Zaguri was *hors de combat*; Terzieff was otherwise engaged; but it did not take Brigitte long to find another gallant knight to be teased into attack. Her new playmate was a member of the cast, Mike Sarne, the Austro-English pop-star-turned-actor, who played the part of a fashion photographer. Mike who does not subscribe to the old Viennese saying, '*Hat der Jüngling ein Vergnügen, sei er dankbar und verschwiegen*' (If a young man has his fun, be he grateful and keep mum) has since talked a great deal about Brigitte and himself.

With his lean and hungry look, a cut above most of Brigitte's casuals, Mike, ambitious, self-possessed, masculine, took her in his stride. Their romance was a movable feast. They went to Paris but Sarne felt out of his depth 'in her territory'. Returning to London he took her to his digs in Chiswick – suburban of suburbs – which he shared with a Chinese restaurateur – hardly the ideal love-nest for a French superstar and wife of one of Europe's wealthiest playboys. Mike was overwhelmed: 'She is irresistible because she has made a careful study of being irresistible,' he opined, 'she thinks only about money, power, her image, happiness.' While the fascination lasted – a few days, no more – Serge Bourguignon had difficulty digging them out of their retreat.

However intent on making a contribution to the analysis of the Bardot phenomenon, Mike Sarne did not come up with any shattering new conclusions. For Brigitte it was a minor affair which she soon brushed aside as if it had never happened. She felt neither loss nor remorse when she returned to Paris to be reunited with Gunter who had taken time off to enjoy the uninhibited Munich October Festival, where beer is imbibed from giant beer mugs in incredible quantities, but which is hardly the 'orgy' which imaginative friends described it as to Brigitte.

They stayed together in Gunter's apartment, four hundred square metres of perfect interior decoration, simple contrasting colours, marble, no faults, not a thing out of place, like an ice-cold clear diamond (his description); not, as he realised too late, 'ideal for a woman from a doll's house with a bird's craving for a warm nest.' Brigitte was prepared to endorse that: 'A fireplace without a fire!' she sneered. 'When I wanted to light it, Gunter was afraid the place would burn down.' She was scathing about the rows and rows of books bound in fine leather which turned out to be spines without pages: 'A decorator's job with nothing personal about it.' She suffered it for his sake. For a while there was harmony: 'Brigitte had to get up at seven a.m. to go to the Billancourt studios,' Gunter told me. He used to sleep on blissfully: 'One morning she returned after an hour. . . .' While he rubbed the sleep from his eyes, she told him that all work at the studio had stopped because the Scottish heather, imported for close-ups of her lying on a Scottish hillside, was not fire proofed. 'She had nothing to do, so we spent the day in the country,' Gunter said.

The next morning she went off as usual but was back by nine: 'What's happened now?' Gunter asked. 'The set has burned down – all except the heather.' While the damage was being repaired, the couple went to Majorca but Brigitte was too exhausted and weak ('No wonder,' said her producer, 'she hardly eats') to enjoy the unexpected holiday. She had a few more days of gruelling work including a total of six hours in a bath-tub for a scene which did not occupy six minutes: 'I never mind retakes,' she said gallantly. 'I am a perfectionist and prepared to work as long as it takes to get it right.' In spite of all the effort, the film was a flop for which Brigitte – with her responsibility for story, director and co-star – could not escape a share of the blame.

Resuming her empty life at La Madrague she found Gunter difficult to manage. Serge and Anka Marquand and the ever-present Philippe d'Exea worked hard to smooth out some rough marital passages – Gunter trying to escape from round-the-clock togetherness into the odd game of boccia with the locals or Brigitte taking umbrage when he invited a young German mannequin to join the house party. Philippe came to the rescue: 'I made it look as if I was interested in the girl' – another crisis averted. Gunter looked on his life with Brigitte as an experiment: 'I was hoping to develop a new style of marriage,' he said. It misfired. Looking back on the slow disintegration, he added: 'We were terribly in love but our love burned too intensely; and when it burns too much it is liable to burn itself out.'

His idea of amusing Brigitte and keeping their flickering love alive was to gather a crowd around them and draw her into his frantic high life when all she wanted was to do nothing except play and talk with her animals. La Madrague was always full of people; she and Gunter were never alone. Her favourite home became the playground of a host of friends like the Marquands, the Dussarts (Jicky was now married), Paul Albou, Gerard de Clery and a changing cast of passing visitors.

Brigitte was upset when Gunter left on business trips to Munich or Paris: 'She married a barefoot boy,' Philippe d'Exea said, 'she does not want to see Gunter in a waistcoat and jacket. That's something she can't understand. If he is preoccupied with serious matters she feels cheated.... Unless it's holiday all the year round, she will leave him....' When Gunter asked her to go with him she was not happy either. Would she join him and some Swiss friends for dinner? She would not. (How famous women hate being shown off to their rich husbands' business associates – it was the same with Aristotle Onassis and Jackie Kennedy.) Brigitte was sceptical when Gunter sponsored a film – about a playboy and a cover girl – in which he proposed to star her opposite Patrice Bauchau, Mijanou's husband. She turned him down and the project died in its infancy.

A roamer by nature – Cannes, Nice, Monte, Venice – Gunter tried to drag his reluctant wife with him. He wanted to go out every evening but Brigitte was only just recovering from a frightening experience when she was recognised by a posse of tourists who surrounded her, pulled at her shirt, reached for her hair, pressed their cameras in her face until she escaped in a little boat whose owner rowed her to safety: 'When I heard this story,' Gunter recalled, 'I began to understand why she hated going out.'

They did go to Rome for Brigitte's next film, *Histories Extraordinaires* based on an Edgar Allan Poe story. It was as well that Gunter was with her because Brigitte's leading man was Alain Delon, whose effect on the opposite sex was almost as notorious as hers. Vadim was there with his wife, Jane Fonda, and working on the script for an episode in the film in which Jane stars. Brigitte tried not to show her resentment of her ex-husband's second wife although the Vadim marriage was as shaky as her own with Gunter. The two couples, an uneasy foursome, went out together making the best of an embarrassing situation.

Back in Paris, Brigitte retreated to her own apartment and spent much of her time pottering around in the dressing-room, experimenting with the jars of cream, phials and tubes which spilled over from her make-up case; looking long and intently in the ornamental circular mirror; or in her sitting-room with the red and green easy-chairs, the solid furniture, some presents from Pilou, others picked up in antique shops; leafing through volumes which filled the bookcases along two walls, gazing on the dozen frameless Bardot paintings and drawings on top. Time and again she returned to the card table and a half-finished game of patience or picked up the guitar, accompanying herself to a low-key song. And there were the animals. . . .

Animals, not only in the apartment and at Bazoches. When she heard that two score or more dogs were condemned to be destroyed at an animal home, she jumped into her Rolls, drove to the home and spent hours choosing fifteen animals worthy of salvation. She took them with her to Bazoches and started thinking up names for them, beginning with one she christened Betterave (Beetroot). It was not long before Brigitte was labelled 'Madonna of the Strays'.

She and Gunter saw little of each other but when everybody

thought that the end of their marriage was nigh, they arranged to spend a week together in Gstaad as the guests of Peter Notz at his sumptious chalet. Gunter and his son Rolf had to wait for Brigitte who was working in Paris on her regular New Year's Eve show, but when she arrived at Gstaad she pooh-poohed stories of a rift: 'We are perfectly happy,' she declared. 'Gunter and I need to be independent but we also need each other.' They went on to St Moritz where the Shah was in residence at the Villa Souvretta, the resort's biggest chalet. Ignorant of the Shah's strong views on Gunter's brief romance with Soraya, Brigitte was convinced her husband wanted her to meet the ruler of Iran. They were, as usual, arguing about Gunter's mania for socialising but Brigitte found a perfect excuse for opting out when she received news from St Tropez that, after a few hectic years of uphill struggles, Raoul Lévy to whom she owed her first big success had come to the end of the road and shot himself. Terrified by the thought of death, mourning Raoul – and the gap his end left in her past – she went into a state of depression which was quite incomprehensible to Gunter.

The prospects for *A Coeur de Joie* looked so poor that Brigitte agreed to help Bob Zaguri drum up interest. She wanted to get away from Gunter for a while, yet was upset when he did not object to her joining Zaguri. She needed to talk, pour out her heart – even to the press. Bob was happy and alarmed at the same time. He warned newspapermen: 'She always says what she thinks, even if it loses her friends. Pretence is totally alien to her.'

In her reflective mood, she mused about things that occupied her mind and, as if looking at herself, talked about her clothes, her make-up, money, sex, marriage. She was not as rash as Bob Zaguri expected, took care not to destroy the Bardot myth but allowed the reality to come through now and then. As an actress and trendsetter, her appearance was important. She said the clothes she wore in her films reflected her personal taste but not always. She like pastel colours best, and loose garments that billowed in the wind (shades of Marilyn Monroe's windblown skirt in *The*

Seven Year Itch), but hated frills, fringes, trimmings. 'Ten or twelves times a year,' she said, 'I have to wear *haute couture* gowns for big parties – I don't like it and never wear the same gown twice; I give them away.' She still did not wear jewellery except for her thin gold chain and, maybe, one ruby ring; or hats, for that matter, except for a bathing cap or a straw hat to protect her from the sun. Shoes – shoes were another story. She loved all kind of shoes, lace-ups, sandals, pumps; she had about seventy pairs.

Hairdressers were her *bête noire*: 'My hair is my treasure – I wash it myself. I will have no coiffeur. Most of them make pastries or Pretzel of our hair.' In spite of her make-up arsenal, she used no skin cream and concentrated on lips and eyes, 'the most important features in a woman's face.' A lot of black around her eyes – too much, most of her directors complained – and a drop of atropin or lemon juice in the eye worked wonders. She left her eyebrows alone but had a lipstick for every occasion – summer, winter, mornings, evenings, indoors, outdoors, sun, rain, swimming, dancing and – kissing.

Being rich enough to survive without ever doing another day's work, she could not understand actors who rushed from one film to another as if driven by a whip. It never occurred to her that they were doing it because they needed the money, that she had done the same thing in the past: 'I am perfectly content doing nothing for months on end,' she said. She was not money conscious and it was untrue that she had invested in all sorts of enterprises, bars in the Champs Elysées, laundries and bowling alleys: 'I have a share in the profits from my films and receive rents from my apartments,' she volunteered, leaving out her impressive portfolio of industrial shares.

Sex? She did not like to talk about it and did not want to see it de-mythologised: 'The less said about sex the better!' She had no wish to see, when they became the vogue, such soft-porn films as *La Grande Bouffe, Last Tango in Paris* or *I am Curious, Yellow* which put private sex on show. But in the privacy of her home she often reached for one of the erotic volumes on her bookshelves; she also loved running around in the nude – no sex involved. Perhaps an element of exhibitionism? She would not admit to that. Marriage was a delicate subject just then: 'I am against a marriage that cannot be ended.' As if dropping a hint, she added: 'Nowadays one can be open when love dies and draw the consequences.'

Was she about to draw the consequences? Gunter Sachs was away publicising his boutiques as skilfully as Brigitte promoted her films but pictures of him nuzzling his mannequins were not conducive to a good marriage. Brigitte challenged him about them when he returned from his tour. 'What about those pictures of you half-nude and being whipped by Alain Delon?' he countered referring to a scene from *Histoires Extraordinaires*.

It was a tortuous business, their quarrels and reconciliations, like one of those television series in which each episode ends with a cliff-hanger – will they part? will they get together again? Brigitte seemed anxious to hang on to her precarious marriage while Gunter wanted the best of all worlds. In spite of his protestations that Brigitte was not his publicity girl, he presented her as the star attraction at a big party at Maxim's in Paris to launch a new boutique; it also marked their wedding anniversary. He lured her back to Munich for the opening of his art gallery and, as usual, overdid the publicity which backfired when he announced that Brigitte – 'to prove her love for me' – planned to take German nationality. 'Not true,' she growled, 'I shall always remain French!' To stress her point she angrily discarded a big bouquet of flowers in the Bavarian national colours of white and blue in full view of Munich's *haute volée* who had come to see Bardot rather than Gunter's art exhibits. Although a little disappointed with her sober, sombre black dress and black stockings they tittered about her youthful features and incomparable hair. She was not in the mood to respond to compliments and glad to escape to the relative calm of Rechenau.

A few weeks later she excelled in the role of a fond mother and stepmother when Nicolas and Rolf, four years older than her boy, joined her for a summer holiday at St Tropez. Bardot's publicist could not resist putting a curious remark into Nicolas' mouth: 'How beautiful you are, *maman*!' He was supposed to have exclaimed on rediscovering his mother.

While Brigitte was playing mother, Euan Lloyd, an intrepid young British producer, was busy setting up a film deal with a small budget and big hopes. His dramatic operation (graphically related by Peter Evans) developed from his plan to make a cheap western to be called *Shalako* with Henry Fonda and the voluptuous Austrian glamour girl, Senta Berger. When the combination failed to excite his backers, Lloyd boldly set his sights higher and approached Sean Connery who was resting on his 007 laurels, unwilling to make another James Bond picture. Connery was interested but Senta Berger was surely not the right choice. Short of cash but not imagination, Euan Lloyd hit on an idea – why not try to get Brigitte Bardot. The name would galvanise the media! Without as yet revealing his plans, he made sure that Brigitte was free at the right time, then called Sean Connery. It was three in the morning.

'What's so desperate that you call me in the middle of the night?' Connery asked.

'I'm going to say two words to you – Brigitte Bardot!'

'Bloody marvellous!' Connery replied and went back to sleep.

When the backers were as enthusiastic, Lloyd approached Brigitte's agent with the bait of a substantial contract: 350,000 dollars plus a share of the profits. He sent the script to Brigitte who read it, liked it, and invited him to St Tropez to discuss details but would not commit herself without testing Sean Connery's vibrations. In an attempt to throw a spanner in the works, the James Bond producers made a counter-bid for Brigitte hoping to match her with Connery's successor, the virtually unknown George Lazenby, but their proposition did not appeal to her. Euan Lloyd's next problem was to tell Sean Connery that Brigitte wanted to see him without giving him the impression that he was 'on approval'. Having accomplished this feat, Lloyd arranged for the two disparate stars to meet on neutral ground – Deauville – where they got on so well that Gunter Sachs celebrated the occasion with a big champagne party but soon began to fear the worst.

Convinced that his wife had found another diversion, he went away and let her stew in her own juice. With Connery gone too, Brigitte felt lonely and did not mind who knew it: 'Gunter cannot be with me,' she said, 'and I am living with memories of my wedding and our honeymoon. God knows why I married when I was so much against the idea of marriage – I thought Gunter and I would live happily for ever after.' She made it sound like a requiem for a marriage.

XV

Too High, Too Dirty, Too Hot

In the South of France, Brigitte was so much in people's minds that they saw her where she was not. There was the crowd of gawkers on the beach at St Tropez scanning the sky to get a good look at the lithe figure dangling from a parachute generously showing her long legs and supple thighs as she floated down. Word had got round that Bardot was at work: 'Brigitte! Brigitte!' the crowd shouted. It was not Bardot at all but a double standing in – or parachuting – for her for a sequence in a television film.

'Brigitte to Mexico!' announced the headline but this, too, was a misconception. Brigitte was going to make *Shalako*, Euan Lloyd's and her first western, the story of a party of aristocrats in the eighteen-eighties going to New Mexico on safari in the style to which rich people were accustomed, taking all their home comforts with them into Apache country where the Countess Irina (Brigitte Bardot) meets Shalako, a rough cowhand (Sean Connery) who sees her washing her shirt in a stream, hence not wearing it, with predictable outcome. Brigitte was not going to New Mexico. The film was to be made in Europe's own wild west – southern Spain and the dusty city of Almeria.

To allow the notion of a grandiose expedition to Mexico to get about was a ruse of the publicists who were beating the drums for *Shalako* long before the first shot had been fired by the Indians or the film cameras. Brigitte was brought over to London and the press encouraged to report that she had come to do her Christmas shopping in Carnaby Street – swinging London and all that – before it was revealed that she was trying on costumes for *Shalako*. Then David Bailey, cockney prince of British photographers, was sent to Paris to photograph her. Surprisingly, they established an instant rapport, thinking and reacting alike in their unorthodox ways. They toured off-beat boutiques to find way-out costumes and spent hours discussing moods and make-up. The result was Bardot in Bailey's 'strident view of femininity.' But it was a rather unfeminine Carnaby-style military tunic with thick gold braid that Brigitte wore when she attended a reception given by President de Gaulle at the Elysée. Attracting as much attention as she was her escort Gunter Sachs. What was going on? Were they still together?

The *Shalako* promoters who looked on Brigitte Bardot in the first place as a publicity asset – 'We pay 350,000 dollars for millions' worth of publicity.' – could take comfort from a poll which revealed that the 'sweet sixteens' of France who were four when *Et Dieu Créa la Femme* was first shown, regarded Brigitte as their ideal. ('Maybe,' she said, 'they like me because they sense I'll never settle down, that like them I am still completely available.') Bardolatry flourished again in the wake of her New Year's Eve appearance on French television. One of her outfits, a very short transparent tricolour, was banned, putting her on every front page. She appeared as Shirley Temple; as Bonnie (of *Bonnie and Clyde*); as a comic strip figure; and, best of all, as a motorcycle moll in the shortest leather dress and the longest leather boots which reached up to her thighs. She looked sensational.

Another Bardot recording caused an even greater uproar. After an animated *tête-à-tête* with her, composer Serge Gainsbourg who waxed lyrical about those boots – 'like two chalices for her beauty' – came up with a song, *'Je t'aime' – 'Moi non plus'* ('I love you' – 'I don't love you any more'). They recorded it in a midnight session, clearing the studio of all not immediately concerned before starting work behind locked doors. Their 'song' was four minutes and twenty seconds of sighs and groans which were suggestive enough even without the text escalating from Bardot's innocuous 'I love you' via Gainsbourg's 'I don't love you any more' to some very explicit lines.

'Two lovers letting themselves go passionately,' was how the sound struck one listener. *France Dimanche* wrote that the words and sounds of the record were not designed to silence the rumours which had been circulating about Brigitte Bardot and Serge Gainsbourg for some time. When Gunter Sachs heard these stories he blocked the release of the record. Eventually Gainsbourg recorded the same song with Jane Birkin who lived with him and, some years later, would partner Brigitte in a much more shocking film sequence.

Brigitte's next stop was Almeria. With the date of their departure for Spain approaching, she grew more and more apprehensive about the prospect of travelling alone and being without a manly shoulder to lean on. Although the risk of her remaining lonely for long was minimal she implored Gunter to come with her. As with Scotland a year earlier, Gunter cried off but promised to visit her on location before long.

Last of the big names to arrive, Brigitte made a grand entrance in the unprepossessing Spanish town. Sean Connery and the rest of the cast (Stephen Boyd, Jack Hawkins, Honor Blackman, Eric Sykes, Peter van Eyck and several imported American cowboys) watched her white Rolls with the black chauffeur approaching at the head of a procession of motorcars carrying a small army of photographers. Euan Lloyd and his director, Edward Dmytryk, rubbed their hands gleefully at the prospect of blanket coverage but Sean Connery was heard muttering something about 'a bloody circus'. Brigitte gave one look at the dismal town and the stony desert beyond, typical wild west country, and exclaimed: 'This is the end of the earth – I want to go home!' She soon thought better of it and played up to the cameramen for all she was worth.

Once installed in her ninth-floor suite of the Hotel Aguadulce – she called it 'my prison' – she tried to be regal and gracious but was so taut that Dmytryk expected her to burst at the seams any moment and gave instructions that she was to be handled with umost care. Work had just got under way when the arrival of Gunter Sachs disturbed the precarious calm. He and Brigitte tried to be discreet but her manner and expression in the morning betrayed the secrets of the night. They had not been making love but war. Three days later Gunter gave his verdict on Almeria – 'too ugly, too dirty, too hot' – and was gone We have it on the authority of Brigitte that she 'cried and cried for days.'

Hopes that the leading lady would now settle down were rudely disappointed when she became embroiled in an 'ugly, dirty, hot' row with Stephen Boyd. American papers were carrying stories of a turgid romance between her and Boyd which were at best ancient history but read as if they emanated from Boyd himself. Was he trying to suggest that it was happening here and now? With a divorce from Gunter on the cards these stories were highly embarrassing. Though Brigitte had disregarded similar rumours in the past, this time she instructed her lawyers to issue a strong denial. Unsure about the damage the unwelcome gossip might have caused she asked for time off to go and see Gunter in St Moritz. He would not say whether she simply explained that there was no truth in the Boyd stories and made an attempt to save their marriage or whether they discussed divorce and a settlement. Brigitte seemed easier in her mind when she returned to Spain.

With a characteristic change of mood, the only member of the company not to be ground down by the dust, dirt and hard work in the hot sun, she started to live it up the moment the cameras stopped turning. She kept open house in her apartment where all comers were welcome to a drink; she danced, sang, played the guitar and did God knows what for the entertainment of the American cowpunchers, the camera crew and actors with a taste for Brigitte's brand of amusement. The parties often went on until it was almost time to start the next day's work.

When it was all over, the unit's publicity man told all and sundry that Brigitte seemed 'obsessed with the idea that she was ageless, a perennial teenager who wanted to show that she could go dancing, singing and whooping it up all night.' She could do all these things and did look like a teenager as she generously revealed when it came to her bare-breasted screen encounter with Shalako. While the camera was allowed to focus on only so much of her – and no more – Sean Connery and the innumerable aides with indeterminate duties who congregate on a film set were treated to a full view of her charms. They were delighted – the shape of Marianne's bosom had not suffered with the years.

Almeria also produced the kind of shaggy dog story which follows Brigitte around like a hungry mongrel running after a bone. As with her beloved Guapa on her previous visit to Spain, she came across a small herd of stray dogs, fed them, and took the most pathetic of them back to her hotel where, according to the inveterate publicist, she bathed and brushed him and fed him with pâté and other goodies. Too far gone and sickened by the unaccustomed luxuries, the dog died. Brigitte was said to have felt as bereaved as if she had suffered a personal tragedy.

Her disturbed state of mind could more likely be traced back to the collapse of her marriage. In these unhappy days she could not keep off the subject. Tearfully and bitchily in turn, and often both at the same time, she talked about Gunter, and nothing else – she could never get accustomed to calling him her husband. Their lives were almost totally separate, she complained, because Gunter would not give up his time to her; they had never set up home as man and wife: 'I haven't even got a key to his apartment,' she said morosely. Gunter had not given her what men are supposed to give a woman – tenderness. Gunter had taken her by storm: 'I was on a flying carpet but when it landed – bang! Gunter was dry, artificial, obsessed with making an impression – exhibiting me to the Shah of Iran or some important businessmen. I hate that!' She hated Gunter's parties, especially the champagne-and-caviar bit.

She would have left Almeria with Gunter but did not want to let the producer down. In the same breath she blamed Gunter for not putting love first: 'With him it's receptions, parties, friends!' Raising a new hare, she said Gunter was as independent as she, so handsome and beautiful that all the girls wanted to be with him which meant that there was a sort of fight between them with neither prepared to change for the sake of the other. His worst crime was leaving her alone: 'When I am left alone, I change my life – yes, by going off with someone else. I must not be left alone!' She had never been unfaithful but had always just left. She needed change, and if this meant that she had a terrible character, she could not help it: 'I have a big appetite for life.' Nor could she love an absent man: 'Other men look at me with tenderness. Why should I go on suffering?'

Apart from a few tantrums, a few late starts after late nights, a few days' French leave, Brigitte gave her employers their money's worth. She was professional, competent, conscientious. The camera crew thought her range of expressions was greater than that of any other actress, her face a sensitive register of the emotions she was expected to convey. Her only dispute with Edward Dmytryk was over the amount of eye-shadow she used but few knew better than Brigitte herself what suited her. Euan Lloyd was euphoric: 'Absolutely fantastic,' he said. 'I adored her!' Only the publicity man remained hostile to the end: 'I cannot remember an actress who was so arrogant, up-stage, rude and off-hand – except Bette Davis,' was his parting shot.

Shalako opened to mixed reviews but although Brigitte came in for some ribbing about her 'Eengleesh' and one critic wrote that Honor Blackman was sexier than she, audiences warmed to her performance. The film came to be acknowledged as one of her best but she gave all credit to Sean Connery: '*Shalako* is Sean Connery's film,' she said. 'He carried the whole weight on his shoulders.'

Now it was the turn of the Germans to agonise over Brigitte's future. The threatened defection of their prized French possession hurt their pride. They worked out that Brigitte and Gunter Sachs had spent no more than a hundred nights together in a marriage which (by August 1968) had lasted a total of five hundred and fifty-seven days but took new heart when the couple met once more: could something be rescued at the eleventh hour from the ruins of their marriage? Their rendezvous in Rome – with Mijanou acting as chaperone or lightning conductor – was hardly propitious for a reconciliation. When *paparazzi* discovered the couple in the garden of their rented villa, Brigitte in a bikini, Gunter in swimming trunks, Gunter was not in a conciliatory mood. In a rare fit of bad temper, he charged the photographers like an angry bull; sprinting two hundred yards he caught up with one of them and sent him away with a sore mouth but too late to undo the camera's work. He and Brigitte parted 'good friends' but the amiable spirit did not survive: 'Don't mention that man to me!' was Brigitte's angry retort when Gunter's name cropped up.

She did not suffer for long. No sooner was she back on her home ground when she saw tenderness in the eyes of one Luigi ('Gigi') Rizzi, a good-looking twenty-three-year-old night club owner and son of an Italian shipbuilder. 'She eats when she is hungry,' Simone de Beauvoir said, 'and she makes love in the same matter-of-fact manner.' Brigitte and Gigi swam together in the sea, she as always without the top of her bikini; in fact, the same issue of Munich's *Quick* magazine which carried photographs of her and Rizzi in semi-nude abandon published a pictorial account of Gunter Sachs cavorting on the nudists' beach at Kampen on the German island of Sylt. The girl with him was, as in the good pre-Bardot days, a mannequin.

Like many people in the public eye, Brigitte blamed her misfortunes not on her own extravaganzas but on the press reports about them. If reporters and photographers had only left her and Gunter to pursue their extra-marital affairs unrecorded all may yet have turned out well. In a similar situation, Onassis once told me he thought the French were right when they said: *'Pour être heureux il faut vivre en cachet.'* For Brigitte this was certainly not practicable; it was, in any case, much too late. As Gunter in a blaze of publicity was taking a bevy of model girls with him on a trip to Rio de Janeiro and New York to open branches of his boutique, Brigitte was 'messing around' with her boat at St Tropez making ready for a jaunt with Gigi Rizzi to the Aga Khan's holiday resort in Sardinia. Work on the boat went ahead very slowly because Brigitte and Gigi stopped every other minute to embrace and remained locked in endless kisses. She was rolling around on deck like a kitten full of the joy of life: 'He is sovereign, stands shoulder-high above things,' she complimented her new man.

On the way to Sardinia they went ashore in Genoa where Gigi introduced Brigitte to his mother which was taken to mean that they intended to get married. Within a fortnight they were back in St Tropez but a day later a dejected Gigi – giving one a distinct feeling of *déjà vu* – emerged from La Madrague carrying his suitcases. He boarded Brigitte's mini-moke, her least pretentious vehicle, and was driven away by her chauffeur in the direction of Monte Carlo and out of her life. 'The whole French nation heaved a sigh of relief,' read one report of the event, 'that Luigi Rizzi has been given the good old heave-ho.' Proud Frenchmen rejoiced that Brigitte had rid herself of a German and an Italian in one fell swoop. The nationalistic fervour was misplaced because Brigitte presently picked up a young American singer and negotiated a contract with a record company for him before sending him, too on his way.

Did she after all still suffer from a Gunter Sachs hangover? It was inevitable that he should be on her mind when she went to Munich for the premiere of *Shalako* but she caused surprise when she said that she hoped to see him. Gunter arrived in Munich the day after she had left for Hamburg where she attended another *Shalako* opening and celebrated her thirty-fourth birthday in one of Gunter's favourite night clubs, hanging on till three in the hope, her friends thought, of bumping into him. No luck. Gunter seemed confused: 'I don't even know whether I'm divorced from her,' he sighed. 'Unhappiness, thy first name is Brigitte.' He was joking, of course. His Swiss lawyers were suing her for divorce on the grounds that 'she had abused the idea of marriage and left home premeditatedly.' Brigitte's only comment: 'That's what he says!'

At last there was a man in her life who was not – and was not suspected of being – her lover. For a few weeks in September and October 1968 she was almost inseparable from the great French seafaring champion Eric Tabarly who had defeated the Atlantic single-handed four years earlier and received the Légion d'Honneur for his feat. Brigitte was taking instruction in advanced sailing techniques at Tabarly's sailing school at St Raphael.

As interest in her flagged at home, she found herself the centre of controversy in Soviet Russia where she was known as the 'rebel' in *Babette*, whose première in Moscow she had attended. Russian film experts argued about her place in the world of the cinema. Her Soviet fans demanding the inclusion of her name in the new *Soviet Encyclopaedia* were, according to *Literaturnaya Gazeta,* opposed by purists who insisted that her popularity was out of all proportion to her talent and built on publicity. 'It is pointless to argue about talent,' Brigitte's supporters countered, 'Popularity is of itself a good enough reason for inclusion in the *Encyclopaedia*.' The argument went on for some time, though Brigitte's fans lost it.

In St Tropez for a respite, Brigitte met a young Englishman, Christopher Wedow, at a party and casually asked him where he was staying. When he confessed that he had not yet found a place he could afford – St Tropez hotel prices being beyond the reach of an English working-class boy from Wandsworth, London – she offered to put him up at La Madrague. Not much was seen or heard of her or Christopher for the next three weeks until his mother appealed to Brigitte via a London Sunday newspaper to giver her back her son. Brigitte obliged.

Resuming the promotion of *Shalako*, she turned up with a different escort in every capital. In Paris – the beginning of a longer association – it was a twenty-three-year-old student, Patrick Gilles, son of a garage owner in St Etienne, a carbon-copy of her previous boy-friends. The situation became confused when she was escorted to London by a 'mystery man,' walked arm in arm with him from the airport and held hands with him in the car which took them to the *Shalako* opening while Patrick Gilles was in his apartment at a Mayfair hotel watching television. Who was the mystery man? No mystery – it was Patrice Bauchau, Brigitte's brother-in-law.

Patrick Gilles was the man who mattered. As he was ten years younger than she, their affair was unkindly compared to the practice of geriatrics of antiquity who took young girls to bed to draw strength from their youthful bodies. Brigitte boasted: 'Every summer I'm getting a year younger,' one of those ominous remarks women make to reassure themselves. Rising thirty-five, she was beginning to show symptoms of advancing years although the time when photographs would expose the first subtle changes in the profile of her body was not yet. Feeling that she needed two summers a year to keep up with the march of time, she escaped the European winter taking Patrick Gilles ('I love him!') with her to the Bahamas.

They took a bungalow on Naked Island, spent the days in the time-honoured Bardot manner riding along the sea front and the evenings listening to calypso bands. Patrick introduced her to his favourite sport, golf, which she took up as avidly as Sacha Distel's guitar a long time ago. At a night club in Nassau she signed the Golden Book – with her lipstick – between the signatures of Douglas Fairbanks and Cary Grant; and at the Aquarium made friends with the dolphins.

Two other contrasting signs of the times. First, Brigitte began to seek the company of old ladies, a drastic switch from her contemptuous rejection of RFCs (those ready for chrysanthemums) which psychologists would diagnose as an attempt to cope with her fear of growing old. As revealing, when it came to publicising her next film, her forty-first, she dug up an old school photograph of herself, class of 1946, a return to her childhood, and asked the publicity boys to release it. It was almost impossible to recognise Bardot in the solemn-faced little girl with spectacles and a ribbon in her short hair.

Next, the ever-alert, never-aging Jean Rook noticed her sudden interest in clothes and asked pointedly: 'Does she, let's be bitchy, now need to get dressed?' Not yet, not yet! In her photographs she still looked like a dreamy child perpetuating the child-woman myth; and she was still alluring enough for a French writer (Jean Cau) to call her 'Aphrodite Bardot.' But the straps of her bikini were pulled a little tighter, and she sued a French newspaper which reported that she had been seen leaving a clinic where she had had a face lift. 'I went to see a friend,' was her explanation. She pocketed damages of around eight hundred pounds.

Gunter Sachs had faded so completely from her life that the dissolution of their marriage went unnoticed. On 1 July, 1969, almost exactly three years after their wedding in Las Vegas, Brigitte and Gunter were granted a divorce, effective 1 October, by Judge Georg Janett in the small Swiss town of Filisur, near St Moritz, in the Albula District where Gunter was domiciled. The terms of the financial settlement were not disclosed – £100,000 made no appreciable dent in the Sachs fortune and was less than Brigitte could expect for a shorter and less arduous scenario. Closing this chapter in Brigitte's life, Gunter Sachs warned me: 'Bardot does not really care what is written or said about her; or what people think of her. Your book will be widely read; the one person, I'm sure, who will not read it is – Brigitte Bardot.'

When the news of the divorce came out, Brigitte happened to be in the company of one of the world's most eligible young men, *Bonnie and Clyde* star Warren Beatty. They were dining at La Cafetière in Paris and Brigitte, hidden behind her huge sun-glasses, her hair tucked into a scarf, remained unrecognised until fans of her friend from Hollywood took a closer look at his companion. To be overshadowed by another star was a novel experience for her, and she did not like it. Gunter Sachs, incidentally, was already 'inseparable' from Mirja Larsson, one of the girls who had travelled with him modelling Micmac clothes. Swedish-born Mirja, healthy, *sportif,* disciplined, down to earth, had little in common with Brigitte Bardot. She and Gunter were soon married and now have a little boy, Christian ('Chri-Chri').

Brigitte would not talk about her divorce; and all Parisians said was: 'Next please!'

XVI

Une Femme de Quarante

As if in need of solitude for the first time in her life, Brigitte dropped out of view. She withdrew to her thatched farmhouse at Bazoches and busied herself with her growing family of pets, Cornichoo, the donkey, the sheep which had just joined her 'zoo,' the goat, the birds, the cats, the dogs – Patapon, the red setter, was her current favourite. Indoors her lively companions were almost outnumbered by the stuffed variety of the species.

Varied and amusing as the inhabitants of her animal kingdom were, she got bored and went to St Tropez where Patrick Gilles joined her. She was getting bored with him, too, but still so dependent on his company that, reversing the old pattern of taking her screen partner as lover, she manoeuvred him into parts in her next films, *Les Femmes* and *L'Ours et la Poupée. Les Femmes* was directed by Jean Auret, the man she had sacked from *La Bride sur le Cou* and restored to favour after he had made a profitable film with Catherine Deneuve, Vadim's former friend, and Sami Frey, her own ex-lover. In *Les Femmes* Brigitte played the part of a secretary and Patrick Gilles her fiancé who has to contend with the attractions of her employer and is left high and dry.

While the cafés in St Germain des Prés frequented by the film fraternity buzzed with whispers about Brigitte's skilful promotion of her lover to *soi disant* stardom, only veteran Bardot experts grasped the significance of a much more piquant addition to the cast of *L'Our et la Poupée.* The young man chosen to play Brigitte's lover on screen was Xavier Gélin, twenty-four-year-old son of Daniel Gélin and Danièle Delorme with whom Vadim had been lodging when he first made love to Brigitte; and with whom Brigitte and Vadim, in very minor roles, appeared – was it really almost twenty years ago? – in *Les Dents Longues*. With her teenager's body, Brigitte at thirty-six did not look a day too old for her young partner but the advent of the new generation on the scene nudged her firmly into her age group.

Before long, alas, Patrick Gilles lost Brigitte altogether and the spectacle of another lover lugging his bags out of La Madrague was once more repeated. Had she, after all, had a secret companion in Bazoches or had she on the way from farmhouse to villa found a new friend in Paris? Wherever the first encounter took place, Michel Engel, a young French publisher, succeeded Gilles and was, in turn, replaced by Christian Kalt, a bartender from Alsace moonlighting as a ski instructor. Kalt ran into her in the snow of Meribel – another recurring feature – and was lured to the milder clime of St Tropez. Eight years younger than Brigitte, he was, in colouring, physique and vacuity, hard to tell from his predecessors.

The arrival of the newcomer did not stop whispers that Brigitte wanted to turn her back on men, that she was like a compulsive smoker who wanted to break the habit but found himself with a new cigarette between his fingers before he had put the old one out. It was another ploy to prepare the fans for her next film, *Les Novices* which, it was suggested, was not so out of character as it seemed. Brigitte was cast as a novice nun who wants to become a prostitute and takes instruction in the arts of the oldest profession from a seasoned woman of the streets, portrayed by Annie Girardot. She and her mentor ply their trade in an ambulance, a bordello on wheels which gives ample scope for titillation as do her sisters-in-faith who exchange their habits for swimsuits and romp around on the beach. But when all was shown, said and done, it was a moral film with a pious ending – Brigitte rejects the men and the old whore turns her back on her past and takes the veil.

The film did not do much to improve Brigitte's box-office appeal. Was she the victim of changing tastes? The thought had barely occurred to her when she accepted a part in *Boulevard du Rhum* which took her back to the congenial permissiveness of the twenties, enabling her to appear with a Suzanne Lenglen bandeau round her head, with a twelve inch cigarette holder in her hand and wickedness in the heavily made-up eyes of the period. Set in America during prohibition, some of the film's scenes were shot on location in Mexico reviving happy memories of her work with Jeanne Moreau and Louis Malle, relaxed evenings with Bob Zaguri and photographers paying homage to her perfect contours. Not this time. Brigitte was not in the mood. She was tired of cameramen, unwilling to pose or talk to Mexican reporters. Their revenge was savage. 'Her sex appeal,' they reported, 'is no match for the visible assets of Raquel Welch' – the new sex goddess. They said she was drinking 'like a Cossack.' Even worse, when she snubbed the photographers once too often, they snatched pictures of her in an unguarded moment when the corners of her mouth were turned down and her breasts, unbelievably, seemed to flop inside her bikini and the skin around her waistline was in a dozen folds.

Had Brigitte seen the photographs, she would have had good reason to despair. It was fortunate that their publication coincided with the resurrection of the Marianne bust which Aslan had modelled a few years earlier on her youthful features and as yet impeccable bosom. Copies of the 'national bust' were put on the market and universally acclaimed as the 'glory of France.' *L'Express* editor Jean-Jacques Servan-Schreiber described it as a symbol of the new society and, with the bust on his desk, basked in Brigitte's reflected glory when offering himself for election to parliament. 'We should be as proud of Brigitte Bardot,' he said, 'as of Roquefort cheese and Bordeaux wine.' André Malraux, the celebrated ex-Minister for Culture, bought a copy and mayors of a dozen cities installed them in their parlours. When the new Marianne was shown on television, public demand swelled the sales (at around fifty pounds a bust).

As the myth of Bardot triumphed over the reality in France, she suffered a set-back in Italy when she briefly visited Rome, met Gigi Rizzi again and was about, much against her principle, to resume where they had left off. 'That's Brigitte who was already a star when I still went to school,' he introduced her to his friends. She turned her back on him and found a more tactful admirer, night club performer Nino Ferrer who sang to her and shared her plate of spaghetti, a typical Bardot gesture signifying intimacy. 'Brigitte Bardot chasing her past,' scorned the Italian press which had never been kind to her. The opposite would have been nearer the truth.

When *Boulevard du Rhum* failed to interest exhibitors outside France, Brigitte could only be persuaded with difficulty to fulfil her contract for *Les Pétroleuses*, a western in which the other woman was played by Claudia Cardinale, 'Italy's Brigitte Bardot.' The two stars were thrown into one of the screen's most bruising fights; and in another scene 'gun-slinger' Brigitte holds up a quartet of rough males and orders them to strip. They obey, turning their backs modestly on her and hiding their shame with their cupped hands. Brigitte gave a splendid performance but the public response was disappointing.

Not far from despondency even in her moments of glory, Brigitte took failure badly. Haunted by the past which she could not recapture, she turned away from it. Tempting as it was to give it all up, she brushed aside the thought of advancing years – advancing, that is, towards her thirty-seventh birthday – and decided to turn over a new leaf. She started with her apartment in the avenue Paul Doumer which hemmed her in and burdened her with too many memories. The old furniture handed down from her parents, the portraits of earlier years staring at her mockingly, the sagging strings of her guitars, the ornaments and souvenirs of bygone expeditions – away with them! In a violent break with the last fifteen years, she put the apartment, furniture and fittings, books, portraits and ornaments on the market asking a hundred thousand pounds for the lot. When no purchaser appeared she advertised in the newspapers – perhaps the place would sell, she quipped, if she included herself in the price.

Her new home was a hyper-modern penthouse in the boulevard Lannes. Alain Demachy, her interior decorator, persuaded her to follow fashion and 'live without furniture' – well, almost. The new Bardot style was a huge salon empty except for a few outsize cushions on the carpeted floor, a bare, purely decorative staircase, two ornamental metal rods reaching to the ceiling and three ultra-modern paintings. Brigitte's more traditional taste reasserted itself in the bedroom's oriental design with the tent ceiling, a dozen cushions on the wide bed, an erotic painting on the wall and – a technical novelty – a concealed dashboard by the bed from which she could operate the television set and the stereo equipment and illuminate the terrace with romantic light patterns. Her circular built-in bath tub was raised window high to enable her to see people promenading in the Bois de Boulogne through the wall-wide window or look at herself in the mirror opposite which was as big.

La Madrague underwent as radical a transformation. Walls tumbled, rooms changed size and shape, the furniture took on an up-to-date hue. Roger Herrera, a young St Tropez architect, worked for seven months to give Brigitte's villa a totally new look. Paradoxically, the new Bardot set frequenting the rejuvenated house was more 'RFC' than in her past. Her new companions were fifty-year-old record producer Eddy Barclay, forty-eight-year-old restaurateur Félix Giraud and sixty-year-old Joseph Soldani, ex-champion of a defunct French ball game. Brigitte and the 'old boys' played cards for hours – she, grimly, almost compulsively. Only the number of beds in the place was a reminder of a livelier past.

Poor, bewildered Christian Kalt seemed lost. Seeing himself already – after travelling with Brigitte as Monsieur and Madame Kalt – as Brigitte's fourth husband, he was stunned by the arrival of Vadim whom Brigitte had summoned urgently to La Madrague. Although unaware of how often Vadim had been on hand when Brigitte changed lovers and had sought his advice before entering into a new relationship, Kalt could see the writing on the wall. For a few weeks he refused to take the hint and tried to brazen it out. It was no use. Sadly, he left La Madrague, returned to his place behind the bar and earned a little pocket-money by writing the inside story of his eighteen months as Brigitte's bedfellow.

But Brigitte expected more from Vadim than his help in getting rid of her lover. She needed her first husband, her first mentor, her most loyal friend and steadfast admirer to take her back to her beginnings. Vadim took one long hard look at her and decided it was time for the legend of the child-woman to be buried. Since she was within sight of her fifth decade with only a couple of years' grace before crossing the threshhold, he gently steered her into a position where she could still say that she was always thinking of men but could yet be suspect of thinking also of – women. It was probably more than a coincidence that she was seen at the opening of a new night club with her lips melting into the mouth of Vadim's current girl-friend, Margret Markow, suggesting something more than friendship. There was nothing to it except a strong pointer to Vadim's next Bardot project.

He had lost nothing of his cunning and ingenuity in promoting his products. When it came to projecting Brigitte in the colouring of his own design he still had no equal. A dash of personal philosophy, a suspicion of popular sociology were the ingredients of his new publicity cocktail. Like Faust imbibing Mephisto's magic potion, those who took a sip of it saw Brigitte as he wanted her to be. He was delighted when the announcement of his new film was followed by predictions that he and Brigitte, 'the scandalous couple of yore,' together again sixteen years after *Et Dieu Créa la Femme,* were preparing another assault on their old enemy: bourgeois morality. His intentions became obvious when the title of his film was revealed – *Don Juan 1973*. But wait! Who would be Don Juan? 'The Don Juan of our day is the woman!' Vadim proclaimed adding for all who had not yet tumbled to it, 'Brigitte Bardot in real life.' The male chauvinist's voyeurist dream, two women in a sexual relationship, which had always interested him and which lurked behind so many of Brigitte's films, was to be deployed in an explicit sequence. To exclude any misunderstanding, the film's sub-title was *Si Don Juan Avait Eté une Femme*.

Brigitte was game. She liked the idea and, as in the past, was more than willing to go along with Vadim. Vadim himself, knowing better than most that she was no lesbian and not even tempted to experiment in this sphere, was anxious to save her from sexual frustration. Without a man, Brigitte was bound to be unsettled and difficult to handle. Something had to be done. In the event it was impossible to say what came first – Brigitte fortuitously meeting a new young man with instant appeal; or Vadim shuffling the cards so adroitly that an acceptable Jack jumped out of the pack. The young man was Laurent Vergez but it is a moot point whether Vadim gave him a part in *Don Juan* because he had caught Brigitte's eye, or had selected him in the first place to fill a vacuum, in Brigitte's life. Be that as it may, Vergez took over where Kalt had left off. While his screen part was confined to an episode to be shot on location in Stockholm, he played the principal character in a passionate interlude with a becalmed Brigitte. 'Laurent saved the day,' Vadim said. He certainly saved Brigitte whose glow almost melted the Scandinavian snow. She and Laurent spent every free minute together but I could find no confirmation of reports that the couple had demoted sex to a spectator sport, spending their evenings at local sex shows.

If Laurent Vergez's role in the film was a minor one, everything depended on Brigitte's female partner. Vadim did not have to look very far before his choice fell on Jane Birkin, the ravishing, boyish *ingénue* with the sensuous mouth and eyes. He was working on the script with Jean Cau whose analysis of Bardot complicated her image. Brigitte, the child-woman, became Brigitte, the boy-girl; Brigitte, the man-eater, was turned into Brigitte, the woman-wooer; Brigitte, who had made so many men happy, was presented as a woman plotting the destruction of her lovers demanding from one as the price of her favour – his life. Symbolically, in the end, her house burns down and she perishes in the flames.

No longer content to excite the public with heterosexual love scenes, however explicit, Vadim, ahead of time, if only just, ahead of films like *Emmanuelle*, expected Brigitte to 'give her all.' In *Don Juan* she and Jane Birkin would appear in full frontal nudity in a lesbian love scene. Happily, the two women liked each other and performed with great gusto – a delightful view. They managed to shock some but others, including a few critics, reacted with an embarrassed giggle. There were those who thought that the bedworthy couple had not gone far beyond a schoolgirlish romp while another school contended that the two bodies were too clean-limbed and near-perfect, that Brigitte and Jane were too natural and uninhibited to heighten the sensation with a little wickedness. Although in the script the all-female performance was designed to stimulate a man, it left some of the audience cold.

The film's other ingredients and characters were provocative – a priest who takes a murderous woman's confession, a ruthless millionaire, Swedish students in an orgy (Laurent Vergez's high spot), wrists cut in an orgiastic climax and the inferno of the burning house. In the centre of these happenings there was Brigitte urged on by Vadim, as in their early days, to achieve total realism. The clever dialogue by Vadim and Cau was tailored to Brigitte's manner of speaking so as to smudge the borderline between her and her screen self. It was a skilful pretence but it distorted Brigitte's real feelings. Who would believe her when she was made to say: 'Men are passé – useless!'?

Laurent Vergez's performance on and off screen earned him a part in Brigitte's swan song, a film with the cumbersome title *L'Histoire Très Bonne et Très Joyeuse de Colinot Trousse-Chemise* which, freely translated, means 'The Happy and Joyous Story of Colinot, the Man who Pulls up Skirts.' The story was set in France in the Middle Ages and Brigitte's part was that of a beautiful, imperious woman well versed in the techniques of love, doing her own thing, taking the initiative in the sex game, a role which could not have been more congenial. Latterly, though, Brigitte was not as dominant as of old. A mere hint from Laurent Vergez that he might leave (before she had finished with him) drove her to distraction. On the few nights they did not spend under the same roof, she took one of his pullovers or shirts with her to bed.

She was as concerned that her animals should have a happy sex life. Mauricette Marcey, her housekeeper, said that her mistress once told her: 'Our hens seem bored. They need a cock!' No sooner uttered, than she was off to market to buy the biggest and proudest cock on sale. Madame Marcey's life with Brigitte was not a happy one although she stuck it out for two years. After that Brigitte's problem was not unlike that of royalty who are frequently embarrassed when servants leave – and talk. In a high moral tone, Madame Marcey voiced her indignation about Brigitte's guests, Michèle Morgan among them, sunning themselves in the nude in her garden, and the odd Italian beau enjoying Brigitte's unadorned company. The break came over money – Madame Bardot would not pay her for a hundred hours' overtime, Mauricette said.

Money, basically, her wheeling and dealing as a landlord, was at the root of a bitter quarrel between Brigitte and sister Mijanou. They first had a little contretemps when Mijanou suspected Brigitte of having an affair with her husband. Although the suspicion was unfounded, another row broke out over one of Brigitte's apartments which was occupied by Mijanou, her husband and their eight-year-old daughter. Offering alternative accommodation, Brigitte asked Mijanou to get out and when the answer was an uncompromising '*Non*!' instructed her lawyers to start proceedings to evict the Bauchau family.

'Brigitte gave me the apartment as a wedding present,' Mijanou declared. 'Not so,' Brigitte's lawyers countered, 'our client just let Madame Bauchau stay there rent free.' Two days before the case was due to be heard, Brigitte changed her mind and asked for an adjournment *sine die*. Since she delivered herself of another tirade against intrusions into her privacy – 'stardom,' she said, 'was like a house without curtains' – Mijanou assumed that she had only relented for fear of adverse publicity. Relations between the sisters were never the same again.

In another angry row, Brigitte's adversary was the Mayor of

Bazoches who felt the lash of her tongue when ten of her dogs, all one-time strays, disappeared within the space of a few months. Brigitte discovered that the local authority had placed chunks of poisoned meat in strategic places in the fields around her estate 'to protect the wild life from ferocious dogs.' 'The cruelty of human beings revolts me,' Brigitte thundered. 'I spent whole weekends in the forest calling for my dogs.' Only two turned up, one violently sick after swallowing poisoned meat, the other with a wire snare embedded in his neck. Both dogs died. 'Madame Bardot should not have allowed the dogs to stray,' was the mayor's defiant defence, 'It was her fault that they perished as a result of my campaign against harmful animals.'

Brigitte was not happy. Vadim said she would not even talk to him: 'She does not want to see anyone. She's bitter, cynical and sad.' He was nearer the truth than on previous occasions. Work with him had drained her; she had given him all she could and reached the limit of her strength. 'I'll soon quit,' she said in a television interview. 'I've noticed signs of aging in the last two years and even feel a little frightened when a new wrinkle appears.' Although she found the strain of looking beautiful from morning to night terrifying she would not dream of having a face lift. She had not lost her sense of humour, though: 'No need to panic,' she added. 'What is more beautiful than an old lady with white hair grown wise with age and able to tell lovely stories about her past?'

It was a prelude to her final announcement: 'I am retiring because if I don't abandon films they may abandon me.' Although Brigitte had threatened retirement so often before, this time her words had the ring of conviction. The French press, echoed all over the world, composed eloquent obituaries on the career of Brigitte Bardot. One of the headlines she did not expect to see was: 'BB grows old so gracefully.' To prove that she was not as old as all that, she showed herself riding pillion with Laurent Vergez on his powerful motorcycle.

It was as if she was riding away from fame and fortune. Her friends realised that for a long time to come nothing and nobody would persuade her to make another film. She never read the fervent appeals from hard-boiled film writers to reconsider. Derek Malcolm implored her to say that all these semi-official announcements were untrue: 'There was never another one like you,' he wrote. 'No, not Garbo, not Monroe, not Loren and certainly not Mansfield. You were, and are, unique . . .!' Giving the lie to the photographs of an aging Bardot, *Colinot Trousse-Chemise,* released just before her thirty-ninth birthday, presented her all but nude body as firm and shapely as twenty years earlier. It was 'revealed' that her statistics, 35–23–35, were exactly the same as when she started in films in 1952, but somebody must have slipped up because the figures suggest that she had put on an inch on her bust and hips and three on her waist. In case anybody thought there was some significance in *Colinot* being an all-woman enterprise – director Nina Companeez, producer Mag Bodard – Brigitte was quick to stress that she was giving up films, not men. A tear of regret percolated through her farewell: 'This is my last film,' she said, 'and the first I shall be sorry to finish.'

Yet, turning forty was traumatic for a woman in whose language expressions like '*une femme de quarante*' and '*une femme entre deux ages*' were used as if they applied to a species with special attributes and qualities or defects. Alas, as the figures of French film stars' financial ratings indicated, Brigitte's fear that films might abandon her was not quite groundless. In the list of the eighteen most highly paid screen performers, headed by Alain Delon who could command £250,000 for a film, Brigitte was in fifteenth place with a current rate of £50,000.

Nor had maturity strengthened her maternal feelings. Nicolas was growing away from her and like most boys approaching their teens found his father's company more congenial. He was at an expensive private school from which he emerged only in the holidays, a tousle-haired youngster, more Charrier than Bardot. His father encouraged him to see films like Charlie Chaplin's *Limelight* but he was too young to be allowed to watch his mother on the screen. He did not see much of her off screen either.

Although Brigitte said she was looking forward to the simple life ('Deep down inside I am a very conventional girl'), this was also a time for looking back: 'Of all the films I have made only five were good' – she did not say which – 'the others were trash!' As if shedding the shackles of her image, she seemed to have lost her pout and looked more real, a woman who had lived and learned and wore the lines around her mouth and chin like badges of wisdom. Her face was growing older just a fraction before her body which she offered to her boy-friend for a series of photographs. Laurent Vergez did not have to be a master of the camera to produce some delightful nude studies. With greater abandon than in many a year, Brigitte put her best bottom forward and arched tantalisingly for a side view silhouette. The photographs aped the techniques of girlie magazines but in the key picture ('Bardot in her fortieth birthday suit') which showed her in the buff, one of her hands was protectively positioned to disguise a slight deterioration in her outline.

Not that she made the smallest attempt to hide her age. At the approach of her birthday, she gave a beach party in St Tropez which made even sophisticates swoon. She danced barefoot and swirled her skirt to show that much else of her was as bare, played the guitar and sang in her low suggestive voice. A flower in her hair, she could take on the rawest flower children. She was in high spirits again at the birthday party at the 55 Club. A smile, a sigh – 'When you get to forty you lose all your puff' – she gave the lie to her own words by blowing out the forty candles on the big square cherry-and-cream birthday cake as twenty-five friends led by Françoise Sagan sang 'Happy Birthday to You!' in English. In her red shirt, blue jeans and red boots she looked like a teenager. Somehow, a bicycle appeared, was put on the table and Brigitte mounted it and held her glass up in reply to the toast.

Was it a flash in the pan? A few days later, the corners of her mouth dropping as they did when she was a little weary, her eyes without sparkle, her face pale, she looked ten years older. She was a different person every day: 'Not so many winters but many more moods,' said a friend. 'She has not lost youth but she has lost joy!' Brigitte who had taken everything and everyone she wanted all her life, had little left to desire. There was a hint of sadness in her smile – a certain smile. The mood was captured by Françoise Sagan who wrote *A Certain Smile* and understood the sentiments behind it. Talking long and earnestly with Brigitte she extracted from her a definition of herself: 'A person who has made a success of her career but not of her life, let's say someone who is incomplete.' They touched on the subject of her fame and money which, Brigitte thought, unbalanced her relationships with less well-known and less well-heeled men.

When Sagan mentioned that she was bored with erotic films, sex, violence and blood, Brigitte said she felt the same; she was against exhibitionists who, she was sure, were repressing feelings of shame, but she did not include herself in that category. For her, love needed mystery, secrecy and silence, strange to hear from a woman who had talked more and more freely than any other about her loves and her lovers. As surprising was her view that 'night is a waste of time' – she liked day-time and sunshine. Her postscript on retirement was: 'The myth of BB is finished!' She hoped that in five years' time – when she was forty-five – people would have forgotten her and she could do the things which amused her and for which she alone was responsible: 'I shall no longer be a beautiful object but a human being.'

Very much a human being, Brigitte moved to her winter residence. She was without a man. At some stage between the hot summer at St Tropez and the invigorating winter at Meribel, Laurent Vergez had slipped away – two years with the same man was about Brigitte's norm. Meribel had always been a promising hunting ground, the slopes alive with adorable snowmen. The one she tracked down this time was Meribel's resident sculptor, Miroslav Brozek, aged thirty-three and of Czech extraction, whose work under the pseudonym Jean Blaise commanded respect in French art circles. Visiting his studio Brigitte examined the artist more intently than his sculptures: 'She looked into my eyes in a way that said more than words,' Miroslav crooned, 'At once we were in love.' It was Take Twelve or Take Thirteen of the old scene and Brigitte had not changed the script. Holding hands in bars, soulful looks, public kisses, strolls in the snow. . . . At least Miroslav did not mind sharing Brigitte with half a dozen animals who followed her everywhere.

Like them he followed her – in the first instance to La Madrague where the love story continued like a carbon-copy of the previous editions. Part of the scenario was the running commentary on the affair from 'close friends', many of whom said things that had been said about Brigitte and every man she had been associated with – she wanted a love-child from Miroslav, one averred, although nothing could have been further from the truth. But Ghislain Dussart noticed 'a momentous change in Bardot' which was probably the familiar glow of a new love. 'The tigress has been tamed,' Ghislain elaborated, 'This time Brigitte will stay happy for ever!'

XVII

Seals of Approval

Miroslav Brozek was lounging on the inflated rubber mattress on the edge of the sea where a dozen or more young men like him had sat at the feet of Bardot. Coming from the villa to join him, Brigitte stood for a moment framed by the white gate. Her life style had changed little but retirement is an emotive word suggesting decrepitude, and even 'retiring young' can saddle a woman in her best years with the stigma of failing powers and failing looks. A fleeting glance at Brigitte taught me how dangerous it was to view a living legend through the filter of a preconceived notion which concentrates the mind on the flaws and scars time leaves on a myth.

Any other woman in her forties would have been proud to look like Bardot although the bosom, bare in St Tropez fashion, could no longer serve as a model for Marianne, and the legs looked fuller and shorter than I remembered them from only two or three years earlier. The lines in the face were not new but the contours had sharpened. No use sycophants pretending that Bardot had not changed. Of course, she had. There was a serenity about her, a poise which had been lacking. She looked beautiful, neither sex-kitten nor child-woman nor tigress but a mature woman superficially no longer perfect yet, without all that gloss and glamour, eminently desirable.

There was sadness in her eyes when she went to visit Pilou, who was gravely ill in hospital with little hope of recovery. Though his death at the age of seventy-nine did not come unexpected, Brigitte mourned him deeply. She had not only lost a father, but part of her own life. This was the final break with her over-extended childhood.

Film scripts were still reaching her by the dozen, ideas, suggestions, propositions continued to pour in (mostly through her agent) but Brigitte would not look at them. When the correspondence was sifted and the approaches scrutinised, her attention was drawn to one inquiry which she found tempting. Would she care to serve France once more – at a suitable fee? She would! France called her into service to publicise France. Who better to lure the tourists, tell them about the claret and the burgundy, the castles of the Rhone valley and the mountains of the Haute Savoie, the beauty of the Dordogne, the beaches of the Riviera? Brigitte went back to the studio and on location to make a television commercial for her country. She was so appealing and seductive that honours were about even between her and the panorama she extolled.

From this venture into advertising (and sponsorship of La Madrague as a trademark for a range of clothes on the lines of Gunter Sachs' Micmac) it was not far to much more profitable publicity assignment. After negotiations which took a year, Brigitte accepted £100,000 to sing the praises of a men's perfume on television. She went about the job with her usual application and thoroughness, insisted on a say in the ingredients of the new fragrance (lest it included substances extracted from animals), vetted the bottle and the pack, chose the director (with whom she had worked on *L'Ours et la Poupée*) and the cameraman (who had photographed her in *Les Novices*) and reserved the right of veto on the finished commercial.

Arriving at nine sharp at the Paris studio where the drawing-room of La Madrague had been reproduced, Brigitte was accompanied by her own hairdresser and make-up expert. She worked for twelve hours non-stop, deftly converting the sound of her inimitable English into a typical French smell. The thirty-second commerical which cost half a million pounds to produce was first shown on independent television in Britain, the only time I have come across the magical Zendiq which Brigitte tried to press on me from the screen. Asked how he had managed to persuade her to undertake this labour (other than by offering her the huge fee) an employee of Goya, the producers of Zendiq, answered:

'If you mention anything about wild life preservation, she almost eats out of your hand.'

It was a clue to Brigitte's thoughts and interests which occupied her in the three hundred and sixty-two days of the year left after her effort on behalf of Zendiq. Miroslav helped her to while away the time and there were the dogs. In Meribel, her day – every day – started with 'walkies' for the dogs. When last seen, the pack yapping around her ankles included four red setters (Nini, Mouche, Mienne and Macho), a mongrel of indeterminate origin who answered (sometimes) to the name of Pichnou, and a friend's canine, Julius, who was not allowed inside the chalet because he worried Belote, her little tortoise-shell cat. The dogs were also in attendance when Brigitte skied down the gentle slopes and demanded a good deal of attention throughout the day when they had to be taken out at regular intervals.

All-pervasive as the dogs were, they were not the animals uppermost in Brigitte's mind. Ever since she had seen the horrendous spectacle of the 'culling' of baby seals in Newfoundland on television and cinema screens – 'culling' (selecting, weeding out) being the euphemism for wholesale slaughter – she had been in a state of agitation. Regarding the death of a stray dog as a personal tragedy, the mass murder of the endearing '*bébés phoques,*' the brutal crunch of clubs on the tiny heads of the helpless little animals, was bound to move her deeply. Brigitte could not talk of anything but '*phoques, phoques, phoques*!' The languorous, lackadaisical, retired sex symbol was transformed into a fury, and fury spawned action. Her telephone worked overtime as she canvassed support for a campaign to stop the barbarous massacre. Naturalists, officials, politicians, diplomats were badgered by the insistent voice at the other end of the wire. Brigitte had stood up to the political gangsters of Algeria, had shamed the French National Assembly into enacting new laws against cruelty to livestock. If her pleas for help remained unanswered she was prepared to wage war on the tormentors of baby seals single-handed.

With the next seal hunt in Newfoundland scheduled for early

April (1976), she stitched together a script for a documentary to expose the pernicious practice. Like the anti-nuclear bomb campaigners sailing into atomic test areas, she set out to be filmed denouncing the seal slaughter at the 'scene of the crime.' She was excited and confident of her power of persuasion with visions of putting the tough hunters to flight by her mere presence, hoping they would refuse to kill under the eyes of their adversary and her cameras. She did not get very far. Arriving at London Airport on the way to Newfoundland her courage failed her although Miroslav Brozek was there to support her. Overcome by the thought of the suffering seals, she collapsed, tears rolling down her cheeks from behind her dark glasses. Miroslav did not know what to say: 'She is sick, very sick,' he stammered. 'She has a fever. . . .' Disconsolately he trailed behind her as she made for the next flight back to Paris.

The fiasco did not discourage her. A few days in the dumps and she was ready to return to the fray. More thought, more consultations led to the next step in her campaign, a direct appeal to the Canadian government within whose jurisdiction the seals were hunted. When it yielded no result she decided to employ a bigger gun to attack her target. She registered a Foundation for the Protection of Distressed Animals wherever and however they were threatened. To help with the organisation, she recruited Philippe Cottereau, Secretary General of polar explorer Paul Emile Victor's Environment Group, to act in a similar capacity for the BB Foundation. Paul-Emile Victor himself and Commander Jacques Cousteau, underwater explorer and television personality, lent their names to her cause. Brigitte said she would stake her prestige and her money on the mission of mercy but reports that she intended to endow the Foundation with a third of her income were misleading – since she no longer worked her income was much reduced and she never mentioned specific amounts. President of the Foundation was, of course, Brigitte Bardot.

Collaboration between the President and her associates was not as trouble-free as the noble purpose required. When the whole bubble burst, Philippe Cottereau was scathing about her part: 'She certainly loves animals,' he said later. 'The only trouble is that she is not prepared to lift a finger personally to help them.' He was angry because, when he arranged for Columbia Broadcasting to donate half a million dollars to the Foundation if she would allow herself to be photographed in an American wildlife park, she refused. She did not like flying, she told him. 'She is just a wealthy lady,' was Cottereau's comment, 'who prefers to play cards with her friends in her villa in St Tropez rather than do something to help animals. . . .'

In such an acrimonious atmosphere, it was surprising that a prospectus about the Foundation's aims and philosophy came into being at all. In the event, its language reflected Brigitte's feelings: 'The planet is in a state of war,' it read, 'and unless there is action by its inhabitants irreversible accidents will put the survival of the species at risk. . . .' The Foundation would sponsor a veritable crusade to denounce abuses in the treatment of wild or domestic animals; promote ecological research, circulate information and propaganda in schools, cinemas, on radio and television; picket fur sales (such as the traditional pre-Christmas fur fair in Paris) and take political action if necessary. The campaign for the protection of baby seals would reach a climax in the spring of 1977 when President Bardot hoped to visit Prime Minister Pierre Trudeau in Canada. There would also be an anti-animal-experiment campaign and an anti-abandon campaign against the practice of leaving pets to their fate. Respect for all animals, a reasonable limit on the time of work, the right to rest and decent food for working animals were other demands. The Foundation hoped to obtain contributions from sympathisers in industry and the arts, and to persuade the public to become members at one hundred francs per head.

The thoughtful prospectus notwithstanding, Brigitte was not really qualified to deal with the mechanics of such a crusade. She cut a sorry figure at the public launching at a restaurant in the Bois de Boulogne. The press was invited to take '*un coup de Champagne*' with her and arrangements had been made for the proceedings to be televised and relayed to the United States by satellite to encourage contributions from animal lovers. Although the press turned up in large numbers, the conference was at best a magnificent flop. There was such a crush of reporters and photographers that Brigitte felt 'intimidated' and seemed struck dumb. Satellite or no satellite, she would not speak and would not stay. Extricating herself from the crowd, she was gone before the press conference had properly started. It never got very far – it was not possible to verify an Iranian journalist's assurance that Queen Farah had promised to support the Foundation with a quarter million dollars.

With the help of a friend, Swiss film producer Franz Weber, Brigitte carried on in the seclusion of her private retreats instructing aides to send out appeals and messages to interested bodies and organise protests against vivisection, the use of rare animal skins for commercial purposes, keeping the baby seal issue well to the fore. She worked on plans for a magazine devoted to her cause and for a film festival of animal pictures, commissioned scripts for what she intended to become regular radio and television programmes. It was all getting a bit too much for her. Volunteers, unable to cope with the correspondence, were replaced by professional secretaries and clerks. Brigitte was not cut out for the administrative work involved and was bad-tempered in her dealings with collaborators who turned against her.

In September, six months after her abortive trip, she threw in the sponge and liquidated the Foundation. In a feeble public explanation, she said the Foundation had raised £7,500 but had spent double that amount on salaries, stationery and postage. She did not want contributions to be used to pay bureaucrats: 'Perhaps I would have done more good,' was her conclusion, 'if I had bought twenty-five thousand tins of dog food and distributed them to strays.' She intended in future to cooperate with like-minded organisations and concentrate on high-level lobbying of international bodies like the Common Market and the Council of Europe.

The sad and sudden end of the Foundation engendered a lot of unpleasantness and squabbling between Brigitte and some of her associates. She instructed her lawyer, Maitre Gilles Dreyfus, to recover monies paid to the Victor Group for rent of an office and salaries, accused Cottereau of all sorts of things – which he strenuously denied – and asked for symbolic damages of one franc for 'injury to the Foundation's image.' The dispute rumbled on with accusations and counter-accusations, claims and counter-claims. What stung Brigitte most was the suggestion that she had been laggard in her efforts. When she asked Maitre Dreyfus to refute it strenuously, he issued a statement that raised several eyebrows: 'Madame Bardot,' he announced, 'fulfilled her obligations but she obviously could not be expected to spend twenty-four hours a day working for the Foundation. That is not her job. As a beautiful woman, she is not prepared to enter the Holy Order of Animals.'

But she was determined to join in when the International Fund for Animal Welfare prepared to stage a protest against seal hunting on the ice-floes of North-East Newfoundland. This time – again on the supporting arm of Miroslav Brozek – she made it a good deal further than at the first attempt. Well-equipped with protective clothing and statistics, she chartered a jet to take her to Canada. Her battle cry could be heard loud and clear: 'At the present rate of killings,' she declared, 'the last of the seals will be finished by 1985.' Challenging the Canadian government again, she warned that Canada faced the risk of diplomatic conflict: 'The whole world has risen up against the seal hunt,' she cried and vowed to go to the end of the earth to stop this barbarity. Would she go as far as other demonstrators who had tried to shield baby seals with their bodies against the club-swinging Canadian and Norwegian hunters? 'I have never seen a baby seal being killed,' she admitted tremulously. The subconscious fear of having to watch the slaughter, so heart-rending that it shocked hardened reporters, dogged her every step.

While she was having talks on the mainland about setting up a fake-fur industry, a helicopter stood by at St Anthony, one of the points from which the hunt could be reached, to take her and International Fund officials to the ice-floes. She arrived half an hour late but insisted on having a meal before going on and lingered so long over lunch that the pilot and his passengers took off without her. Retreating to the village of Blanc Sablon on the Quebec-Labrador border – and the only house with a bed (the villagers sleep on the floor) – she called a press conference but the reporters felt that Brigitte, 'in full coiffure and make-up,' was drawing more attention to herself than to the seals, and compared her unfavourably with Yvette Mimieux, another actress interested in conservation, who went out to the most forward areas. Brigitte was in one of her moods: 'All this is too badly organised,' she told the reporters, 'I am tired and want to go back to Paris.'

Even her departure was beset by trouble. Because her pilot had failed to clear his landing, Customs held up the jet, then the weather closed in and Brigitte was forced to spend three days in the highly uncongenial surroundings: 'Everything seems to be against me,' she sighed. At last, with Chou-Chou, a baby seal, in her arms, she took off for France. She posed with the pup on arrival in Paris and took him on to St Tropez where he made friends with the dogs and started to bark like them. Chou-Chou ended up at the Marine Zoo in Antibes. The press was highly critical of Brigitte's antics, and in Newfoundland by this time some fifty thousand baby seals had been killed and another quarter of a million were doomed.

Licking her wounds, Brigitte waited for a more propitious time to resume her campaign and vowed she would go back to Newfoundland again and again until the evil of seal hunting was stopped. However jaundiced the press, the publicity she had generated was world-wide and conservationists everywhere were happy to capitalise on her name. How much weight it still carried was amply demonstrated when the publicity-conscious Council of Europe invited her to Strasbourg to attend a debate on seal hunting (24 January 1978), the first time such an invitation had been issued to a private person.

Concern for thousands of baby seals did not blunt her compassion for individual animals. She was moved to tears by a pathetic scene she witnessed in a Paris park where she saw an old donkey who had been giving children joy-rides for many years sitting down too exhuasted to get up and carry on with the job. Brigitte contacted the owner, paid a handsome amount for the donkey and had him taken to Bazoches to join her menagerie.

Her visit to Strasbourg turned into a personal triumph. They did not actually roll out the red carpet for her as they had done for the French President but Brigitte's reception by the Council of Europe was no less ceremonial than his. There were quite as many reporters and photographers awaiting her and snapping away as she was conducted to a private audience with the Council's Austrian president, Professor Karl Czernetz, who said: 'I believe it is not out of place for a parliamentary assembly to salute someone who, like Madame Brigitte Bardot, interests herself in this cause' – the protection of seals against cruelty. In her place of honour in the public gallery later in the day, Brigitte listened open-mouthed – with parted lips, anyway – to the debate on a motion to secure a two-year moratorium on seal hunting.

Presenting the Regional Planning Committee's report to the Assembly, Frau Magda Hubinek (Austria) drew attention to 'the famous film star' who had been to see for herself what occurred in practice and was now present. A Dutch member, M Cornelisson, went out of his way to give credit to her: 'Largely because of the action taken by Brigitte Bardot whom I should like to congratulate,' he told the Assembly, 'the public was particularly incensed by the massacre of the baby seals in the Atlantic. . . .' Much had been achieved, he said; discussions were taking place in many countries on measures to prohibit import and trading in baby seal skins and the Dutch fur trade had already stopped it.

In a counter-attack, opponents of any restriction on seal hunting, concentrated on Brigitte. Turning the tables on her, they suggested that Madame Bardot's campaign could well be a publicity stunt in preparation for her return to the screen. A Belgian Socialist, Claude Dejardin, complained that her presence had turned the debate into a circus and demanded that greater attention be given to humans and to protests against child massacres in Vietnam and Africa: 'I hope there will be as many delegates and members of the public present when we discuss human rights!' Brigitte would not be drawn into a political argument. As she had said before: 'Politics don't interest me.' She thought politicians were ambiguous. 'They are not bad but as soon as they make politics they are possessed by ambition and want to be popular at any price. . . . They resort to tricks to become popular and forget to deal with the important things in life.' The accusation was promptly hurled back at her.

Brigitte felt that her day in Strasbourg was well spent. The immediate result was the adoption of the recommendation to the Council of Europe to press for the two-year moratorium on seal hunting. Her joy would have been greater had she not been handed 'an open letter' from Prime Minister Trudeau telling her that the seals were killed more quickly and in a more humane manner than most domestic animals in civilised countries, and that Canada would not bar seal hunting. Speaking on her behalf, Franz Weber told the press that she would be putting a complaint against Canada before the International Court at The Hague. Her campaign was far from finished. Back in Meribel, celebrating the third anniversary of her association with Miroslav Brozek, she praised him for standing loyally by her in her efforts to protect animals and in the hard battle against shocking indifference, contempt and hate.

Her personal life? She said she inspired Miroslav in his work as a sculptor: 'I believe I have at last found profound stability.' Was she trying to convince herself? Her relations with Miroslav had reached an intensity such as had previously signalled an imminent decline if not the end of an affair. As Gunter Sachs remarked: when love burns too intensely it threatens to burn itself out. At forty-five, love was a more complicated state of mind than the involvements which had fulfilled her in earlier years; and for Miroslav ministering to a woman of her age the problems grew apace.

For the first time since her retirement, people close to her detected signs of restlessness as if animals, after all, did not engage her so much that there was not room for other causes. Indeed, she presently took up a new one and backed it with a vehemence which seemed out of proportion with the issue. Her latest *bête noire* was a plan to build a big office block and four hundred and sixty flats on the outskirts of St Tropez. Although a leading French architect was responsible for the designs, she protested violently against the 'implantation of a cancer city' in a place where she had found 'protection, charm and freedom'; she joined a rally to 'save St Tropez from disfigurement' and threatened tempestuously to sell her house and leave the resort if the authorities approved the project. The Mayor of St Tropez found himself in the unenviable position of having to weigh the benefit of the new buildings against the enormous publicity value of Brigitte's presence which he subsidised with concessions on rates and other charges.

The fervour with which she went into the new battle – any battle – revealed something about her state of mind. She was desperate to employ her nervous energy, to find an outlet for her cascading emotions, to feed her active brain with creative thoughts; lest it seemed that she was only concerned with animals, her friends recalled her successful intervention on behalf of Josephine Baker's model children's village in the Dordogne which she saved from closure. Her mind was like a high-powered, finely-tuned machine going at full blast but producing nothing. Though only dimly aware of it, idleness which she craved for short periods suddenly loomed ahead like an endless, empty desert. Now and then a casual remark betrayed that she was conscious of the diminishing assets of her face and her body and that all that remained was the legend which she had long wanted to destroy.

Money was not a consideration, she did not seek new fame but she needed reassurance beyond one man's desire and adoration. She was looking for a new challenge. Like other stars who owed their reputation to 'sexploitation' films (or like clowns anxious to play Hamlet), Brigitte had one more peak to climb – to prove herself as a serious actress but only in harness with a director like Ingmar Bergman, a subject worthy of her vocation and a script amenable to her individual talent. Her spirits were low until she heard a distant voice whispering that such a combination was already under discussion although it might take a year or more to produce a proposition sound enough to bring her back into the business.

The news transformed her mood at a stroke. Although Brigitte had at one time graciously conceded that General de Gaulle was much bigger than her, his ghost stalked her villa. The atmosphere at La Madrague was reminiscent of Colombey-les-Deux-Eglises where '*le grand* Charles' had spent his temporary retirement. Like de Gaulle twenty years earlier, Brigitte Bardot was waiting for the Call.

The Films of Brigitte Bardot

1952 *Le Trou Normand* (The Norman Hall)
The story of a dumb villager who inherits an inn and defends it successfully against his acquisitive aunt Augustine with whose daughter (Brigitte) he is in love.

1952 *Manina, la Fille Sans Voile* (The Lighthouse Keeper's Daughter)
Student and smuggler in partnership raising a Phoenician treasure-trove. While the student dallies with the lighthouse keeper's daughter (Brigitte), the smuggler gets away with the loot – almost.

1952 *Les Dents Longues* (The Long Teeth)
In walk-on parts – Brigitte Bardot and Roger Vadim (soon to be man and wife) act as witnesses at the screen wedding of real-life marrieds, Daniel Gélin and Danièle Delorme. A young provincial journalist using his long teeth gnaws his way to the top in Paris.

1953 *Le Portrait de Son Père* (The Image of His Father)
A young farmer who inherits his natural father's wealth, turns down the advances of his step-sister (Brigitte), gives up the glamour of Paris and returns to the land and the girl he loves.

1953 *Quelque Part Dans le Monde* (Act of Love)
Brigitte Bardot plays the maid in a Paris hotel where love between an American GI and refugee girl ends in tragedy.

1953 *Si Versailles M'Était Conté* (Versailles)
As a courtesan, Brigitte flits briefly across the stage which is peopled with the élite of French and American performers who bring to life the history and glory of Versailles from the Sun King to present times.

1954 *Tradità* (Haine, Armour et Trahison, or Treachery)
Two brothers on opposite sides in the First World War contest between Italians and Austrians with Brigitte (in her first Italian film) as a nurse in the Austrian Red Cross in love with one of the brothers who crosses lines in a confusing story which ends happily – for Bardot.

1954 *Helen of Troy*
The Trojan Wars seen through a Hollywood-coloured camera lens with Brigitte Bardot just missing the leading part as antiquity's most beautiful woman in a minor role as Helen's servant girl, Andraste.

1954 *Le Fils de Caroline Chérie* (The Son of Caroline Chérie)
The victorious military and amorous advance of the adventurous son of an enterprising mother (heroine of popular novels and successful films) with Brigitte as one of the girls he conquers at the time of the French occupation of Spain.

1954–55 *Futures Vedettes* (Future Stars, *or* Sweet Sixteen)
Based on Vicky Baum's novel set in Vienna where an operatic tenor turned professor of music has the time of his life with two girl students played by Brigitte Bardot and Isabelle Pia. When his wife returns the girls suffer but their music profits from the painful experience.

1955 *Doctor at Sea* (Rendez-Vous à Rio)
Professional and personal complications ensue when a young medical man signs on as ship's doctor on a cargo vessel which, surprisingly, carries two women passengers, one of them a French *chanteuse* played by Brigitte Bardot. Result predictable.

1955 *Les Grandes Manoeuvres* (Summer Manoeuvres)
Directed by René Clair, the master of French cinema, Brigitte, in a subsidiary plot, is overshadowed by the film's delicately presented main theme of a young officer courting a handsome milliner to win a wager and falling in love with her only to be rebuffed when she learns of his base motive.

1955 *La Lumière D'En Face* (The Light Across the Street)
Disaster which haunts Brigitte in many films overcomes her when her marriage cannot be consummated while her husband recovers from an accident. She falls for the guy on the other side of the street – with fatal result for the hapless husband.

1955 *Cette Sacrée Gamine* (Mam'selle Pigalle, *or* That Crazy Kid)
Sensitively speaking Vadim's lines, Brigitte plays the daughter of a night club owner in trouble with the police and is comforted by the club's resident singer who falls in love with her much to the chagrin of his fiancée. But all ends well.

1956 *Mio Figlio Nerone* (Les Week-ends de Neron, *or* Nero's Weekend)
As Emperor Nero's girl-friend Poppea, Brigitte – who bathes in asses' milk and takes part in the odd orgy – becomes involved in plot and counter-plot when her lover plans to murder her mother and mother in turn puts poisonous vipers into Brigitte's bed. All escape – except Rome which burns while Nero fiddles.

1956 *En Effeuillant la Marguérite* (Plucking the Daisy, *or* Mam'selle Striptease)
The practised Vadim-Allegrét team does Brigitte proud. As Agnès, a general's daughter who has written a naughty novel, she escapes her father's wrath to Paris where she runs out of money and tries to recoup by entering a strip-tease contest. After some Fledermaus-type deception at a masked ball, Agnès is forced to discard her disguise and face father and music.

1956 *Et Dieu Créa la Femme* (And Woman was Created)
In the film that made Bardot a world star (and made St Tropez), Brigitte plays a sexy orphan who becomes involved with a wealthy shipowner and two brothers causing upheaval and bitter fights among them.

1956 *La Mariée Est Trop Belle* (The Bride Is Too Beautiful)
Overtones of the real BB as Chouchou, a cover-girl, who poses for a wedding photograph with the wrong guy and finds happiness with the right one, the archetypal handsome French lover, Louis Jourdan, in the end.

1957 *Une Parisienne*
As the French Premier's daughter, Brigitte is found in bed with his principal secretary and obliged to marry him. The young husband's roving eye is matched by his wife's amorous interest in a visiting Queen's consort (with newsreel shots of the Queen's and the Duke of Edinburgh's visit to France injudiciously shown). The straying wife and the prince consort both catch colds before reverting to their lawful spouses.

1957 *Les Bijoutiers du Clair de Lune* (Moonlight Jewellers, *or* Heaven Fell That Night)
Ursula (Brigitte) on holiday with her uncle, the Count, falls for Lambert who is beaten up by the Count's men, then kills the Count and flees with Ursula. She learns about the seamier side

of sex and is killed in a shooting match between her lover and the police.

1957 *En Cas de Malheur* (In Case of Adversity)
Street girl Yvette owes her acquittal in court to middle-aged Parisian lawyer whom she offers her body in lieu of payment. The affair of the incongruous couple ends in death for Yvette – Brigitte once more coming to a sticky end – who is stabbed to death by a casual lover.

1958 *Le Femme et le Pantin* (The Girl and the Puppet, *or* A Woman like Satan)
As a young dancing girl in a night club, Eva keeps rich admirer dangling. He follows her on provincial tour and is consumed by jealousy of her partner until she succumbs to him after all.

1959 *Babette S'En Va-t-En Guerre* (Babette Goes to War)
Brigitte with a dark wig, bordello maid, turns resistance heroine in World War Two, is parachuted into Nazi-occupied France by London-based Free French, interrogated by the Gestapo but, an irresistible bait, helps to capture German General and in the process captures the heart of Gérard (Jacques Charrier) on and off screen.

1959 *Voulez-Vous Danser Avec Moi?* (Come Dance With Me!)
Brigitte, amateur-sleuth, in a web of blackmail and murder, proves her husband innocent of the death of Anita Flores whose previous victims make a colourful gathering of rogues. Much suspense and some comedy until a drag artist is unmasked as Anita's murderer.

1959 *Le Testament d'Orphée*
Jean Cocteau's surrealist fantasies projected on to the screen.

1960 *L'Affaire d'une Nuit* (It Happened At Night)
Brigitte, her husband and the producer occupy a table in a Paris-

by-night scene to provide background to the real action (without getting as much as a credit on the screen).

1960 *La Vérité* (The Truth)
The sordid but gripping story of two unequal sisters, Brigitte playing the profligate one who seduces and kills her sister's lover. Told in flashbacks as her trial proceeds, the action affords Brigitte a rare opportunity to show her dramatic talent. The final scene of her suicide becomes, if anything, too realistic. Brigitte includes *La Vérité* among the few valuable films she has made.

1961 *La Bride Sur le Cou* (Please Not Now!)
Sexual romp with interchangeable infatuations which takes Brigitte, as a cover girl who wants to make her lover jealous, to a wintersports resort; when she has been seen as an uncover girl, it all ends very much as it started.

1961 *Les Amours Célèbres* (Famous Loves)
The sad story of a humble, beautiful girl who marries a Bavarian prince but is hounded by jealous women at court and finally drowned as a witch. Brigitte, as ravishing as the part demands, makes the plot credible. It ends with the prince following her into death.

1961 *Vie Privée* (Private Life)
Thinly disguised allegory of Bardot's real-life problem of preserving her privacy. She plays a highly successful model and cover girl who becomes a film star suffering from the pressure of an existence in the limelight. Nervous breakdown followed by romance which brings brief happiness, new fame and tragic death.

1962 *Le Repos du Guerrier* (Warrior's Rest, *or* Love on a Pillow)
Brigitte as Geneviève in the centre of a sordid tale, in love with a suicidal drunkard whose talent for sculpture she encourages until he leaves her for a street woman. Finally he returns to her.

1963 *Le Mépris* (Contempt, *or* A Ghost at Noon)
Hauntingly beautiful story about the making of a film with Camille (Brigitte) married to a writer who feels unequal to his task. Contemptuous of him she leaves with the American producer Prokosch – both are killed in a motor crash. German-American director Fritz Lang plays himself and Godard appears as his assistant.

1963 *Paparazzi*
Photographers photographed – the work of *paparazzi*, bane of Brigitte's life, observed by Rozier and his crew while *Le Mépris* is being made in Rome.

1963 *Tentazioni Proibite* (Forbidden Temptation)
Yet another short film, this time purporting to depict Brigitte's private life, made while work on *Le Mépris* was in progress.

1963 *Une Ravissante Idiote* (A Ravishing Idiot, *or* Adorable Idiot)
Light-hearted story of Ninotchka-type Russian spy who falls for adorable, light-headed seamstress (Brigitte). While working for the wife of the Admiralty chief, she helps the Russian to steal important secret files.

1964 *Marie Soleil*
Walk-on part for Brigitte in story of humble engineer who falls in love with promiscuous Riviera beauty (Danièle Delorme). Ex-husband Charrier as the engineer caught up in events reminiscent of his own experiences.

1965 *Dear Brigitte*
Erasmus, eight-year-old mathematical genius, predicts results of horse races and has an abiding passion for Brigitte Bardot to whom he writes fan letters. He meets her face to face in a brief scene, Brigitte's only contribution to the film. Tricksters take

advantage of the boy who yet turns his gift to good account for himself and his family.

1965 *Viva Maria!*
On the death of their revolutionary hero, two travelling circus ladies, Maria I and Maria II, carry on the liberation struggle of Mexican peasants against wealthy landlords and become involved in a series of intriguing adventures, inventing the strip-tease on the way. Heroines of the revolution, the two Marias end up in Paris with their act.

1965 *Masculin-Féminin* (Masculine-Feminine)
Confused story of young people (Jean-Luc Godard called it 'a concerto on youth') in confusing cohabitation and fast-switching jobs which ends in death. Brigitte's appearance in an interlude lasts less than two minutes.

1966 *A Coeur Joie* (Two Weeks in September)
Brigitte as French model girl Cécile who comes to London to work and to work out her relationship with her lover; becomes embroiled with two admirers, makes love in the Scottish heather and has difficulty in deciding with whom to share her life. By the time she makes up her mind the man of her choice has gone off without her. Another film which mirrors Brigitte's personal woes.

1967 *Histoires Extraordinaires* (Tales of Mystery and Imagination)
Brigitte appears in one of the film's three episodes based on Edgar Allan Poe stories (while Jane Fonda appears in another scripted by husband Roger Vadim). Set in nineteenth-century Italy, the story revolves around a tough officer who has a strange encounter with Giuseppina, cheats at cards and, confronted by his *Doppelgänger*, his better self, takes his own life.

1968 *Shalako*
In the eighteen-eighties, a party of European aristocrats, Countess Irina (Brigitte) among them, goes on safari in New Mexico but is taken into Apache territory where cowhand Shalako (Sean Connery) saves them from the wrath of the Indian chief. Some of the aristocrats are killed and the rest return to Europe – except Countess Irina who stays behind with Shalako.

1969 *Les Femmes* (The Women)
Dissatisfied with her job and her lover, the latter portrayed by Patrick Gilles who occupied that position also in her life, Brigitte Bardot looking stunning (with nothing on), as secretary Clara, explores new territory, encounters writer Jérome who requires professional and personal services which Clara supplies. Having triumphed over two other women in Jérome's life, she gets over-emotional and leaves him while he consoles himself with another secretary.

1970 *L'Ours et la Poupée* (The Bear and the Doll)
A motoring accident in which Gaspard is hit by Félicia's Rolls is symbolic of the clash between the two. Brigitte as the 'Doll' is wealthy, elegant, seductive; Gaspard, a devoted musician without social graces. The two incompatible characters meet again and take a dislike to each other but Félicia cannot resist the challenge of Gaspard's obduracy.

1970 *Les Novices* (The Novices)
As Sister Agnes, Brigitte quickly sheds her nun's habit, escapes Mother Superior, swims to freedom, reaches Paris and teams up with Mona Lisa, an old prostitute who tries to instruct her in the tricks of the oldest profession. The two women ply their trade in an ambulance but Agnes turns against men and Mona Lisa is converted to the faith. Both end up in the convent.

1970 *Boulevard du Rhum*
Brigitte in a twenties' romp. Rich liquor smuggler at the time of the American Prohibition falling for big star Linda, sees every one of her films. He meets her and takes her on a cruise but she falls in love with a lordly fellow traveller and the poor rich rum-runner is reduced to watching her on the screen forever after.

1971 *Les Pétroleuses* (The Oil Girls, *or* The Legend of Frenchie King)
In New Mexico in the eighteen-eighties, two women in fierce rivalry – Brigitte as one of the four daughters of the late gang leader Frenchie King carrying on father's bad works; and Claudia Cardinale who rules her four brothers with an iron hand. It's all about an oil find on Frenchie King's land but when the battling four sisters and four brothers are arrested, the sheriff marries them off. The screen characters portrayed by Brigitte and Claudia become one happy family and at the head of their clans are off on new adventures.

1973 *Don Juan 1973/Si Don Juan Etait une Femme* (Don Juan/If Don Juan Were a Woman)
Another rather sordid tale made reasonably attractive by Vadim's flair for titillation when, at long last, he shows Brigitte 'as God created her' in bed with another woman (Jane Birkin). The lesbian tryst is designed to excite a nasty millionaire, one of the men Bardot leads to destruction. A bewildered priest listens to the confession of her deeds which include murder. Symbolically the evil character Brigitte portrays dies in the inferno of her burning house.

1973 *L'Histoire Très Bonne et Très Joyeuse de Colinot Trousse-Chemise* (The Happy and Joyous Story of Colinot, the Man Who Pulls Up Skirts)
For her last film, Brigitte, produced and directed by women, returns to a costume role in a story of fifteenth-century France

and a man who delights in pulling up women's skirts and proceeding successfully from there. In pursuit of his kidnapped bride he becomes involved with all manner of characters until he meets the proud Arabelle who – like Brigitte herself – makes the pace in matters of sex and love. Underlining the point, Brigitte's own devoted lover, Laurent Vergez, also serves her on screen. What an appropriate exit for the star whose name is synonymous with sex!

Index